Scottish Emigration
and
Scottish Society

Scottish Emigration
and
Scottish Society

Proceedings of the
Scottish Historical Studies Seminar
University of Strathclyde
1990–91

Edited by
T M DEVINE

JOHN DONALD PUBLISHERS LTD
EDINBURGH

ISBN 0 85976 370 6

British Library Cataloguing in Publication Data
A catalogue record for this book is
available from the British Library.

Phototypeset by The Midlands Book Typesetting Company
Printed and bound in Great Britain by
Hartnolls Ltd., Bodmin, Cornwall

Contributors

Jeanette M Brock
Formerly Teaching Assistant in Scottish History, University of Strathclyde

Edward J Cowan
Professor of History and Chairman of the Scottish Studies Programme,
University of Guelph, Canada

T M Devine
Professor of Scottish History and Chairman of the Department
of History, University of Strathclyde

Ian L Donnachie
Senior Lecturer in History, Open University in Scotland

Malcolm Gray
Formerly Reader in Economic History,
University of Aberdeeen

Isobel Lindsay
Lecturer in Sociology, University of Strathclyde

Michael E Vance
Assistant Professor of History, St Mary's University,
Halifax, Nova Scotia.

Contents

1

INTRODUCTION:

The Paradox of Scottish Emigration

T.M. Devine

European emigration to overseas destinations in the nineteenth and early decades of the twentieth centuries was both extensive and widespread. One authoritative estimate suggests that between 1821 and 1915 about forty-four million emigrated from Europe or about a quarter of the natural population increase on the continent over this period.[1] Scottish emigration was one part of this broader movement and shared many of its features but also possessed certain distinctive characteristics. Most importantly, Scotland lost a much higher proportion of her population than most other European countries through outward movement. In the eight decades before the First World War, M.W. Flinn estimated that somewhat more than half of the natural increase of population in Scotland left the country of their birth.[2] In addition, within the United Kingdom, the Scottish rate of population growth in the later nineteenth and early twentieth centuries was significantly lower than in England and Wales and this can be largely attributed to a rate of emigration about one and a half times that of the two other countries.[3] What is more, the Scottish haemorrhage persisted longer. When UK emigration in general was decelerating, outward movement from Scotland remained very high. Indeed, over the whole period 1861 to 1930, net Scottish emigration reached its greatest ever levels in the decades between the two world wars.[4]

The scale of the exodus from Scotland also stands out in an international context. Dudley Baines has compiled a table of comparative emigrations from European countries between 1861 and 1913.[5] Of sixteen western and central European countries, three, Ireland, Norway and Scotland, consistently headed in most years the league table as the source areas of proportionately most emigrants. Ireland, not unexpectedly, led the list over most of the period. Norway and Scotland fluctuated in their relative positions. However, in no less than three decades, 1851–60, 1871–80, and 1901–10, Scotland was second only to Ireland in this 'unenviable championship' and in 1913 had an even higher rate of emigration than either Ireland or Norway.[6] It should also be noted that these rankings specifically exclude Scottish migration to England.

This comparative context brings into particularly sharp focus the essential paradox of Scottish emigration. Almost all the European countries with significant losses were agricultural economies. Not surprisingly, they included in addition to Norway and Ireland, Italy, Spain and Portugal. But in the nineteenth and early twentieth centuries, Scotland's industrial pre-eminence was well established. Already by the census of 1841, only a quarter of her workforce were still occupied in agricultural or related employment. By 1910 it had fallen to just over 10 per cent. From an existing base in linen, cotton and woollen textiles, massive diversification had occurred from c.1830 into iron, coal, engineering, steel, and shipbuilding. Undeniably by 1900 the heart of the economic system in the west of Scotland deserved the designation 'Workshop of the British Empire'. With industrialisation had come rapid urbanisation. By the end of the nineteenth century, the typical Scot had become a town dweller. In 1911, almost 60 per cent of the population lived in concentrated settlements of more than 5,000 people, while, in a 'Rank Order of European Urbanisation' for 1910–11, covering fifteen countries, Scotland was second only to England and Wales.[7]

Herein lies the puzzle of Scottish emigration. Heavy outward movement from backward and poor rural societies such as Ireland and Italy was not unexpected. As their populations rose in the nineteenth century, these agrarian economies remained relatively sluggish, transatlantic transportation improved, and opportunities increased in North America. Accelerating emigration from these countries could therefore be anticipated. Yet the economic circumstances were entirely different in Scotland. Emigration did already exist in the early nineteenth century but it expanded rapidly just as indigenous employment opportunities became more available and standards of living rose moderately in the later nineteenth century. The transformation of the economy enabled additional numbers to be fed, clothed and employed. Scottish population as a result rose from 1,265,380 in 1755 to 4,472,103 in 1901. But it was precisely in this period that more and more decided to leave. Between 1825 and 1938, 2,332,608 people departed Scotland for overseas destinations.[8] No other industrial society in Europe experienced such a haemorrhage.

Three further aspects deepen the puzzle. First, as the Scots were moving out in larger numbers, so migration into Scotland was on the increase. This was a clear and unambiguous sign that opportunities were not only available in the Scottish economy but were also expanding at a considerable rate. The number of Irish-born had reached 7.2 per cent of the population in 1851 and was still 5.9 per cent as late as 1881.[9] Second, a sampling of Scottish immigrants to the USA in the later nineteenth century indicates that some 77 per cent came from towns rather than from rural areas, a significantly higher proportion than that of the urban proportion within the total Scottish population. Charlotte Erickson has also shown from her examination of American passenger lists that 58.9 per cent of Scottish male emigrants were from 'industrial' counties while, by 1885–8, this ratio had risen to 80 per cent.[10] In her paper printed on p.104, Jeanette Brock confirms these results.[11] These are significant findings. Even allowing for the possibility of inmigration from rural areas to towns and industrial centres being concealed within the data, they strongly suggest that increasingly after 1860 most emigrants came from the new manufacturing and urban economy and not from distressed or declining country districts in the Highlands or rural Lowlands.

Third, many Scottish migrants in the later nineteenth century and thereafter were possessed of marketable skills. Brinley Thomas has produced figures which show that over the period 1875 to 1914 some 50 per cent of Scottish male emigrants to the United States were 'skilled' and that Scotland also provided the highest proportion of professional or entrepreneurial emigrants from the four UK countries.[12] Interestingly this finding ties in with Isabel Lindsay's conclusions in chapter 8 about Scottish graduate emigration in the later twentieth century. Similarly, as many as 55 per cent of adult men leaving Scotland in the early 1920s had skilled trades while in 1912–3 no less than 21 per cent came from the middle-class category of 'commerce, finance, insurance, professional and students'. Only 29 per cent in these years were labourers.[13] Throughout the decades from the mid-nineteenth century, then, a significant number of those who left Scotland were members of the new 'aristocracy of labour' and the business and professional classes. This was again a pattern which was distinctively Scottish. Inevitably the social composition of emigration from most other European societies where agricultural activity remained dominant differed considerably. But the Scottish variant also contrasted with the occupational structure of English emigrants in which common labourers predominated and relatively few were skilled craftsmen.[14] The fact that a substantial number of those who left Scotland had marketable skills helps to account for the remarkable success of many in the New World. Such skills were at a premium in these developing societies and the Scots were often among the minority who possessed them. This is the essential background to Ian Donnachie's survey in this collection of Scottish business and economic success in Australia.[15]

Recent research has helped to identify, describe and clarify the distinctive features of emigration from Scotland. Yet, as the inherent paradox becomes clearer, its resolution remains difficult and challenging.[16] Essentially two linked problems come into focus: the reasons why more people left Scotland as the country became increasingly prosperous and the related issue of the forces which lay behind the sheer scale of Scottish emigration which placed it close to the top of the European emigration league. In the state of current knowledge no definitive or entirely convincing answers can be given to these major questions although some clues are provided in the papers which follow. The purpose of the remainder of this introduction is to advance a general interim interpretation of the issues by trying to identify those key features of Scottish society which may help to explain the volume of the exodus. It should be stressed that the exercise is basically speculative and suggestive, an agenda for future research and discussion rather than the setting out of any final thesis.

There is no doubt that the nineteenth- and twentieth-century movement of Scots was very great. However, this fact has tended to obscure the scale of emigration in preceding periods. One of the most important features of modern Scottish emigration was that it was built upon an extensive exodus in earlier times. Inevitably statistics for the pre-1800 phase are even more elusive and less precise than those for later periods. But a recent survey has confirmed that Scotland was then already a society with very high levels of emigration.[17] Between 1600 and 1650 the net emigration outflow may have been between 85,000 and 115,000 and in the second half of the seventeenth century between 78,000 and 127,000. The emigration of mercenary soldiers was very significant but most movement even in this period consisted of civilians. The Scottish colony in Ulster absorbed about 30,000 from the south-west counties in particular by the 1640s. A further 50,000 may have moved across the Irish Sea during the terrible harvest failures of the 1690s.[18] Until the middle decades of the seventeenth century probably more Scots moved to Poland than any other European location but Scandinavia was also a significant point of attraction. Overwhelmingly, Scots emigrants to these destinations were small merchants, pedlars and soldiers while Ulster drew farmers and servants.[19]

Before 1700 there was much greater emigration from Scotland than from England and the country was already losing considerably greater numbers than most European societies.[20] The trend continued in the eighteenth century. Bernard Bailyn's analysis of movement to the thirteen American colonies from Great Britain in the 1770s confirms that proportionately more Scots than English were likely to emigrate.[21] What is also striking is that relative to England, Scotland before 1800 produced a disproportionate number of skilled and educated emigrants: doctors, teachers, ministers, and merchants. As Ned Landsman has succinctly commented:

> In commerce, Scots formed prominent commercial cliques in the Chesapeake, the port cities of New York, Philadelphia, and Charleston, and throughout the backcountry, extending into Canada. In medicine, more than 150 Scottish doctors emigrated to America during the eighteenth century, and almost the whole of the colonial medical profession was Scottish émigré or Scottish trained. In religion, Scots and Scottish trained ministers dominated both the Presbyterian and Episcopal Churches in America. So did Scottish educators, not only at Princeton, under Witherspoon, but at the College of Philadelphia, the many Presbyterian academies in the middle and southern states, and as tutors in Carolina and the Chesapeake.[22]

The professional and entrepreneurial emigration of the nineteenth and twentieth centuries was therefore nothing new. The so-called 'brain drain' has been a feature of Scottish emigration from at least medieval times. Many talented and gifted people left the country even in the eighteenth century which was the great age of Scottish intellectual achievement and remarkable economic improvement. Those critics who see the haemorrhage of indigenous ability as an obstacle to Scottish progress in more modern times need to consider this historical record. The exodus of the able has been a constant theme in Scottish history, even in the most dynamic phases of the nation's development.

This brief survey of the period before 1800 has several implications for an analysis of nineteenth-century movement. It is clear that mass emigration was a continuum; the great diaspora of the Victorian and Edwardian decades was a further stage in a process which had been going on for centuries. The extent of early modern emigration may also have established or extended a 'culture of mobility' in Scottish society. The nineteenth century did, of course, differ from earlier times in one crucial respect. Most Scots in the modern period emigrated to North America and, to a lesser extent, Australasia and South Africa. Before 1700 Ireland, England and Europe were the common destinations. There was therefore little scope for the continuation of 'chain migration' over the centuries. However, in the eighteenth century, important linkages were indeed established between the Highlands and parts of Canada.[23] These became conduits of continuing emigration in subsequent decades. One reason why movement was later so extensive from the western

Highlands was the attractive power of these eighteenth-century Gaelic settlements.[24] They provided information and assistance on arrival for new emigrants and so helped to lower the threshold of risk for those contemplating the hazards of the transatlantic journey. Scotland's long record of heavy emigration, however, does still leave the paradox unresolved. In one sense the early modern movements are easily explicable. Scotland before 1700 was undeniably a poor country on the periphery of the European trading system with a climate and topography which were not well suited to the regular production of food surpluses. Recurrent phases of heavy emigration were just as likely in such a society as the harvest crises and failures which punctuated the agrarian economy. In the second half of the sixteenth century, there was grain shortage in some areas of the country in about one-third of the years of the period.[25] But when material conditions measurably improved in the eighteenth century emigration did not recede. On the contrary, it not only persisted after 1750 but accelerated in the second half of the nineteenth century when, by the common consent of historians, standards of life for the majority of people were manifestly becoming better. To understand why this was, a closer focus on this later period is necessary.

To a significant extent the very nature of Scottish economic trans-formation in the period after c.1780 became the vital context for extensive emigration. Far from restraining outward movement by providing new employment and material improvement, industrialisation actually stimulated a continuing exodus of people. Basic to the Industrial Revolution in Scotland was profound change in rural social and economic structure. In the Lowlands, farms were consolidated, subtenancies removed and the terms of access to land became more rigid and regulated.[26] Over time fewer and fewer had legal rights to farms as consolidation accelerated and subdivision of holdings was outlawed. As numbers rose through natural increase, mobility of people became inevitable. Peasant proprietorship in Scotland was unknown and by 1840 most Lowland rural Scots were non-inheriting children of farmers, farm servants, country tradesmen, textile weavers or day labourers. The Scottish Poor Law before 1843 was notoriously hostile to the provision of relief for the able-bodied unemployed though, in practice, modest doles were often given. In this context, the majority of the population of the Lowland countryside relied mainly on selling their labour power in the market to survive. The ebb and flow of demand for labour inevitably enforced movement upon them. Before 1800 such domestic mobility was already present and probably gave Scotland a higher incidence of internal migration than most areas of such countries as France or the German states.[27]

In the nineteenth century this certainly intensified. There were at least five reasons for this. First, population was rising while both agricultural and industrial opportunities in rural areas were stagnant or, especially after c.1840, contracting rapidly. In consequence the proportion of natural population employed in agriculture declined markedly from 24 per cent in 1841 to 10 per cent in 1911. Second, most permanent agricultural workers on Scottish farms were 'servants' hired on annual or half-yearly contracts who received accommodation as part of their labour contract. The unemployed farm worker who inevitably had lost his home, had no choice but to move to seek a job.[28] Third, Scottish urbanisation was notable for its speed and scale.[29] The proportion of Scots living in settlements of over 5,000 rose from 31 per cent in 1831 to almost 60 per cent in 1911. The vast majority of the new urban populations were from the farms, villages and small towns of the Lowland countryside.[30] Fourth, the first phase of industrialisation down to c.1830 had extended manufacturing employment, especially in textiles, in rural areas. During the coal, iron and steel phase, production concentrated more intensively in the central Lowlands, the Border woollen towns, Dundee, Fife and Midlothian. Indeed one of the most striking features of Scottish industrial capitalism was its extraordinary concentration. This process ensured a rapid shedding of population from areas of crumbling employment to the regions of rapid growth in the Forth–Clyde valley.[31] Fifth, in the last quarter of the nineteenth century, clear evidence emerged of a growing rejection by the younger generation of the drudgery, social constraints and isolation of country life. The towns had always had an attraction but now they seduced the youth of rural society as never before.[32]

The interaction of all these influences produced an unprecedented level of mobility. The 1851 census shows that no less than a third of the Scottish population had crossed a county boundary. Recent demographic research has demonstrated also that in the 1860s the vast majority of parishes in all areas were experiencing net outmovement of population.[33] Heavy losses in the Lowlands were especially pronounced in the south-west region and in many parts of the east from Berwick to Moray. The only areas attracting people were in the central zone and the textile towns of the Borders: 'The conclusion must be that almost the whole of rural Scotland (and many of the more industrial and commercial areas also) were throughout our period, unable to provide enough opportunities at home to absorb even quite modest rates of population increase.'[34]

This demographic pattern is crucial to an understanding of the roots of Scottish emigration. The Scots were mobile abroad partly because they were increasingly very mobile at home.[35] No comparative index exists of national rates of European internal migration. If it did, it would probably put the Scots near the top. Emigration, then, was but an extension of migration within Scotland, which was much less painful after 1860 with the revolution in transatlantic travel associated with the steamship. Such a suggestion is entirely consistent with the point made earlier that most emigrants in the later nineteenth century were urban in origin. Almost certainly concealed within this category are many who had been born into an agricultural or industrial background in the countryside and moved to the towns before emigrating. At the same time, one must be careful not to see the process of internal movement as a simple relationship between rural and urban society. After 1860 there was much greater migration between cities and towns of varying size, prosperity and occupational structure than there was between urban areas and country districts.[36]

The direct and indirect links between Scottish emigration and Lowland mobility helps to place the well-known contribution of the Highlands in perspective. But the significance of Highland emigration as an important part of the Scottish exodus as a whole should not be underestimated. Until the middle decades of the nineteenth century the region contributed disproportionately to the total outflow. In more precise terms the western Highlands and Islands did so; most of those who left the parishes of the southern, central and eastern fringes in the first instance made for the Lowland towns.[37] The factors explaining the Highland exodus are far from simple. The far west was a poor, conservative peasant society where, through subdivision, access to land, albeit in minute holdings, was still possible for the majority. The regional society most closely comparable within the British Isles was the west of Ireland which was broadly similar in its poverty, peasant social system and tenacious attachment to peasant values. For these very reasons, however, emigration from this area was limited compared to Ulster and the eastern districts of Ireland.[38]

In part what made the western Highlands different was the incidence of soldier emigration from the region. This not only established a tradition of mobility and spread knowledge of overseas destinations but the military settlements created after the Seven Years' War and the American War also acted as foci of attraction for successive waves of Highland emigrations.[39] Scottish Gaeldom was also much more subject to intense levels of commercialisation than the communities of the west of Ireland. The rent inflation of the post-1760 period, the 'modernisation' of the social system through the destruction of the old joint tenancies, the imposition of the croft system and the clearances for sheep all represented the powerful impact of 'improving' ideology and Lowland market forces on traditional society. Up to c.1820, the Highland emigrations can be regarded as attempts to resist the forces which were transforming the old ways so painfully and rapidly. Internal protest was muted but emigration was extensive and was preferred to migration to the south because of the independence which came from holding land and because the preservation of traditional values could be more easily ensured.[40]

But the mass outward movement of Highlanders only occurred after 1820 and especially in the famine of the 1840s and 1850s.[41] Essentially that can be seen once again as a process intimately associated with Scottish industrialisation. This is a connection which reinforces the thesis under discussion: the economic transformation itself was in the final analysis a major influence on emigration. It was the stimuli of southern industry which produced buoyant demand for Highland cattle and kelp and encouraged landlords to subdivide land among the population to boost output of these commodities. But this inevitably led to an imbalance between the number of inhabitants and existing resources which was rendered even more acute after 1820 when Lowland textile and chemical industries found cheaper alternatives to Highland kelp. At the same time the now 'redundant' population in the north-west was further squeezed by clearances designed to extend sheep farming, which because of changing external demand remained the only significantly profitable specialisation.[42]

The emigration of the Highland population therefore indicates how a society can experience very heavy outward movement despite the growth of a modern economic system. Industrialisation brings increased wealth but its benefits are usually spread unevenly. Growing poverty in one region is entirely compatible with plenty in another, especially as the dynamic industrial growth ensures the destruction of formerly viable subsistence and semi-subsistence economies in peripheral areas. As manufacturing concentrated ever more in the central zone the mass exodus from the poorer rural areas of the south-west and the north became inevitable.

Yet, as indicated earlier, specifically 'rural' factors cannot explain the later nineteenth-century emigration which derived predominantly from the industrial and urban regions and eventually mainly comprised those with industrial skills. The dynamism of the manufacturing economy had for some time created stresses and tensions which squeezed out certain groups of worker. The classic example was the impact of changing technology on the handloom weavers.[43] One of their responses was the formation of emigration societies which gave support to those in declining crafts to seek a new life overseas. This phase in Scottish emigration forms the background to Michael Vance's essay in this volume.[44] But the movement of the handloom weavers was never numerically significant and was over in large part by 1850. The large-scale emigration of craft and industrial workers after that date cannot be explained in terms of technological unemployment. If many emigrants were 'victims' of Scottish industrial society their condition was dictated by more subtle forces than this.

Two features of Scottish industrialism may have promoted significant levels of emigration. First, for much of the period, Scotland was a low-wage economy. Indeed, it was generally recognised that Scottish industrial success in large part rested on low labour costs, the result in part of mass inward migration from the rural areas and Ireland to the industrial centres. There was considerable variation between areas and occupations but in 1860 Scottish wages were often up to 20 per cent lower than for equivalent English trades.[45] Scholarly debate continues over the extent of convergence thereafter but when real wages are considered the most recent estimate suggests that Scottish manufacturing earnings were still 10 to 12 per cent less than in the industrial areas of England on the eve of the First World War.[46]

There is no inevitable correlation between low wages and emigration. What is crucial is the relative differential between opportunities at home and overseas. In the second half of the nineteenth and early twentieth centuries that differential between western Europe and the New World became greater. Wages and opportunities were increasing at home but they were doing so with even greater speed overseas because the American economies were very rich in resources but grossly underpopulated. Those with industrial skills and experience were especially in demand.[47] The scenario for mass emigration from societies such as Scotland was clearly emerging as the previous constraints on movement crumbled. Ignorance of conditions across the Atlantic and in Australasia diminished as information was disseminated more widely through the press, government sources, emigration societies and previous emigrants. Emigration therefore became available to many more as income levels rose in the later nineteenth century. The sheer cost had been a significant obstacle to many in previous times. Detailed analysis of migration in Scottish rural society after 1870 has suggested a marked increase in social expectations, a change partly related to higher wages but also to expansion in educational opportunities after 1872.[48] It would seem likely that there were similar attitudinal changes among many urban and industrial workers and these may have intensified their awareness of greater opportunities overseas.

Above all, the transport revolution was critical.[49] The steamship did not so much lower the costs of transatlantic travel as radically increase its speed, comfort and safety. In the 1850s it took six weeks to cross the Atlantic. By 1914 this had fallen to a week. In 1863 45 per cent of transatlantic emigrants left in sailing ships. By 1870 only a tiny number travelled in this way.[50] By drastically cutting voyage times the steamship removed one of the major costs of emigration, the time between embarkation and settlement, during which there was no possibility of earning. In North America itself the unprecedented expansion of the railway from the 1850s further facilitated rapid movement. All in all, what was being created for the first time was a truly efficient international transport system. The essential infrastructure for the formation of a transatlantic labour market was evolving.

That the Scottish labour market had now become internationalised was apparent in three ways. First, it is shown in the way that heavy phases of emigration were very closely related to boom conditions in the North American economy.[51] Second, it is illustrated by the seasonal emigration across the Atlantic of particular groups of workers, such as Aberdeen granite tradesmen, who were recruited in Scotland by agents for American companies.[52] Third, and most importantly of all, the process can be seen in the increasing frequency of return emigration. Transport constraints in the era of the sailing ship ensured that emigration was virtually permanent exile for most. The steamship made return not only more possible but very common. One (probably) conservative estimate suggests that by the later nineteenth century around one-third of those who left, sooner or later returned.[53]

In this period, then, the habitual and historic internal mobility of the Scots could be translated fully into international movement. In the same way as they had compared wages and employment within Scotland, it was now easier than ever before to evaluate opportunities in New York, Toronto and Chicago in relation to Glasgow and Edinburgh. The income differentials were often so enormous and the skills shortage in the New World so acute that many thousands could not resist the lure, especially since, in the event of failure, the return journey home was the price of a steamship ticket. The temptation was also there, of course, for the skilled of that other advanced economy, England. But it is hardly surprising that the Scots found it more irresistible. Scotland was still a poorer society than England and the difference between opportunities at home and abroad was greater for the Scots. Quite simply, they had more to gain by emigration. The proof of this was the enormous migration from Scotland to England before 1900. For the period 1841 to 1911, according to one estimate, about 600,000 Scots-born persons moved to

England and Wales.[54] This was around half of the total net emigration from Scotland in the nineteenth century and was not paralleled by any similar significant movement from the south to the north. This was eloquent testimony of the perceived differences in standards of life between the two societies, especially when it is remembered that from the 1870s many Scots who moved to England were skilled and increasingly settled in the mining and heavy industrial areas of England and Wales.

But it was not simply because the rewards of industry could not compete with those abroad or in England. Scottish emigration also attained such high levels *because* of the peculiar economic structure of the society. It had a higher proportion of its inhabitants employed in industrial work by 1871 than any other country in western Europe apart from England. But unlike England, the majority of the employed male population in Scotland was heavily concentrated in the capital goods sector of shipbuilding, coal, metals and engineering. In addition, to an unusual extent, many of these activities were heavily dependent on the export market. The Scottish economy lacked the cushion of a strong service sector and a range of industries catering for the domestic market.[55] After 1830 the British economy as a whole became subject to more extreme fluctuations in the trade cycle but in Scotland the amplitude and duration of cyclical change was more violent because of the tight interrelationships within the heavy industrial structure, the bias towards foreign markets, which were inherently fickle, and the relative weakness of domestic demand. This economic insecurity was basic to emigration. Violent fluctuations in employment were integral to Scottish industrial 'prosperity' even in the heyday of Victorian and Edwardian expansion. Their scale and frequency can be seen in the building industry which employed about 7 per cent of the occupied male labour force in the 1880s. Between 1881 and 1891 the numbers employed fell by 5.1 per cent, rose by 43.4 per cent during 1891 to 1901 and contracted again by a massive 21.4 per cent over the years 1901–11.[56] Not surprisingly emigration was at its height at the bottom of these cycles. Because fluctuations were probably more savage and longer lasting in Scotland it is reasonable to assume that the volume of outward movement would be greater than south of the Border. The dramatic peaks in Scottish emigration, the later 1840s and early 1850s, the mid-1880s and 1906 to 1913 all took place in periods of serious industrial depression at home.

Similarly, the continuation of heavy outmigration from Scotland in the 1920s and 1930s at a time when it was decelerating elsewhere in the United Kingdom is itself largely attributable to her characteristic industrial structure. Because of the peculiar mix of heavy, export-orientated industries, Scotland's most populated areas were a good deal worse off than elsewhere. At the bottom of the slump in 1931–3 more than a quarter of the Scottish workforce was without a job compared to a little over a fifth in the UK as a whole.[57] The Scots suffered disproportionately and not surprisingly tended to emigrate when they could in greater numbers. *Plus ça change, plus c'est la même chose.*

There was therefore an unfortunate and depressing parallel between the continuing haemorrhage of the twentieth century and the large-scale emigration of Scots in the early modern period and thereafter. The essays in this collection seek to clarify some aspects of that phenomenon which is so central to an overall understanding of Scotland's historical development over the last four centuries. They do not pretend to be exhaustive or definitive. The serious study of Scottish emigration is in its very early stages. This collection will have achieved its aim if it gives further momentum to that very necessary task.

NOTES

1. I. Ferenczi and W.F. Willcox, *International Migrations* (New York, 1929–31), pp.236–88.

2. M.W. Flinn (ed.), *Scottish Population History from the Seventeenth Century to the 1930s* (Cambridge, 1977), p.448.

3. M. Anderson and D.J. Morse, 'The People' in W.H. Fraser and R.J. Morris (eds.), *People and Society in Scotland, 1830–1914* (Edinburgh, 1990), pp.12–14.

4. Flinn (ed.), *Scottish Population History*, p.449.

5. Dudley Baines, *Migration in a Mature Economy* (Cambridge, 1985), p.10.

6. Flinn (ed.), *Scottish Population History*, p.448.

7. R.J. Morris, 'Urbanisation and Scotland' in Fraser and Morris (eds.), *People and Society in Scotland*, p.74.

8. Flinn (ed.), *Scottish Population History*, pp.441–2.

9. R.H. Campbell, 'Scotland', in R.A. Cage (ed.), *The Scots Abroad* (London, 1985), p.13.

10. Charlotte J. Erickson, 'Who Were the English and Scots Emigrants to the United States in the Late Nineteenth Century?' in D.V. Glass and R. Revelle (eds.), *Population and Social Change* (London, 1972), pp.360–2.

11. See pp.104–126.

12. B. Thomas, *Migration and Economic Growth: A Study of Great Britain and the Atlantic Economy* (Cambridge, 1973), p.62.

13. Flinn (ed.), *Scottish Population History*, p.453.

14. Baines, *Migration*, p.51.

15. See pp.135–153.

16. R.H. Campbell was one of the first to indicate the paradox in print. See Campbell, 'Scotland', pp.29–45.

17. T.C. Smout, N.C. Landsman and T.M. Devine, 'Scottish Emigration in the Seventeenth and Eighteenth Centuries' (forthcoming).

18. M. Perceval-Maxwell, *The Scottish Migration to Ulster in the Reign of James I* (London, 1973), pp.311–14; L.M. Cullen, 'Population Trends in Seventeenth-Century Ireland', *Economic and Social Review*, 6 (1975), pp.154–7.

19. A. Bieganska, 'A Note on the Scots in Poland, 1550–1800', in T.C. Smout (ed.), *Scotland and Europe, 1200–1850* (Edinburgh, 1986), pp.157–161.

20. Smout, Landsman and Devine, 'Scottish Emigration'.

21. B. Bailyn, *Voyagers to the West* (London, 1986).

22. Smout, Landsman and Devine, 'Scottish Emigration'.

23. J.M. Bumsted, *The People's Clearance: Highland Emigration to British North America, 1770–1815* (Edinburgh, 1982).

24. *Ibid.*

25. S.G.E. Lythe, *The Economy of Scotland in its European Setting, 1550–1625* (Edinburgh, 1960), ch.1.

26. The most recent examination of this process is by M. Gray, 'The Social Impact of Agrarian Change in the Rural Lowlands' in T.M. Devine and R. Mitchison (eds.), *People and Society in Scotland, 1760–1830* (Edinburgh, 1988), pp.53–69.

27. R.A. Houston, 'The Demographic Regime' in Devine and Mitchison (eds.), *People and Society in Scotland*, p.20.

28. T.M. Devine (ed.), *Farm Servants and Labour in Lowland Scotland, 1770–1914* (Edinburgh, 1984), *passim*.

29. T.M. Devine, 'Urbanisation' in Devine and Mitchison (eds.), *People and Society in Scotland*, pp.27–9.

30. *Ibid*, pp.41–7.

31. Malcolm Gray, *Scots on the Move: Scots Migrants, 1750–1914* (Dundee, 1990), pp.14–23.

32. T.C. Smout, *A Century of the Scottish People, 1830–1950* (London, 1986), pp.81–4; Devine (ed.), *Farm Servants and Labour*, pp.251–3.

33. Anderson and Morse, 'The People', pp.19.

34. *Ibid*, p.22.

35. Campbell, 'Scotland', p.10.

36. J.M. Brock, 'Scottish Migration and Emigration, 1861–1911', unpublished PhD thesis, University of Strathclyde, 1990.

37. T.M. Devine, 'Highland Migration to Lowland Scotland, 1760–1860', *Scottish Historical Review*, lxii (1983).

38. C. O'Grada, 'Irish Emigration to the United States in the nineteenth century', in D.N. Doyle and O.D. Edwards (eds.), *America and Ireland, 1776–1976* (London, 1980).

39. Bumsted, *The People's Clearance*, pp.67–9.

40. See pp.92–5.

41. T.M. Devine, *The Great Highland Famine: Hunger, Emigration and the Scottish Highlands in the Nineteenth Century* (Edinburgh, 1988).

42. *Ibid.*

43. N. Murray, *The Scottish Handloom Weavers, 1790–1850: A Social History* (Edinburgh, 1978), pp.142–7.

44. See pp.37–60

45. Smout, *Century of the Scottish People*, 112; R.H. Campbell, *The Rise and Fall of Scottish Industry, 1707–1939* (Edinburgh, 1980), pp.76–101.

46. R.G. Rodger, 'The Invisible Hand: Market Forces, Housing and the Urban Form in Victorian Cities', in D. Fraser and A. Sutcliffe (eds.), *The Pursuit of Urban History* (London, 1980), pp.190–211.

47. J.D. Gould, 'European Intercontinental Emigration, 1815–1914: patterns and causes', *Journal of European Economic History*, 8 (1979).

48. Devine (ed.), *Farm Servants and Labour*, pp.119–20, 251–3.

49. Baines, *Migration*, p.279.

50. M. Harper, *Emigration from North-East Scotland* (Aberdeen, 1988), I, p.96.

51. Brock, 'Scottish Migration', p.410.

52. Harper, *Emigration from North-East Scotland*, pp.254–9.

53. Anderson and Morse, 'The People', p.16.

54. Flinn (ed.), *Scottish Population History*, p.442.

55. Clive Lee, 'Modern Economic Growth and Structural Change in Scotland: the Service Sector Reconsidered', *Scottish Economic and Social History*, 3 (1983), pp.5–35.

56. J.H. Treble, 'The Occupied Male Labour Force' in Fraser and Morris (eds.), *People and Society in Scotland*, pp.195–6.

57. Smout, *Century of the Scottish People*, p.114.

2

The Course of Scottish Emigration, 1750–1914: Enduring Influences and Changing Circumstances

Malcolm Gray

From the later eighteenth century, Scotland's industry and consequently her towns were growing rapidly. Yet, as the previous chapter has shown, at the same time the country never ceased to lose part of the natural increase of her population in a process of emigration. Such loss of population has been, indeed, an abiding characteristic of Scottish development and in the nineteenth century it was mounting to a scale that could not be matched in any other industrial country.

The paradox of people streaming out of a country in which industry was ever hungry for more labour can be explained by concentrating on the situation that lay behind both movements. Each must be set in the context of a society whose members had a high propensity to move in search of opportunity. It is true that some of the emigration can be seen as a series of particular movements generated by highly specific sets of circumstance, as it were, as autonomous changes. But the more general aspect is of a mobile force that might move, now in one direction, now in the other (at least in terms of relative weight). The common source of these streams was an increasingly turbulent rural society, but flight must not be represented as an undirected flood of poverty-stricken and driven victims of agrarian change. The causes of such movement were complex, lying not only in the rural condition but also in attractions elsewhere, whether in the growing towns or in settlements overseas. The tradition of overseas settlement developed a force of its own, continuing through changes of fortune and social arrangement in the countries being fed by immigration. But the pull thus generated always worked into the complex forces of rearrangement within the country of emigration, with results that varied in the relative balance of numbers going to the towns, on the one hand, and leaving Scottish shores, on the other.

Scottish emigration, subject to interruption by the wars of the eighteenth and early nineteenth centuries, remained irregular, although unremitting through the years up to 1914. But, considering the matter in rather longer periods of time, certain definite trends, mainly of increase, do emerge.

Until 1825 scale has to be judged from knowledge of particular episodes, except over the short period 1773–5 when an attempt was made at detailed official record. Certainly until 1815, emigration was intermittent and very varied estimates have been made of numbers involved. Even after 1825 when an unbroken annual series begins, the method of counting was such that there must remain doubts about the numbers of emigrants who were truly Scottish. However, the broad outlines are clear enough. Certainly, the tendency was for growth from one broad period to the next. Thus most of the years in the quarter-century from 1825 recorded figures well below 10,000; in the following quarter the typical figure was not far below 20,000; from 1875 to 1900 numbers fluctuated between 20,000 and 30,000; and by 1914 they were reaching up to 60,000.[1]

On certain aspects of the emigration process we remain ignorant. We can but guess at how, until 1860, rates of emigration related to natural increase of population. In the nineteenth century we have, of course, the evidence of the decennial census but, until 1871, this gives no indication of births and deaths and therefore of natural increase. However, only in the first three decades of the century does it appear that the realized growth of population approached natural increase.[2] Still, in these decades there was also heavy immigration from Ireland and the superficial figures of increase must have concealed some erosion.

Year by year, then, the drain of population persisted, but at an unsteady rate. It cut into natural increase but did not threaten to bring actual decline at least over the ten-yearly periods of the census record. In the end it was to deposit nearly two million Scots in the new countries of expanding settlement, particularly in North America and Australasia.

The emigrants had three main destinations—USA (after 1783), British North America (to become the dominion of Canada in 1867) and Australia. Throughout, North America was the main choice but the balance swung between the USA and British North America, with the former taking the larger number from 1840 onwards, while the first decade of the twentieth century saw Canada become once again the main choice for the Scots. In the 1850s for a period Australia was taking more than each of the two North American countries, considered individually.[3]

Scotland, particularly in the nineteenth and early twentieth centuries, was participating in a westward movement that entangled various countries, mostly losing their populations from an impoverished agrarian base. Yet Scottish emigration was both exceptionally heavy and derived from social circumstances that were peculiar to the country. One such particular condition, which was to set a pattern and a framework for further growth of emigration, was the situation in the Highlands and Islands as it was beginning to emerge in the eighteenth century.

Briefly, through the greater part of the eighteenth century, Highland society was being forced from a patriarchal into a commercial mould. One recurring theme in the transformation was the removal of tacksmen from positions of influence. They had played an important part in a society organised for military, or quasi-military action. But they stood as a barrier to landlords who, in more peaceable times, wished to extract in fullest measure rents which had been milked by the tacksmen as middlemen in the letting of land. Consequently, tacksmen, feeling threatened or being positively removed, led a movement of those who had been their subtenants to settle on undeveloped land in America.

It was in the nature of such a movement of compact groups of people, who were often kin to one another, to begin to set in place a framework for settlement which would encourage later emigrants. Those from the Highlands and Islands moved as family units along with known people of their locality and often of their own kin or at least clan names.[4] Thus were sustained family, kinship and neighbourhood links. Such forms of compact grouping gave peculiar importance to the location and continuing Scottish domination of certain settlements in America.

One result, then, of early Scottish emigration was to form solid communities or even whole areas with dominating representation of Scots, indeed of Scots from particular areas or kinship groups. The first notable example was the settlement of areas of North Carolina by groups of Highlanders, led by former tacksmen. The colony of New York, too, saw early developments of this ethnically compacted type. The influence of these moves of the period before 1775 was to be wrenched but not fractured by the American War of Independence. Many of the Scottish settlers, who on the whole remained loyal to the British Crown, transferred to British North America.[5] There they came to form part of a spreading array of settlements, through which transatlantic connections and mutual bonds would be sustained even into the twentieth century.

The settlements that were thus taking shape in British North America were in part the result of spontaneous surge, of a flight from threatening economic conditions and crumbling status. Such economic pressures were particularly strong in the Highlands and Islands and they contributed to the spread of settlement along the northern shores of the Maritime Colonies, from Cape Breton to the western boundary of Nova Scotia. Other communities were planted with less well-defined connections as a result of wars and accommodation of ex-service men, many of whom were Scots: the Seven Years' War, the War of Independence, the war of 1812 all left their residue.[6] In addition, the United Empire Loyalists included a substantial Scottish contingent. These Scottish interests were more diffused than were to be found in the original Highland settlements but they did spread a conscious Scottish feeling westwards to the Ontario peninsula. Similar in effects were the efforts of the imperial government after the war of 1812 to create a solid line of settlements as a strategic barrier along the St Lawrence. Group settlement was continued into the nineteenth century. A well-documented case is that of the Glengarry settlements of Upper Canada which served as haven for refugees from one troubled area of the Highlands.[7] A special instance is that of the settling of handloom weavers in Lanark County in Upper Canada.[8]

The record of movement which supported these developments of the earlier period is fairly plain, particularly where the Highlanders were involved. The implications and the tangled relationships of group movement also emerge with some clarity. Less obvious were the movements of the Lowlanders but they also, in more dispersed fashion, took part in the emigration surge. Relationships within the groups they formed and links between emigrants and the relatives and neighbours they left behind were probably looser. But they still showed, if more faintly, the forms of linkage and communication typical of the Highland communities. The Maritimes had been the area in which Highlanders had first shown the firmness of group connections which could stretch across the Atlantic. But in other parts of North America Scots of Lowland origin were to nourish similar feelings about the communities they had left behind, although the traces may be fainter.[9] Lowlanders as well as Highlanders gathered in widely spread but recognisable groups. Often the Scots were a few among people of other origins but they would still retain a sense of separate identity. Scattered individuals, self-consciously Scottish, might determinedly choose marriage partners of like tradition, might indeed even limit themselves to such as came from the same district of Scotland.[10] Individual attachment and communal feeling formed the connecting strands of a network which gives reality to the idea of a Scottish community of interest interlacing the broader transatlantic connections.

Communication brought sensitive interaction between widely separated groups. Scots could be informed with fair accuracy of conditions on the other side of the Atlantic; they could compare the facts of living as they knew them at home with what they might expect in a new country. They might receive remittances of money to help them on their way. And they would constantly be reminded of the old links of kinship and neighbourhood.

Accurate information might, of course, act as a deterrent as well as a stimulant to moving. There were agencies at work to spread an over-favourable notion of life in the Americas. Shipping and land companies were active to that end. Articles in the local press, usually optimistic, about the emigrant's prospects were particularly influential.[11] A letter from a relative struggling with the problems, say, of life on the frontier was a strong corrective to the rosy promises of the professional booster.

Indeed, in spite of the basic facts in the new country of plenitude of land, of high wages, of diverse and growing employment, the newly landed immigrant faced a hard time unless he had the means of purchasing developed land or had a much-needed skill. But, on the whole, there can be little doubt that the flow of urging, of information and possibly of money stemming from past emigration tended, cumulatively, to build up the emigration totals.

The emigration which was based on these feelings of allegiance was in the main planned, ordered and self-financed at least in terms of extended family connections. An autonomous force was generated which pulled people into the migrant stream whatever might be the surrounding circumstances. This was given added power by a long-term and persisting condition that was favourable to the shift of population westwards across the Atlantic. Determination to emigrate was necessarily based on the comparison of living conditions within economic systems of divergent type. On the one hand Scotland had a large and densely settled country population and a rapidly growing industrial sector. By the nineteenth century the rate of natural increase of population was high, which was bound to create problems in the countryside where there was little land for new settlement. As for the towns, as T.M. Devine has already shown, the surge of population and the congestion of the labour market tended to keep wages low.

North America, on the other hand, had vast stretches of land capable of settlement. The rapid development of land of high potential brought much related commercial activity and employment together with an active industrial sector to serve the expanding market. High rates of natural increase added to heavy immigration were tending to double the population in every twenty-five-year period. Yet the various growth factors brought benefit not only to the agriculturist with land to spare but also to wage-earners in every sphere. Compared with Scotland, North America was a land of unbelievably high wages.

The economic facts seemed to be conclusively in favour of emigration from the older country. Yet there were also dampening influences.

One lay in cost. In spite of much discussion about alleviating poverty by encouraging emigration, little government aid became available to meet the costs of passage and of settlement. The former had been raised by the Passenger Acts.[12] Limitation of numbers that could be carried on ships of given size meant inevitably that more had to be charged for each passenger. This, indeed, was the main aim of the Acts. They deliberately raised a barrier against emigrants. However, such cost-raising effects were soon neutralised by the rise of the timber trade between Britain and British North America during the Napoleonic Wars.[13] The large timber fleet was threatened with empty holds on the westward run. Cargo space could be turned to the use of passengers and the shipping interest became active in promoting the emigrant trade by offer of cheap passages. The cost of crossing the Atlantic to the nearest American ports (St John and Quebec) was brought down to £3 or £4.[14] Conditions for the passengers were atrocious and the risk of disease high but the low cost opened the possibility of emigration to people of quite modest means. However, in a system which depended largely on self-finance the truly destitute had little chance of making the crossing.

For the intending settler the costs of passage were only the beginning of a sequence of expense and difficulty. Until the 1840s most Scottish emigrants landed in the first instance in British North America although some might move on to the USA.[15] Lower Canada (Quebec) presented a truly alien social and land system and had little attraction for the British. For them the settlement areas of Upper Canada (Ontario) were more attractive but they lay at the end of a journey that would cover hundreds of miles. If they did not find land in the Maritimes where opportunities were limited the settlers had to face a costly and arduous move from tidewater to inland areas. In the USA, too, new land was to be found at growing distances from ports of entry.

Even more daunting were the problems of settlement on virgin land. Hardwood forest which covered most of the available fertile land could only be brought into cultivation by slow stages and by systems of clearance that had to be painfully learnt. Sustenance during a period of clearance depended either upon having capital to spare or upon taking wage-work. In areas where most were engaged in similar tasks of initial clearance few would be in a position to give employment. It was possible, of course, to purchase developed land. Indeed, a class of professional frontiersmen had grown up. They would acquire uncleared land cheap, work it into condition, then sell and move on. But such land was relatively expensive for the more permanent settlers who followed. Here again possession of substantial amounts of capital appears as a precondition of successful settlement. A period of working for wages in the towns that lay further back in the east might be the only answer.

This argument has presented the case of the emigrant as an intending settler, probably in British North America or Canada, rather than as a prospective industrial worker or town-dweller. In the eighteenth and early nineteenth centuries to hold land on easy terms probably represented the ambition of most emigrants and they could most easily fulfil their desire in British North America. But there were always some whose skills and ambitions were industrial or mercantile and as time wore on, as indeed the town and industrial population increased within Scotland, fewer would come from agricultural occupations and aims were correspondingly more varied. Yet the prospect of cheap, or free, land always bulked large among the promises made to attract immigrants. Canada, where public land was still being allocated on the easiest of terms in the early twentieth century, continued to attract great numbers with agricultural leanings, even while the majority of entrants to the USA could be classified as industrial.[16]

While emigrants might come immediately from the towns they were constantly being replaced, even to excess, by migrants from the country districts swarming into the towns. Strains within the rural community were a main precipitant of decisions to emigrate. From the middle of the eighteenth century the stability of Scottish rural communities was being challenged by the tendency of population to grow beyond the capacity of the agrarian system and of rural employments generally to accommodate additional families. Particularly acute were the problems of the north-west Highlands and Islands. Up to 1815 population increase was welcomed by Highland landlords. The result was the division of land into ever smaller holdings, particularly since so much of the higher land was being taken into large sheep farms. However, by the third decade of the nineteenth century landlords' attitudes had swung decisively. Yet they were unable to reverse the proliferation of small holdings over a limited land surface. In many parishes population was beginning to turn down by the 1830s because of the very fact of outward migration.[17] There was little relief for the hard-pressed population that remained. Pressure for further emigration was intense in some quarters but was often resisted by the potential emigrants themselves. Indebtedness in the form of arrears of rent, inadequate and precarious supply of subsistence and virtual disappearance of available money income remained a normal condition. In the 1830s and 1840s the subsistence crises were to become acute.

Pressures were less obvious in the agricultural Lowlands but they were pervasive and they acted on a population much more willing to move than were the Highlanders. Amidst a population that was increasing slowly in the eighteenth century drastic changes were being made in agrarian organisation. The fashionable doctrine of improvement involved the creation of larger farm units. Not only were smaller tenancies absorbed in larger but also numerous subtenants and cottars were entirely dispossessed. And in any case the loss of status coupled with demands for increase of rent suffered by many were enough to set some of the smaller farmers moving. The population in many rural parishes actually declined in this period of the later eighteenth century and in few did realised growth match the natural increase that we must assume.[18]

The strength of the pressure on the Lowland rural population becomes clearer in the nineteenth century. Reorganisation was still in full swing and was penetrating parts of the country that had remained stagnant. In fact, the new forms of agriculture were often labour-intensive and the number of waged employees increased even as smaller farms and subtenancies were being absorbed by the larger. But the rates of natural increase were now well over ten per cent per decade and jobs newly created could not match the threatened increase of population.[19] In any case many of the servants finding employment were unmarried men, whose place on the farm would disappear when they married, probably in their mid-twenties. The growth of population was overflowing the rural opportunities.

Nor is it simply a matter of numbers seeking and failing to obtain employment or land. The sense of insecure and falling status pervaded groups that were challenged even marginally by reorganisation. It is often among such people, particularly of the small tenant class, that we find the emigrants carefully planning their move and providing themselves with needed funds.[20] Disposal of stock could well be the basis of ordered movement. Acting thus, lesser farmers made up at least a substantial proportion of Lowland emigrants in the years of the nineteenth century that were free of catastrophe.

By the middle of the nineteenth century the agrarian system of the Lowlands had settled in a mould that was not to be substantially disturbed until the twentieth century. But this did not remove the pressure on sections of the farm population. From around mid-century employment on farms began to fall and after 1870 declining grain prices turned farmers' thoughts to less intensive, more pastoral forms of agriculture. There began a marked and irreversible trend of decline in rural population although not all types of farm worker were equally affected.

In sum, migration out of rural parishes in the Lowlands removed only a part of the natural increase until the middle of the nineteenth century. Then growth limited by some net outmigration turned to actual decline.[21] The turning point came at different times in particular parishes but in the end decrease of population became the common continuing experience of almost all purely rural areas.

Pressure on the rural population, and particularly on the holders of land in Scotland set against plenty of land promised cheap in the Americas seemed likely to result in massive migration across the Atlantic and indeed much of the emigration of the nineteenth century conforms to this model. But the forces at work were vastly more complicated than the simple pull of cheap land on the land-hungry. The bulk of the migrants from the rural Lowlands and at last from the southern part of the western Highlands moved, not overseas, but to nearby towns.[22] It is evident that there were strong local forces pulling on the country people as well as heavy pressures driving them on. Indeed the movement of farm wages and the comparatively low incidence of unemployment among farm servants who remained in the rural community suggest the strength of these forces of attraction.[23] Cost would sometimes be the determinant of the migrants' destinations. The student of emigration must take good note of the pull to alternative, and in some ways easier, destinations than overseas.

Since cost was so important a consideration for the intending emigrant we might expect some differentiation in the composition of the migrant streams as they turned to domestic or to overseas destinations. The poorer were forced to accept town conditions while those with some means had at least the possibility of reaching the New World. The distinction was by no means absolute or invariable. But it is clear that when no catastrophe or official interference had disturbed the recurring pattern, emigrant parties from both the Highlands and the Lowlands were composed largely of those with some capital, although not all such migrants would move out of the country.[24] In fact, the balance was continually shifting between the numbers respectively of internal migrants and of emigrants. Consequently, the scale of emigration must be seen as partly dependent on general economic conditions, and particularly on employment conditions in the towns, as well as on prospects overseas.

We must see emigration as but part of a total pattern of migration in which the elements interact. It is true that the forces of demography and of sectional development created an unremitting flow of emigrants. But it was by no means a steady flow. Some of the changes from year to year were erratic and inexplicable; or they might be due to sudden changes of economic condition. But it evident also that the economic systems which encased the restless individuals of the migrant body developed through slower rhythms which altered in a more patterned and predictable way both the pressure to move and the relative attractiveness of specific destinations. Cycles of development are an obvious fact of economic life through the nineteenth and much of the twentieth centuries. How far did they penetrate the emigration process and can we proceed to assign economic causes both temporary and patterned to the ups and downs of the emigrant total?

Some clues may be found in the figures for net loss of population from the country as a whole. These may be calculated from the census reports for the decades from 1861 onwards. The figures, of course, include movements between Scotland and the other parts of the UK and, since the balance between Scotland and the remainder of the UK was normally one of loss, they are bound to overstate the scale of net emigration. Numbers crossing the land boundary and moving into Ireland might amount sometimes to almost half of all outmigrants.[25] Since the relationships between movements within the UK and departures for overseas were by no means steady, the calculations for net loss overall may somewhat distort the figures for fluctuation in net emigration. However, such was the normal weight of emigration it is likely that the fluctuations that we will see emerging are a reflection of net losses overseas, although they cannot be taken as entirely accurate.

A mere glance at the figures for net outmigration in the decades since 1861 suggests a very definite regularity. There is an alternation between decades of high and of comparatively low loss of population, although loss never turns to gain.[26] This regularity extends over five decades. Moreover, the differences between high and low points are very wide. This measure is of course, rigidly held to the timings of the decennial census. They can indicate but roughly the deeper rhythms of economic life. However they can be fitted, if crudely, to at least one scheme of economic development.

The best explanation of differences between adjacent decades seems to run in terms of cyclical processes within the various Atlantic economies. But trade cycles as generally understood were each of shorter duration than a decade and can in themselves scarcely explain differences between successive decades. The cycle called in explanation must be something less obvious than the procession of crises that dot the nineteenth century. Longer cycles, however, can be brought into view by smoothing fluctuations of the shorter that are so obvious in the raw figures. The smoothing seems to reveal a succession of cycles lasting each for a period of around twenty years. They run through both the American and the British economies. (Canada's experience,

in this respect, conforms to the pattern of development in the USA.)
But, significantly, the cycles on the two sides of the Atlantic stand
in an inverse relationship. Periods of secular stagnation in Britain are
associated with periods of prosperity in the USA and Canada.[27]

These inverse relationships work on the migration totals by forces
coming from both sides of the Atlantic. Prosperity in the USA attracts
immigrants to that country while accompanying depressed conditions in
Britain turn thoughts there to emigration. Conversely, British prosperity
improves job prospects at home and attracts migrants to British towns
while the overseas prospect fails somewhat in attraction. Thus, there
emerge contrasting periods favourable, at the one time, to emigration,
at the other to growth at home and to slowing of the emigrant stream.

These are conclusions based on the processing of statistics drawing
on various economic indicators. The figures for gross emigration may
be regarded as part of the evidence. More importantly from our point
of view they can also be seen as the result of the behaviour of the
economies as traced by the other variables.

Here we must take care about some of the steps in the argument. In
the first place: how well does Scotland conform to the movements in
the British economy considered as a single entity? After all, Highland
emigration makes up a significant proportion of the Scottish total
especially before 1860 and was not likely to move strictly in time with
that generated by the parts of the economy more closely involved with
industry. The extent of this divergence may well have altered through
time. Brinley Thomas, who developed the theory of long cycles moving
in inverse phases, argues that a change of structure in the America
economy in the late 1860s altered the balance of forces dictating the
movement of population. In the earlier period push elements originating
in demographic fluctuations resulted in surges of emigration. The
demographic history of the Highlands might fit in with such a grading
of causes but would only accidentally fit into a scheme where changing
birth-rates were the deciding factor. Altogether there seems little
evidence to allow us to fit the cyclical model to the period up to 1861.

In the latter decades of the nineteenth century, Thomas argues,
the pull from America becomes decisive in determining the scale
of immigration into the country and, therefore, of emigration from
Europe. The non-industrial character of the Highland sector then
becomes irrelevant. We can begin to fit Scotland securely into the
interpenetrating development influences on the two sides of the Atlantic.
The alternation of decades of high and of low emigration from the
country fits in with the scheme of long cycles as far as restriction to
the use of census dates as measuring points allows.

Statistical processing can, of course, become manipulative and slanted towards certain conclusions and is full of pitfalls as regards timing and cause. There may well be criticisms of Thomas's choice of method. However, certain conclusions are scarcely deniable from his massive collection of evidence. One is that migration, of whatever sort, is much affected by developments in other economic sectors, such as investment and exploitation of particular industrial techniques. Second, regular developments within the American economic system are in some way related to converse movements in Britain. Scale of investment, export and import of capital, commodity exports and imports in the two systems interact and throw off influences that bear upon migration. And, third, there is an undoubted connection between emigration from Britain and migration within the country. This last relationship is more firmly established for England and Wales than for Scotland. But there is evidence of some strength for Scotland. It shows in a comparison between rates of growth in the Glasgow conurbation and rates of national outmigration. The decades of relatively low outmigration were also decades of high urban gain within Scotland, and vice versa.[28] A certain proportion of migrants would choose, according to the circumstances of the time, between moving to towns and emigrating overseas. And these decisions had to be taken within the framework of the countervailing movements of the British and the American economies.

The evidence that the long cycles were a strong influence on emigration from Scotland before 1860 is tenuous. But that there was cyclical influence in the earlier period is beyond doubt. Regular fluctuations were a feature of the British economy throughout the nineteenth and into the twentieth centuries. These fluctuations ran to peaks and troughs in fairly regular time sequences but the development from peak to trough and back to peak took generally less than ten years. How, then, if at all, did these cycles affect emigration?

The effect on emigration of such short-term changes in economic conditions can be argued from first principles but with ambiguous results. The basic question must be: is large-scale emigration more likely in time of prosperity or in time of depression? A case can be made out for either proposition. The coincidence of bad times with heavy emigration we have seen in the longer cycles may not apply for the shorter. In the former case it might be prosperity in America that helped emigration out of a Britain in a phase of relatively long-term stagnation. In the case of the shorter, 'ten-year' cycle America and Britain move in phase with one another. Booms and slumps tend to occur at the same time on the two sides of the Atlantic.[29] Emigration from Britain might well be favoured by the common prosperity not only because the pulling power of America was great but also because funds would be abundant in all countries to aid the emigrant. On the other hand, depression at home supplied a particular spur to emigration because it could be seen as an escape from hard conditions even though times might be almost as hard in America.

Anecdotal evidence was generally in favour of the view that depression brought increased emigration. There is some more sophisticated and thoroughly worked confirmation of this view. Rostow, Gayer and Schwarz in their massive work on British business cycles establish from a whole swathe of economic indicators a scheme of reference cycles which sum up the interweaving of specific series to give a composite view of the behaviour of the whole economy. When the figures for British emigration are fitted to these reference cycles it is found that there is a strong correlation between the trough turning points of the cycles and short-term peaks.[30] These calculations relate only to the period up to 1850. They cannot be carried confidently into the time when the longer cycles are seen to be exercising strong influence. And they relate to Britain as a whole. They can only be regarded as faintly suggestive of conditions in Scotland. Much more detailed study is required before anything but tenuous generalisation can be used to describe the relation between trade cycles and emigration in the distinctive Scottish economy.

It can scarcely be doubted that recurring trade cycles forced the emigration totals from year to year into a semblance of regular and repeated pattern. Such regularity fits in with the idea of continuity, of the sustaining effects of underlying causes. Running through it all we find a particular type of emigrant—that is, the individual with the power and will to move himself and his family. It is people carefully planning to join earlier emigrants because of family and neighbourhood links who sustain the continuity. This is to be seen most clearly in the rural context, particularly in the earlier period, but the wider catchment of the later emigrants need not be regarded as introducing a fundamentally new type of emigrant, although the evidence for the later decades is more flimsy.

Thus it came about that for most of the nineteenth century emigration totals were sustained by annual complements drawn from groups who might be discontented but yet had the means to plan their moves on an individual basis. Mostly, they made for the nearest and best-known land of new settlement, North America. But on occasion and in particular circumstances the pattern of essentially individual striving was obliterated by masses captured by other systems of emigration. In particular, there were three situations in which larger schemes and pressures overtook the complicated interweaving of individual plans and efforts. First, there were the efforts made to alleviate the lot of the handloom weavers of west-central Scotland in the second quarter of the century; second the situation in the north-west Highlands deteriorated to a point where joint effort was required; and third the problems of finding a labour force from distant sources for the pastoral industry of Australia brought public aid to the emigrant.

One of the bitter results of the rush into a mechanised textile industry was the displacement and long-drawn-out agony of the handloom weavers who had held a proud position within the older industrial order. The problem concentrated mainly in the western areas of the central Lowlands but the suffering of the weavers and their families excited a more widely spread concern. One solution, it seemed, was emigration. The removal of suffering families in large numbers had to depend not only on the necessarily limited resources of the weavers themselves but also on the mobilisation of governmental and charitable aid. The chosen instrument for organising aid and effort was the emigration society. Numbers of these were formed in the 1820s, each consisting of a small group of intending emigrants. Some government aid was added to charitable collections and to the small resources of the weavers themselves. Some eighty societies were formed in the 1820s and they effected the movement of more than 2,000 persons to settlements in Canada where they received grants of land. Then, by the end of the decade the members had either emigrated or dispersed. In the 1840s the movement revived with the formation of a further fifty societies and the movement of at least some of their members. Whenever such emigrants departed and whatever their numbers they went in controlled fashion, moving as groups into settlements that had been prepared for them.[31]

The problems of the inhabitants of the north-west Highlands and Islands were much more lasting and much less tractable than those of the weavers and for long the device of emigration hung over the scene as a supposed, but unrealised remedy. This was an area with the most critical land shortage and the deepest rural poverty to be found anywhere in Britain. It was also an area where the people had played a major part in the founding of the American settlements of the eighteenth century and where, therefore, there were continuing links with relatively flourishing overseas communities with all that this might have been expected to mean for further emigration. Yet through the first four decades of the nineteenth century emigration was held back, in particular by two factors.

The chief sufferers were, of course, the mass of the people of the region. But, in general, they lacked the means and very often the will to engage for a journey overseas. Such emigration as took place was largely in the mode of Scottish emigration generally, consisting of the departure of small groups of such as could gather the means to finance themselves.[32] The help that came from earlier emigrants desiring to help members of their kin to an American settlement did not serve to bring about mass emigration.

Even landlords could not escape a wounding involvement with the problems of overpopulation. The condition of the people on their estates, struggling to live on tiny fragments of land, led many of the old aristocracy into debt and into large-scale selling of ancestral property. The outward face of overpopulation was the division of the arable land surface into minute portions. With the fall in prices that occurred after 1815 rents came to be paid only intermittently and arrears mounted.[33] And the arable land, even when turned to the growing of potatoes, could not provide full subsistence. The bill for imported grain was added to the demand for rent. Landlords suffered doubly from lack of income coming in from rent payments and from the need to sustain a dependent population in years of scarcity. The source of these mounting problems seemed to be the existence of a numerous class of poverty-stricken subtenants and squatters. Yet landlords did not generally operate by the direct encouragement or finance of outmigration. Movements of population were the outcome, the by-product, of the main drive of estate policies which was to clear land for sheep. Few of these removed from their holdings were given aid to emigrate.[34] Some were accommodated in small coastal holdings but most were allowed to drift. The clearance of some of the land merely added to the severity of the overcrowding on the recipient areas and in particular to the growth of rural slums housing poverty-stricken and landless groups.

The failure of the potato crop in 1846 and the onset of desperate famine worsened the problems of overpopulation while seeming to remove further the possibility of remedy by emigration. The last pools of ready capital among the people were drying up. In fact, famine served to concentrate the attention to long-existing Highland problems and brought some rescuing funds to the scene. In the first place, landlords now accepted that encouragement of outmigration must be an end in itself and not merely the by-product of other policies. Clearances continued, indeed in some places occurred on a scale that had seldom been known before. But they were now linked with a positive effort of organisation by which large numbers could be carried overseas. The money for this organisation came out of the pockets of landlords, some of them newcomers to the area, who had sources of funds outside the Highlands. Such determined action had been accompanied by some increase in the willingness of the Highland poor to accept emigration as a remedy for their pitiful condition. The emigrant ships could in part be filled by volunteers. But in other cases those willing to move were too few to fill the ships. In any case, the volunteers were not always of the type that landlords wished to force away from their estates. Emigrants were then found by a process that amounted to compulsion. Devastating clearances were effected so that, stripped of their livelihood, the victims could only take passage.[35]

Famine also brought other forms of aid. The Free Church of Scotland was quick to organise collections for relief, while committees in Edinburgh and Glasgow concentrated the philanthropic effort of their areas. Government, too, was forced into some effort at rescue. None of these bodies considered that the task was merely one of handing out the means of averting starvation. All looked to some form of social reconstruction. The emphasis was very much on the imposition of a discipline of work but it was also recognised that the pressure of population on resources must be diminished. Thus, the various bodies came together to form the Highlands and Islands Emigration Society. It was to Australia, where by the 1840s the pastoral economy was in rapid expansion, that the society directed its emigrant beneficiaries. The society in fact, drew on funds from three sources—from the Colonial Land and Emigration Commissioners (who disbursed the proceeds of sale of public land in Australia), from the Destitution Committees of Edinburgh and Glasgow, and from landlords. These last could obtain a passage for each nominee from among their tenantry at the cost of £1.[36] Conditions were stretched to allow the selection of the poorest for the long and expensive passage and landlords found this a means by which, with relatively little expense, they could clear their lands of unwanted subtenants and squatters. But it was only late in the famine period that this opportunity arose.

Altogether the events and efforts of the famine brought such a surge of emigration from the Highlands and Islands over the ten-year period following the first impact of potato failure that departures exceeded those of the previous four decades. One part of this flood consisted of an increase in numbers of emigrants of traditional type, that is families of the better-off crofters, who had the stock to sell and finance their moves.[37] But the funds that were gathered from outside and the compulsions that were exercised by some landowners deepened the social levels from which the bulk of the emigrants were now drawn. Possibly for the first time there were now great numbers of the very poorest among the passengers collected for the moves both to North

America and to Australia. For the first time, too, the machine of charity, with its focused social aim, was dragging along many who had been unwilling to leave the old form of life, percarious as it might have been.

The peopling of Australia also brought into being new forms of organisation in the emigrant trade. Novelty was enforced by the unavoidable expense of long-distance travel and also by the nature of the social order that was emerging in Australia with a consequent demand for a supply of landless labourers. By the 1820s the old convict settlement of Botany Bay was expanding in a burst of pastoral development into colonies of economic promise. The first boom was set on a tiny population base but the prospect of acquiring land was virtually limitless. Conditions were promising enough to draw in immigrants who were prepared to meet the high costs of the long voyage from Britain and also to buy substantial amounts of land.[38] But at this stage no aid was forthcoming from public sources and the British emigration, of which Scots formed a considerable part, was confined to people of some wealth. They might, however, take with them a following of servants and labourers. By the 1830s the prospect of expansion was such that it could not be realised by the inevitably small trickle of unaided immigrants. The cry for labour was answered by a scheme in which the sale of public land was linked by the grant of subsidies—or bounties—to immigrants who might be expected to work as labourers on the land. So, it was hoped, a balanced society would grow which would include both the capitalists to invest in the purchase and management of the land under the developing pastoral system and the landless labourers who would staff the vast sheep-runs.

For nearly two decades, until the discovery of gold brought in hundreds of fortune-seekers, aided immigration had to meet the population needs of the growing colonies. And even in the 1850s public schemes still had their place. In fact, a necessary key to understanding the way in which the use of the fund derived from land sales impinged upon the British public is to examine the system of selecting emigrants. There were two procedures for assigning bounties to individuals, giving possibly different results. First, choice might be made by the public agency, the Colonial Land and Emigration Commissioners; they were likely to bear in mind the function of emigration as a relief to distress in Britain as well as the needs of the developing colonies. In the other case, selection was made directly by colonial interests; then it was the fitness of applicants for a vigorous colonial life that determined decisions. On the whole, it was the second principle that prevailed, even though the bulk of Scottish emigrants departed under the auspices of the

Commissioners, for they proved less than whole-hearted about selecting those most in need.[39] With the Highlands and Islands Emigration Society it was another matter. Here the needs of the very poorest were paramount and numbers running into thousands of the most needy were shipped to Australia.

The course of Scottish emigration in its fluctuating growth was in part determined by forces and events but loosely connected—the dismantling of the old Highland social order, the aftermath of eighteenth-century war, the vigorous reorganisation of Lowland agriculture, the agony of the displaced handloom weavers, the accumulating pressure on the Highland crofters and cottars, the interlocking fortunes of British and American industry, land policies in North America. Yet emigration took a remarkably consistent form over the decades. It remained throughout largely a movement by individuals uncontrolled and largely unaided by governmental or more diffused social authority. Government and the socially influential had, it is true, a developing attitude to emigration. Until 1815 the main concern was to stop movement out of the country, but by the third decade of the nineteenth century emigration was being seen as a solution to pressing social problems. Yet action other than by individual families was half-hearted and discontinuous. Until the 1840s aid for emigrants came in small trickles and from time to time. One form of government help was in the settlement of ex-service men transported to America for military operations. After the Napoleonic Wars some experiments were made in the policy of 'shovelling out paupers' but the total funds made available were small and the duration of the schemes short. The bounty schemes for peopling Australia were more determined and more durable, but they did not greatly widen the social catchment beyond what was achieved by individual effort. In addition, a trickle of charitable aid was entrusted to the emigrant societies and there were occasional small-scale efforts by landlords to deal with their problems by supplying the means for emigration. But in total these efforts can have accounted for only a small proportion of the numbers leaving Scotland. After 1846, however, the application of larger sums to the solution of Highland problems were concerted and determined. By the use of funds collected through the Lowlands and by the disbursements of some of the more affluent landlords, together with greater involvement by the government, some thousands of the poorest were enabled, or in some cases forced, to leave the country. But this was an effort late in the day and confined to the ten-year period after 1846.

The lack both of large-scale planning and of outside aid tells much about the process of emigration and the composition of the emigrant parties. There was little planning in terms of groups any larger than the family or, at the most an association formed from neighbourhood or clan. The family, in fact, was the common unit of planning and it is a particular characteristic of Scottish emigration that families were held together. Emigrant parties would contain representatives from all age groups from the young to the elderly. The assembly of such groups was in the hands of individuals, heads of families, making their bargains with private shipping interests. Thus the typical emigrant emerges as a person of some means, independent in thought and action, or the member of the family of such a person. Emigration for such persons required sustained effort, a consciousness of purpose, and personal force to gather the necessary funds.

Yet the freedom to plan and to choose was necessarily constricted by the social forces that beat upon the individual. A wider perspective must bring in the deep-running causes that give some uniformity to the thousands of individual decisions. These causes we have already seen in action. They operated both within Scotland and within the receiving countries. In Scotland, the major forces were a growing population, a land at the limits of its cultivation and under tight social control, an industry with a demand for labour which grew in intermittent surges and left trails of unemployment in between. On the American and Australian sides, there was land in plenty but it was contained within a system with its own periods of advance and stagnation, periods in which funds abounded or became scarce, in which jobs were plentiful or hard to find. Nor could the land in the new countries ever be picked up without expense. As these social forces worked themselves out the potential emigrant was carried along by the surges of opportunity or held back by scarcity and pessimism. On the whole they worked towards the increase of numbers but only in very fluctuating patterns.

NOTES

1. M.W. Flinn (ed.), *Scottish Population History from the Seventeenth Century to the 1930s* (Cambridge, 1977), pp.446–7. From 1825 to 1853 official figures for emigration relate to departures from Scottish ports. From 1853 emigrants of Scottish birth are enumerated and in 1912 the criterion for inclusion was changed to the residence (of more than one year) in Scotland.

2. *Ibid.*, p.302.

3. M. Harper, *Emigration from North-East Scotland*, vol.1, *Willing Exiles* (Aberdeen, 1988), pp.40–1.

4. B. Bailyn, *Voyagers to the West* (London, 1986), pp.103, 137; J.M. Bumsted, *The People's Clearance: Highland Emigration to British North America, 1770–1815*

(Edinburgh, 1982), appendix B, pp.230–87; M.L. McLean, 'In the New Land a New Glengarry: Migration from the Scottish Highlands to Upper Canada, 1750–1820', unpublished PhD thesis, University of Edinburgh, 1982, p.186.

5. Bailyn, *Voyagers*, pp.399–503; Bumsted, *People's Clearance*, pp.55–80, 224–9; H.I. Cowan, *British Emigration to North America. The First Hundred Years* (Canada, 1961), pp.6, 20–7.

6. Bailyn, *Voyagers*, pp.586–8; Bumsted, *People's Clearance*, pp.67–9; Cowan, *British Emigration*, pp.3–17.

7. McLean, 'New Glengarry', *passim*.

8. J.M. Cameron, 'A Study of the Factors That Assisted and Directed Scottish Emigration to Upper Canada, 1815–1855', unpublished PhD thesis, University of Glasgow, 1970, pp.32, 88–105.

9. Cameron, 'Scottish emigration', p.441; M. Harper, 'Emigration from North-East Scotland, 1830–80', unpublished PhD thesis, University of Aberdeen, 1984, pp.382–6.

10. Harper, *Emigration from North-East Scotland*, I, pp.251–2.

11. *Ibid.*, I, pp.50–3.

12. *Ibid.*, I, pp.105–7.

13. *Ibid.*, I, pp.86–9.

14. *Ibid.*, I, pp.100–2.

15. *Ibid.*, I, p.39.

16. G. Donaldson, *The Scots Overseas* (London, 1966), pp.114–20.

17. R.S. Barclay and F. Fraser Darling, 'Population', in F. Fraser Darling (ed.), *West Highland Survey* (Oxford, 1956), pp.80–3.

18. M. Gray, 'Scottish emigration: the social impact of agrarian change in the rural Lowlands, 1775–1875', in *Perspectives in American History*, VII, 1974, p.103.

19. *Ibid.*, pp.145–74.

20. Harper, *Emigration from North-East Scotland*, I, p.156.

21. M. Gray, 'Migration in the rural Lowlands of Scotland', in T.M. Devine and D. Dickson, *Ireland and Scotland, 1600–1850* (Edinburgh, 1983), p.114; J.A.V. Collett, 'Population and employment', in W.A. Illsley (ed.), *Third Statistical Account. The County of Angus* (Arbroath, 1977), pp.49–59; K. Walton, 'Population', in H. Hamilton (ed.), *Third Statistical Account. County of Aberdeen* (Glasgow, 1960), pp.40–1; C.P. Snodgrass (ed.), *Third Statistical Account. The County of East Lothian* (Edinburgh, 1953), p.69.

22. Flinn, *Population History*, pp.472–5; M. Gray, *The Highland Economy, 1750–1850* (Edinburgh, 1957), pp.65–6; Gray, 'Scottish emigration', pp.95.

23. Gray, 'Scottish emigration', pp.154–6.

24. Bailyn, *Voyagers*, pp.196, 597; Bumsted, *People's Clearance*, pp.74, 78, 80; Cameron, 'Scottish emigration', pp.541, 550; T.M. Devine, *The Great Highland Famine* (Edinburgh, 1988), pp.20–1, 199; Harper, *Emigration from North-East Scotland*, I, pp.156, 182–3; McLean, 'New Glengarry', pp.185, 212.

25. Flinn, *Population History*, p.442.

26. *Ibid.*, p.441.

27. B. Thomas, *Migration and Economic Growth* (Cambridge, 1973), pp.86–90, 109–13.

28. A.K. Cairncross, *Home and Foreign Investment* (Cambridge, 1953), p.23.

29. R.S. Sayers, *A History of Economic Change in England, 1880–1939* (Oxford, 1967), p.43.

30. A.D. Gayer, W.W. Rostow and A.J. Schwarz, *The Growth and Fluctuation of the British Economy, 1790–1850*, 2 vols. (Oxford, 1953), II, p.951.

31. Cameron, 'Scottish Emigration', pp.32, 88–105.

32. Bumsted, *People's Clearance*, pp.74, 78, 80; Devine, *Highland Famine*, pp.20–1, 199; McLean, 'New Glengarry', pp.185, 212.

33. Devine, *Highland Famine*, p.25.

34. Cameron, 'Scottish emigration', p.299; Devine, *Highland Famine*; E. Richards, *A History of the Highland Clearances*, vol.2, *Emigration, Protest, Reasons* (London, 1982), pp.241–4.

35. Cameron, 'Scottish emigration', pp.345–79; Devine, *Highland Famine*, pp.212–23; Richards, *Highland Clearances*, II, pp.241–4.

36. Devine, *Highland Famine*, p.261.

37. *Ibid.*, p.200.

38. D.S. Macmillan, *Scotland and Australia, 1788–1850* (Oxford, 1967), pp.79–103.

39. Macmillan, *Scotland and Australia*, pp.271–98, 303.

3

The Politics of Emigration: Scotland and Assisted Emigration to Upper Canada, 1815–26

Michael E. Vance

In August 1820 Mr Jamieson, a Paisley provost, described the membership of the Paisley Townhead Emigration Society in the following manner:

> they are Industrious Tradesmen . . . [and] . . . Their object in leaving the country is solely with a view of bettering their condition in life and in no respect connected with any pursuits of a political nature.[1]

The majority of scholars studying nineteenth-century emigration would concur with Jamieson's appraisal. Like the Paisley provost, most twentieth-century investigators see the exodus across the Atlantic as the product of economic forces. More specifically, prevailing interpretations argue that periods of severe economic depression in conjunction with high population growth rates 'pushed' emigrants from their homelands. On the other hand, economic opportunity, often in the form of cheap or gratis land, 'pulled' individuals across the oceans.[2]

While the importance of economic and demographic conditions in the emigration process cannot be denied, it is necessary to consider the political context if the motives for promoting or desiring emigration in early nineteenth-century Scotland are to be fully understood. This chapter will demonstrate that political considerations were particularly important in the early government-assisted emigrations conducted from Scotland to Upper Canada. Three different levels of political relationship will be examined. The investigation will begin with a brief discussion of the ministerial decision to provide aid to emigrants. The focus will then shift to the particular political concerns of the local Scottish élite in the sending districts. Finally, the chapter will conclude with an evaluation of the role which popular politics played in shaping emigrant attitudes and behaviour.

I

Between 1815 and 1821 approximately 4,000 individuals received government assistance in order to emigrate to the Bathurst district of the Ottawa valley in Upper Canada. Although this figure represented only a fraction of the estimated 91,000 who left the United Kingdom for British North America over the same period, government involvement with emigration on this scale was unprecedented.[3] The Addington administration had interfered with the emigration process in 1803 by introducing the first Passenger Acts but this legislation was designed to curtail emigration not aid it.[4] The decision to reverse earlier policy, and initiate government support for emigration, was taken by Lord Liverpool's Cabinet at the urging of the Earl Bathurst.

As Secretary of State for the Colonies, Bathurst believed that the promotion of assisted emigration to British North America was necessary in order to strengthen Britain's position on the continent. The attempted American invasion of 1812 had highlighted the precarious British hold on Upper Canada and Bathurst hoped that by settling emigrants in strategic areas the colony would be better equipped to deal with any future attack from the United States. It had also become clear that thousands of individuals, particularly in Ulster, were planning transatlantic journeys once the Napoleonic War ended. If the government failed to direct emigration to British North America, it was very likely that settlers would proceed to the United States and thus strengthen a potential enemy.[5]

This preoccupation with imperial defence underlay all early Colonial Department initiatives in favour of government-assisted emigration. In 1817, shortly after the first emigrants were settled in Upper Canada, Bathurst approached Lord Charles Somerset, governor of the Cape Colony, with a similar proposal. The Colonial Secretary believed that British settlers, placed on that colony's frontiers, would act as an effective deterrent to native African incursions and thus strengthen British control. Despite the governor's keen interest, the scheme was not undertaken until 1819.[6]

Surprisingly, imperial concerns no longer dominated official discussion of emigration once the government-assisted scheme to the Cape was under way. Government members had become concerned with the desirability of continuing assisted emigration as a method of poor relief rather than bolstering the defences of the empire. In fact, the first parliamentary committee on emigration, which met in 1826, hardly concerned itself with imperial questions—despite hearing the testimony of colonial administrators from Upper Canada, the Cape Colony and New South Wales. A great deal of attention was, however, given to the proposals of Wilmot Horton, the new Colonial Department Under Secretary, who advocated systematic colonisation as a method of relieving the distress in Britain's towns and cities. In the end the committee rejected the idea, arguing that the restriction of Irish emigration to Manchester, Liverpool, London and Glasgow would be more effective.[7] Nevertheless, the deliberations of the committee demonstrate the extent to which the issue of government-assisted emigration had been divorced from the context of imperial policy.

This development can best be explained by the fact that debate on the issue had been quickly extended from inside the Colonial Department to the regions supplying the emigrants. This was particularly true in Scotland where assisted emigration soon featured in the responses of the landed and commercial élite towards the economic and political crises which materialised at the end of the war.

II

At the turn of the century many members of the Scottish élite had been hostile towards emigration. Despite the publication of Malthus's *Essay on Population*, there was a persistent belief that emigration would weaken the strength of the nation. Many continued to hold to the eighteenth-century notion that a county's strength lay in its population and leading Scotsmen such as Lord Glengarry, the Earl of Breadalbane and Charles Hope, the Lord Advocate for Scotland, had warmly supported Addington's Passenger Acts. One Scots gentleman suggested that without such measures Britain would have to recruit her future armies from Prince Edward Island.[8]

According to John Campbell, the Edinburgh lawyer appointed by Bathurst as the government agent for the 1815 scheme, hostility towards emigration persisted among several Highland landowners. He was able, however, through personal visits to many magnates, including the Earl of Breadalbane and Lord MacDonald, to assure them that the government merely intended to redirect to Upper Canada emigrants already proceeding to the United States, and were not intent on further depopulation of their estates. Campbell claimed that after his private meetings the scheme was accepted by most 'intelligent men as a wise policy' and that the only reservation expressed by the large landowners was that the proposed emigrations had been 'too abrupt to give time for future arrangements on [their] estates'.[9]

The conversion of the Highland magnates was not entirely due to Campbell's persuasive abilities. In the aftermath of the war, several landowners did indeed find themselves with 'redundant populations'. During the conflict, the Earl of Breadalbane had taken advantage of the large number of tenants in military service by consolidating small holdings into larger farms. On his Loch Tay estate traditional forms of communal agriculture designed to support the trade in black cattle, and subsistence for the inhabitants, were replaced by a system of large farms designed to produce the maximum number of sheep. Many displaced tenants were subsequently resettled in crofter towns. It soon became apparent, however, that this new agricultural system, which employed former tenants as agricultural labourers, was less labour-intensive and required fewer hands.[10] Elsewhere in the Highlands, particularly in the western Isles, the trend had been in the opposite direction. Large holdings were subdivided in order to provide crofts for returning soldiers and a rapidly increasing population. This fragmentation placed greater demands on the limited arable land at a time when secondary industries, such as kelping, were in dramatic decline.[11] As a consequence, west Highland magnates, such as Lord Glengarry, along with improving landlords, like the Earl of Breadalbane, had good reason for being less hostile to the idea of at least some of their tenants being assisted to Canada in 1815.[12]

Nevertheless, when embarkation records revealed that emigration was not to be limited to a few hundred Highland tenants, but was spreading to the rest of Scotland, concerns were expressed. In 1817, a correspondent with the *Dumfries-Galloway Courier* deplored the renewed 'spirit of emigration', citing the departure of over 500 emigrants from Dumfries, and held the government-assisted scheme responsible.[13] The *Scotsman* also regretted the increase in emigration, but for the implied criticism of the British political system rather than the permanent loss of population. The Whiggish *Scotsman* linked the increased interest in emigration with the Liverpool administration's refusal to adopt electoral reform, claiming that:

> political feelings induce many to emigrate, who have no reason to complain of their worldly circumstances. [A] great deal of discontent (and well-grounded discontent too) finds its escape through this channel.[14]

Although other Scottish newspapers were certainly pessimistic in their appraisal of the opportunities which emigration could afford, the *Scotsman*'s attempt to turn emigration into an expressly political issue was not emulated.[15]

Despite these early protests, by 1820 opposition had faded and Scottish Whigs and Tories had in fact achieved a remarkable consensus in favour of further emigration. The MPs for the Lowland constituencies of Glasgow, Lanarkshire and Renfrewshire all presented arguments to the Commons calling for renewed government-assisted schemes from Scotland[16] and the Scottish press had reached a similar unanimity. Even the *Scotsman* no longer deplored emigration but argued, after Malthus, that migration was the 'natural remedy for a redundant population'.

The paper's change of heart was apparently due to the further deterioration of Scotland's economy. The post-war depression was at its worst point yet and thousands were out of work, particularly in the weaving districts of the west of Scotland. The editors argued that:

> Though the emigration, to afford any sensible relief to the whole country, would require to be upon an extensive scale, it is obvious that even upon the smallest scale it is beneficial. If six labourers are withdrawn from a small village, or fifty from a country town, the situation of either will be improved.[17]

The politicians professed to be more concerned with relieving the distressed in their constituencies than implementing emigration as a long-term solution to Britain's economic woes. Their interest was based on immediate local problems, for which they desired short-term solutions. Assisted emigration would be one method of relieving the west of Scotland's unemployed artisans, just as other 'temporary' measures such as canal-digging and road-building had sought to do.[18]

Artisan-led emigration societies had been forming in Glasgow and Lanarkshire since the spring of 1819, calling for assistance to emigrate to British North America. Late in April 1820, Lord Archibald Hamilton, the Whig Member for Lanarkshire, brought together other local MPs and leading members of the local landed élite in order to co-ordinate and supervise the activities of the various emigration societies. A large number of the members of his Glasgow Committee on Emigration were drawn from his own circle. Robert Brown, factor for the Duke of Hamilton, took a leading role as did John Maxwell the Whig MP for Renfrewshire. These men were joined by Colonel Mure, the Vice-Lieutenant of Renfrewshire and close correspondent with the Lord Archibald's brother, the Duke of Hamilton. Nevertheless, the Glasgow Committee was not the exclusive preserve of Hamilton and his associates. The ultra-Tory cotton manufacturer Kirkman Finlay, along with several of his conservative mercantile colleagues in Glasgow, had been persuaded to join the group. Together Finlay and Hamilton pleaded the case for further assisted emigration in the House of Commons and, as a member of the governing party, Finlay was able to convince the administration to listen to Hamilton's arguments. In May 1820, as a consequence of their concerted efforts, the Cabinet reluctantly agreed to provide assistance for 1,100 members of the emigration societies who wished to proceed to Upper Canada.[19]

The Liverpool administration had been horrified by the costs of the first scheme and were hesitant, particularly as it was clear that emigrants were proceeding to Upper Canada on their own accord. The government were much more interested in encouraging emigration to the less popular Cape Colony.[20] The success of Hamilton and Finlay in persuading them to reconsider would appear to have been a consequence of their local concerns overriding party animosity. Hamilton was one of the Whigs' leading spokesmen and a constant advocate for electoral reform, while Finlay was a stalwart government supporter who had been rewarded with the pocket borough of Malmesbury when he lost his Glasgow seat in 1817.[21] It had been the co-operation of these two unlikely allies which had persuaded the government to reconsider their stand.

According to Robert Lamond, the secretary of the Glasgow Committee on Emigration, the basis for this remarkable co-operative effort between political opponents was a shared sense of philanthropy. In his *Narrative of the Rise and Progress of Emigration from Lanark and Renfrewshire . . .*, published in 1821, after the completion of two seasons of government assistance to the emigration societies, Lamond argued that a great debt was owed by the emigrants to the charitable dispossession of the committee members and that one day their activities would 'find a place in the annals of Britain'.[22] Such a reading, however, glossed over differing political considerations which motivated both Lord Archibald Hamilton and Kirkman Finlay and masked the central basis for their co-operation—a shared fear of radical activity among the west of Scotland's distressed.

Hamilton's advocacy of assisted emigration must, however, first be seen in the context of both his parliamentary career and the local concerns of his constituency.[23] As a leading Whig, he had been a constant critic of Lord Liverpool's Tory adminstration and throughout the post-war period had continually deplored the government efforts to combat radicalism. According to Hamilton, the increased disaffection among the lower orders was not due to the activities of provocateurs but to the widespread distress which had characterized the years up to 1820. He made frequent calls for a parliamentary enquiry into the distressed conditions of the west of Scotland and championed the cause of those arrested in Glasgow under the suspension of habeas corpus.[24] Immediately after the 'Radical War', in April 1820, he suggested that the government ministers:

had ascribed a larger portion of the disturbances to disaffection than to distress, and had applied force to quell disturbances which would have been more effectually suppressed by furnishing the means of subsistence.[25]

Lord Archibald's advocacy of assisted emigration not only enabled him to criticise the government's handling of the crisis, but also allowed him to offer the gentlemen of his own constituency a solution to what appeared to be an insoluble problem of artisan unemployment and distress. Hamilton was aware that other methods employed by Lanarkshire's heritors, during the severe depression in the winter of 1819–20, had proved inadequate.

During the summer of 1819 many of the county's unemployed had been occupied in the construction of roadworks and Robert Brown believed that further turnpikes should be constructed the following autumn, claiming that it was more sensible 'to *employ* our people than *fight* them'. However, Lanarkshire's roadwork projects, as with neighbouring Renfrewshire's canal-digging efforts, were only able to employ a fraction of the unemployed during the winter of 1819–20. All of the public work projects had been hampered by the refusal of the local landowners to assess themselves for the necessary funds.[26]

Lanarkshire's heritors were fearful of creating a dependent poor, which they believed was the necessary result of establishing English-style assessments.[27] As a consequence, they attempted to shift responsibility for the region's distressed to the central government. In December 1819, the Duke of Hamilton forwarded a request from the 'Gentlemen of Lanarkshire to the Treasury Board' requesting government assistance for the region's inhabitants.[28] In return for his pains he received a rebuke from Lord Liverpool which suggested that his efforts might be better spent on correcting the defects of the Scottish Poor Law:

> Your grace does not seem to be aware that the government of the country has no fund at its disposal for the relief of the distress of the poor . . . the people of England provide for their poor by local assessment, and . . . it never could be expected in reason or justice that they should be called upon gratuitously to provide for the poor of the other parts of the United Kingdom (where no assessment exists) in addition to their own.[29]

While this debate between Westminster and Lanarkshire's landed élite raged, the County Meetings called to deal with distress began to receive petitions from artisan societies asking for aid to emigrate to British North America. As a result, requests for sums to facilitate emigration were added to appeals to the Treasury since, in the heritors' view, emigration was a national matter. The Treasury did not agree and refused their appeals.[30] Under no circumstances were Lanarkshire's élite prepared to foot the bill for assisted emigration themselves and the idea was dropped until May 1820 when Lord Archibald and his Glasgow Committee on Emigration revived it.

In taking up the cause of assisted emigration, Hamilton added his voice to those from his constituency calling for aid from the central government. Indirectly, he also endorsed their stand on the Scottish Poor Law.[31] Nevertheless, by May, Hamilton was also aware that the overriding concern of Lanarkshire's élite was no longer the assessment issue but the volatile political situation caused by their inability, or unwillingness, to deal with the widespread distress. Although the Radical War had been suppressed, Lord Archibald believed that the danger still persisted. Given that the government refused to provide aid to the distressed in the west of Scotland, Hamilton argued that assisted emigration was the best method of attaining 'the ultimate object which ought to be kept in view—the suppression of the present disturbance in Scotland'.[32]

Lord Archibald Hamilton's advocacy of assisted emigration was, therefore, motivated by Whig political opportunism, and necessitated by the local position on poor relief. Ultimately, though, it was the fear of a further radical insurrection which induced him to support the assisted scheme. A fear which Kirkman Finlay shared.

It is clear that the two men had few other common concerns. Unlike Hamilton, Finlay had heartily supported the government's repressive measures to combat radicalism.[33] He had been preoccupied with monitoring artisan radical agitation, particularly among the weavers, since at least 1812, when he had served as Glasgow's provost. The activities of workers' organisations within his own cotton mills had heightened Finlay's awareness of potential trouble and he had been intimately involved in breaking the organisation behind the 1812 weavers' strike. In Finlay's estimation, workers' combinations and treason were largely inseparable and he sought information on as many groups as possible.[34] He was particularly concerned with individuals 'who under pretence of National Distress . . . and . . . Parliamentary Reform, are engaged daily in intruding their connections and generating every species of mischief'.[35]

By 1819, Finlay had become much more anxious as a consequence of the widening depression in the weaving trade and increased radical activity in the wake of the 'Peterloo Massacre'. As one of the leading citizens of Glasgow, Finlay had been involved in raising subscriptions for poor relief and, in the summer of 1819, helped organise the public work project for unemployed weavers on Glasgow Green. Instead of relieving the tension, by the autumn of that year he saw the work schemes themselves as sources of potential trouble. In a letter to the Home Secretary he expressed the belief that the agitation exhibiting itself in Glasgow 'may be partly be owing to the assembling of the workers in bodies for the purpose of affording them employment'.[36]

Given Finlay's preoccupation with the political activities of weavers' groups up to the spring of 1820, it is hardly surprising that he became concerned with the Glasgow emigration societies. The original Glasgow societies recruited their members from Bridgeton and Calton—the same areas which had provided the support for the 1812 weavers' strike and had been the scene for several demonstrations and secret meetings subsequently.[37] Any group, whatever their purpose, organising in these districts would have attracted Finlay's attention.

Peterloo, the Cato Street conspiracy and the Radical War, all occurring over the year stretching from 1819 to 1820 and all involving artisans, particularly unemployed weavers, justified the fear of insurrection and made assisted emigration a more attractive idea. The two principal members of the Glasgow Committee on Emigration, Lord Archibald Hamilton and Kirkman Finlay, while opposed on most issues debated in the Commons during the winter of 1819–20, had independently come to the conclusion that assisted emigration was the best method of dealing with radicals in the west of Scotland. The *Glasgow Chronicle* suggested in the aftermath of the Radical War that emigration, 'would do more service in thinning the ranks of Radicalism than all the military array of the country' and Finlay, at least, would have agreed with their assertion that it was 'in the interest of all ranks to get rid of such persons as soon as possible.'[38]

Certainly, after the first vessels had departed, Finlay believed that the main benefit of the scheme had been its effect on encouraging more peaceful conditions in the west of Scotland:

> In my opinion [the scheme] has been attended with many important beneficial consequences here, and has contributed much, with other favourable circumstances, to restore that part of the Country to a state of perfect tranquility, if not entire satisfaction and contentment.[39]

The *Glasgow Herald*'s notices regarding the emigrant departures concurred with Finlay's appraisal of the effect on radical activity:

> The late disturbances in the west may have had no small share . . . in increasing the number of emigrants, many implicated in these

proceedings have quietly 'left their country for their country's good'—a determination, by the by, which, however excellent of its kind, some will be inclined to think would have been greatly improved if it had been a few months earlier.[40]

III

The conversion of Scotland's political élite from hostility to endorsement of assisted emigration, in order to combat popular radicalism, only partially explains the Liverpool administration's decision to proceed with further schemes after 1815. The parliamentary pressure exerted by the combined efforts of Finlay and Hamilton was far from inconsequential, but this alone does not account for the administration's decision. A crucial factor in the adoption of the second scheme in 1818, and the third scheme in 1820–1, was the pressure applied from below.

Colonial Department hesitation was demonstrated in less generous terms being offered to the second group of Scottish emigrants who left for Upper Canada in 1818. The department's decision not to advertise the scheme, and restrict participation to large groups who had independently approached the government, also meant that only a few hundred individuals from the Earl of Breadalbane's Loch Tay estate were aided.[41]

Bathurst was only persuaded to adopt this further limited assistance by the numerous petitions which he and John Campbell, the former government agent, continued to receive long after the completion of the first scheme. The particular petition which prompted Colonial Department aid to the Breadalbane emigrants came to Bathurst by a circuitous route. The eighty families who signed the original document had emulated the parliamentary reform movement by sending their petition to the Prince Regent. Although it would be erroneous to suggest that the use of such tactics made the Breadalbane emigrants popular radicals, their actions demonstrated that the initiative for the 1818 scheme came from the tenants and not from the factor, the earl, the government agent or the Colonial Department. In fact the petition caused a stir among Lord Breadalbane's associates and John Campbell, as the earl's 'man of business', was quick to denounce the signatories as malcontents. All the same, Lord Breadalbane soon resigned himself to the loss of another 300 tenants.[42]

Despite the success of the Breadalbane petitioners in encouraging further government assistance, popular pressure was most apparent in the activities of the west of Scotland's emigration societies. Their petitions began to arrive at the Colonial Department in the spring of 1819—long before Lord Archibald Hamilton formed his Glasgow Committee. The societies boasted artisan membership, primarily weaver, and were located in the western Lowlands with the highest concentrations appearing in Lanarkshire and Renfrewshire. The first group to contact Bathurst was the Bridgeton Transatlantic Society who sent a petition in July 1819 but by 1821 there were another thirty-six Scottish emigration societies in contact with the Colonial Department. The first societies were formed in the artisan areas of Glasgow—Calton, Anderston, Bridgeton and the Gorbals all had at least one group by the autumn of 1819—but the organisation quickly spread to the weaving centres of Lanarkshire and Renfrewshire, with Cambuslang and Paisley boasting some of the largest memberships.[43]

The exact origin of the emigration society concept is harder to trace. Artisans had been exposed to the 1815 assisted emigration scheme, though few actually participated, and small groups of Lowland weavers were petitioning for aid to emigrate as early as 1817. Many of the associations included the terms 'union', 'co-operation' and 'friendly' in their titles and some, such as the Glasgow Wrights' Emigration Society, made specific reference to their occupation. There can be little doubt that the organisation employed in the craft and friendly societies was adapted for use in these emigration societies. It is possible, then, to see these groups as a continuation of the self-protective trade guilds which had an extensive history in the west of Scotland; however, there is reason to believe that the contemporary political context exerted an important influence on these groups.[44]

In June 1819, the *Scots Magazine* reported that an association of Carlisle weavers were seeking aid to emigrate, but had reinforced their plea with a strike in which 3,000 took part, taking an oath 'not to return to their looms' until their demand for a rise in wages was met by their former employers.[45] Although the direct combination of industrial action with an appeal for assisted emigration did not occur in Scotland, a meeting of Glasgow weavers held on the Green during the same month did link the issues of ill-paid work and assisted emigration. A motion was passed resolving to petition the Prince Regent for the 'amelioration of their distress' and the means to transport themselves to 'His Majesty's Dominions in North America'.[46] Radical influence was also apparent at the Glasgow Green meeting. One critic in the crowd expressed surprise at the idea of petitioning parliament and the Prince Regent for assistance to emigrate:

> He thought it a hardship that men should be obliged to petition the
> very persons who existed by their industry to be transported from their
> native country . . . He moved, as an amendment to the resolutions,
> that there should be annual parliaments, universal suffrage, and a
> diminution of taxation . . . [and that] . . . the only persons who
> should emigrate to Canada were the borough members, sinecurists,
> and 150,000 of the clergy.[47]

A follow-up meeting on the Green was organised in September by
those interested in emigration and, again, the radical platform was
recited. Orators treated the gathering to a Scottish interpretation of
Peterloo and stressed the need to remain informed of developments
in radical politics:

> . . . the proceedings at Manchester were declared to have no parallel
> except the massacre at Glencoe . . . [and] . . . the meeting concluded
> with a resolution relative to the establishment of an independent
> newspaper; till the accomplishment of which . . . it was resolved to
> support Wooler's *Black Dwarf*, the Manchester *Observer*, the *Statesman*,
> and the Belfast *Irishman*.[48]

Glasgow's press noted the hardened radicals' aversion to emigration
and lampooned their intransigence, especially after the fiasco of the
Radical War.[49] All the same, the élite did fear radical influence on
the emigration societies, and the likelihood of those with radical views
having joined the groups does appear to have been high, given the
similarity of organisation and the areas of recruitment.[50]

In Lanarkshire, it is possible to identify at least one emigration
society leader who had been implicated in earlier artisan agitation.
Robert Beath, the secretary for the Kirkfieldbank Emigration Society,
had been arrested for 'Illegal Combination' in December 1812 as part
of a general assault against the weaver associations. As with many
others rounded up at that time, Beath was released without a trial but
his position as secretary of the local weavers' union strongly suggests
that he was indeed involved with the strike. Given his history of local
leadership, Beath must have appeared a natural choice for secretary
of the Kirkfieldbank Emigration Society when it formed early in
1820.[51]

Although he declined to depart with the emigrants at the last
minute in 1820, Robert Beath continued to play an important role
in petitioning for aid for the second season, corresponding directly
with the Colonial Secretary. His communication provided a less than
deferential critique of the scheme:

Owing to the Depression of Trade it is impossible for us to avail ourselves of the Grand offer which government made us. Instead of relieving the Distresses of the lower Classes it had the reverse effect—as the Grant is only given to those who can transport themselves across the Atlantic we have used every lawful means in order to obtain our Desired object but without effect.[52]

The inability to gain redress through legal means would have been familiar to one who had experienced the disappointment of the weavers' strike, but it is likely that Beath's frustration was shared by members of his society. That the Kirkfieldbank Society was a well politicised group was demonstrated by one of their number upon arrival in Upper Canada. The emigrant found it remarkable that since the departure from Scotland 'Politics have never been spoken of', but argued that this was due to the fact that the settlers' time was 'taken up with their own affairs'.[53]

The records are not sufficiently complete to assess the degree to which radical political ideology influenced the members of the emigration societies; however, it is clear that they were conscious of the élite's fear of political instability and did address this in the petitioning process. The Paisley society believed it necessary to obtain the provost's endorsement, while the president of the Glasgow Canadian Society went further by distancing his group from the Radical War:

We hope by our united labour to subsist ourselves and familys [in Canada] as becomes a British Subject. We would further State that we have preserved our characters as Loyal British Subjects during the late insurrection and that we will continue so to do while under his Britannic Majesty.[54]

The president of the Alloa Emigration Society offered similar reassurances, and claimed that the members were all 'lovers of peace and soberness'. All the same, George Abercromby, in his certificate of character, stated that the society's emigration would help to alleviate a local situation which was 'not free of political contamination from Glasgow'.[55]

Although there is no conclusive evidence regarding the extent of popular radicalism among the emigration societies, it clear that the authors of the petitions were conscious of political developments and tried to manipulate these to their own advantage. This was equally true of national politics as it was of local affairs. The emigration societies raised the issue of assisted emigration with both the Colonial Department and local gentlemen. After these initial contacts they continued to apply pressure and monitor the results of their efforts.

The records of Lanarkshire County Meetings reveal that the heritors were receiving requests for aid to emigrate late in 1819. The inhabitants of Lesmahagow pointed to their inability to save themselves from 'starvation or becoming a burden on the parish' during the 'stagnation of trade' and requested the gentlemen of the county of Lanark to:

> . . . devise some means (either by applications to government or otherwise) of conveying us out to the Colony of Upper Canada and supporting us the[re] until such time as we could provide ourselves with the necessary means of subsistence.[56]

The distressed artisans also kept in direct contact with Lord Archibald Hamilton, as a letter from Charles Baillie, representing 'a few of the inhabitants of Hamilton', demonstrates. The 'wretchedness and misery' of their condition was described and Baillie asked Hamilton to exercise his 'influence and intervene to obtain relief':

> We . . . earnestly intreat that your Lordship will as early as possible, in the House of Parlement, propose some plan whereby we may be carr[i]ed out free of expense to some of the British settlements . . .[57]

In addition, members of the emigration societies keenly followed the Commons debates and attempted to influence the key figures. On 4 May 1820 Lord Archibald received a letter from William Granger, chairman of the Anderston and Rutherglen Society, responding to the views of the Chancellor of the Exchequer, Nicholas Vansittart, which he had read 'in the public prints'. Vansittart had stated that weavers were not required in Canada as the colony was suffering from the same depression in trade as the mother country but Granger assured Hamilton that:

> our view [has] never be[en] to carry on any branch of the cotton-manufacture there [in Upper Canada] but rather agriculture in such a degree as to gain an ordinary living for ourselves and our families . . . [as far as] Upper Canada being overstocked with people we may say with the edition of the *Glasgow Chronicle* that if Upper Canada be overstocked at all it is with trees.[58]

Hamilton, Finlay and John Maxwell, the MP for Renfrewshire, all received petitions from emigrant societies while the issue of assisted emigration was being debated in the Commons. There is evidence that the groups were co-ordinating these lobbying efforts. In his communication with Lord Archibald, William Granger referred to a letter sent by Kirkman Finlay to the Bridgeton Transatlantic Society intimating that there was shortly to be a conference with the ministry on the subject of emigration. As president of the Anderston and Rutherglen Emigration Society, Granger wished Hamilton success in this meeting and expressed his hope that 'Kirkman Finlay, the Lord Register and Maxwell of Pollock will assist you according to promise.'[59]

The petitioning campaign, to which the local élite, MPs and Colonial Department were subjected, demonstrates a high degree of organisation and sensitivity to the debates of the political élite among the emigration society members. Less obvious are the motives behind the artisans' push for further assisted emigration. The severe distress among the trades was frequently cited in society petitions, but the desire for emigration was not based solely on economic considerations. The artisans had clear expectations regarding life in the colonies.

The first of these was, indeed, that emigration would provide an escape from hardship in Scotland. As one former weaver, who emigrated with the assisted scheme, expressed it:

> I am very pleased to handle the axe, instead of the shuttle, and would not, for a good deal give up my present for my past employment. I have to struggle here for a year or two; I had to do so always at home . . . [but here] . . . I am relieved from taxation, rent and crushing ill-paid work.[60]

This was an intentional critique of the home society. Another assisted emigrant expressed the view more forcefully, stating that there were 'no landlords nor tax-gathers' in Upper Canada.[61]

Testimony given by Glasgow weavers before the 1826 Parliamentary Committee on Emigration highlighted a further aim of artisan emigrants. This was the desire to become 'independent'. The witnesses claimed that the object of the emigration society members was to obtain a grant of colonial land 'so as to become independent by their own industry'. They cited the example of a Mr Carswell, an 1821 society emigrant, who had settled in Ramsey Township in Upper Canada. Although Carswell was not accustomed to 'out-doors labour' and was fifteen pence in debt when he arrived on his land, he had 'with government assistance, and with his own perseverance . . . accumulated a good stock on his ground' and was 'almost independent'.[62]

This tale, with slight variations, was frequently repeated in the correspondence from the colony. One letter reprinted in Lamond's *Narrative* claimed that:

An industrious man can soon make himself independent. This is a country I can advise my nearest friends to come to, as there are so many advantages to be had in it . . . as for the weather, it was the best I ever saw . . . by no means so cold as some winters I have seen in Scotland.[63]

In 1827, after six years' residence in Upper Canada, John Gemmil wrote to his son in Glasgow with similar advice for his former tradesmen associates:

I am extremely grieved to hear of the distress that prevails in Scotland . . . if any of our friends are labouring under the present calamity, I would advise such of them to embrace the . . . opportunity of emigrating to this country . . . for in the course of a few years hard labour they would find themselves independent of their fellow creatures.[64]

The emphasis on 'independence' was not the product of novel Canadian circumstances. The Glasgow emigration societies had emphasised its importance in their petitions. Members of the Bridgeton Society claimed to 'have always supported themselves by honest industry' and had been conditioned to look upon 'independence as their chief pride'. It was the fear of indigence which led them to seek emigration as the 'only means of alleviating their distress and making them useful members of Society'.[65]

'Independence' was not, however, a neutral term. Although many heritors were pleased to see the removal of 'dependent' weavers from their parish rolls, others saw 'independence' among the lower orders as potentially threatening. In Canada the 'independent' behaviour exhibited by many emigrants was seen by some contemporaries as an affront, or even challenge, to the existing social order. John Howison, a gentleman traveller with pretensions, reported with obvious shock the lack of deference among the newly arrived immigrants:

Many of the emigrants I saw had been on shore a few hours only, during their passage between Montreal and Kingston, yet they had already acquired those absurd notions of independence and equality, which are so deeply engrafted in the minds of the lowest individuals of the American nation. On accosting two Scotsmen, whom I had seen at Montreal, instead of pulling off their hats, as they had invariably done before on similar occasions, they merely nodded to me with easy familiarity.[66]

A correspondent with the *Glasgow Chronicle* complained of more

serious political consequences of the immigrants' independent attitude
and the Upper Canadian form of government:

> A common labourer from Scotland is entitled to a lot of land.
> Whenever he finds he can subsist upon his farm, he becomes as
> high as the best in the Township, and has full liberty to speak
> at every meeting. It is nothing uncommon to see a poor Glasgow
> weaver, who came among us with scarce a stitch to cover his
> nakedness, strutting between the stumps of his trees as pompous
> as an Edinburgh Magistrate.[67]

A.C. Buchanan, the first government emigration agent in Canada,
was very concerned about the transference of political extremism from
Britain. In his *Emigration Practically Considered*, one of the first in a
long line of nineteenth-century emigrant advice books, he offered a
warning to his readers:

> I beseech you, if you have any party feeling at home, if you wish
> to promote your own prosperity, or that of your family,—wash your
> hands clean of it, ere you embark. Such characters are looked upon
> with suspicion in the colonies; and you could not possibly take with
> you a worse recommendation.[68]

There is further evidence suggesting that radical attitudes were transferred to the districts in the Ottawa valley settled by the members
of the Scottish emigration societies. The Bathurst District became
notorious for raucous poll days and the region developed into a centre
of radical and reform politics during the 1830s.[69] Nevertheless, more
work is necessary before firmer conclusions can be drawn as to the
extent of radical influence among the Scottish immigrants in the
Ottawa valley.

IV

Whether the topic is examined at the Colonial Department, County
Meeting or emigration society level, political concerns were significant
in shaping the government-assisted emigrations from Scotland. Despite
the claim of the Paisley provost, quoted at the beginning of this
paper, Scottish emigrants who participated in early nineteenth-century
government-assisted emigration were 'connected' with pursuits of a
political nature. This is true both in terms of their organisation and
their stated objectives in participating.

In fact, emigration from the west of Scotland is distinguished from that of the rest of the British Isles by the collective society approach and these groups continued to exert their influence well into the nineteenth century. As the decades progressed rules were devised and membership strictly controlled, in order to remove any taint of radicalism by excluding all but the upright tradesman. By the 1850s attention had shifted from Upper Canada to New South Wales, New Zealand and British Columbia. Nevertheless, these societies retained the structure and artisan character of the first groups formed between 1819 and 1821.[70]

Nowhere else in the British Isles did the idea of the emigration society enjoy such enthusiasm. It was this idea, born out of the popular political context of the west of Scotland, which was the most enduring legacy of the government-assisted emigrations.[71] The government failed to offer any further assistance for emigration to Upper Canada after 1826, and once the immediate political crisis of 1820 had faded the local élite lost interest, but the emigration societies persisted and continued to offer their members the possibility of obtaining 'independence' in the colonies well into the century.

NOTES

1. Jamieson to Earl Bathurst, 15 August 1820, Public Record Office (Kew Gardens, London) hereafter PRO, CO 384/6 f.1225.

2. H. Jerome, *Migration and Business Cycles* (New York, 1926), B. Thomas, *Migration and Economic Growth* (Cambridge, 1954), and C. Erickson, 'Emigration from the British Isles to the USA in 1831', *Population Studies*, no.35, 1981, are the most explicit general studies in this regard. While James M. Cameron 'A study of the Factors That Assisted and Directed Scottish Emigration to Upper Canada, 1815–55', unpublished PhD thesis, University of Glasgow, 1970; Dallas L. Jones 'The Background and Motives of Scottish Emigration to the United States of America in the Period 1815–1861', unpublished PhD thesis, University of Edinburgh, 1970, and David S. Macmillan, *Scotland and Australia 1788–1850; Emigration, Commerce and Investment* (Oxford, 1967), provide a similar analysis for Scottish emigration to Canada, the United States and Australia. Marjorie Harper's two-volume, *Emigration from North-East Scotland* (Aberdeen, 1988) is the most recent addition to this school.

3. See Appendix, pp.59–60.

4. There has been a protracted debate among historians over which of two concerns, the appalling conditions on board emigrant vessels or the potential loss of military manpower at a period of fragile European peace, inspired the Passenger Acts but there is no doubt that they were designed to restrict movement overseas. K.A Walpole, 'The humanitarian movement of the early

nineteenth century to remedy abuses on emigrant vessels to America', *Trans. Royal Hist. Soc.*, fourth series, XIV, 1931, pp.197–224; Oliver McDonagh, *A Pattern of Government Growth 1800–60* (London, 1961), ch.3; Barbara C. Murison, 'Poverty, Philanthropy and Emigration to British North America: Changing Attitudes in Scotland in the Early Nineteenth Century', *British Journal of Canadian Studies*, vol.2, no.2, 1987.

5. The government's own statistics demonstrated that earlier legislative restrictions placed on emigration had failed to stop the flow across the Atlantic and many now believed that if the process could not be halted at the very least it should be directed to where it would provide the most benefit to the mother country. Helen Cowan, *British Emigration to British North America* (Toronto, 1961); Hugh Johnston, *British Emigration Policy 1815–1830* (Oxford, 1972).

6. A small party of Scots led by Thomas Pringle, one-time editor of the *Scots Magazine*, participated in the scheme. Johnston, *British Emigration Policy*, pp.26–7, 41.

7. John G. Malcolm, *An enquiry into the expediency of emigration, as it respects the British North American* (London, 1828); Select Committee on Emigration from the United Kingdom, PP, 1826, (404), IV; Second Report of Select Committee on Emigration from the United Kingdom, PP, 1826–27, (88), V.

8. Charles Hope to the Duke of Portland, 2 June 1801, Scottish Record Office— hereafter SRO, RH 2/4/87 f.53; Lord Glengarry to Lord Pelham, 21 March 1802, SRO, RH 2/4/87; Eric Richards, *A History of the Highland Clearances*, vol.II: *Emigration, Protest, Reasons* (London, 1985), pp.201–27; Amicus, *Eight Letters on the Earl of Selkirk's Observations on the Present State of the Highlands of Scotland* (Edinburgh, 1806).

9. Campbell to the Colonial Office, 5 April 1815, PRO CO42/165 f.135.

10. M.E. Vance, 'Emigration and Scottish Society: The Background of Three Government Assisted Emigrations to Upper Canada, 1815–1821', unpublished PhD thesis, University of Guelph, 1990.

11. M. Gray, *The Highland Economy* (Edinburgh, 1957); R.S. Barclay and F. Fraser Darling, 'Population', in F. Fraser Darling (ed.), *West Highland Survey* (Oxford, 1956); T.M. Devine, *The Great Highland Famine: Hunger, Emigration and the Scottish Highlands in the Nineteenth Century* (Edinburgh, 1988).

12. Bathurst's original intention was to provide assisted passage to Upper Canada, implements for cultivation and 100 acres of Canadian wilderness to 2,000 individuals from Scotland, 2,000 from Ireland and a few hundred from England. The return of Napoleon from Elba, however, occupied the transport ships intended to take the emigrants to Quebec and the scheme was scaled down. In the end the majority of the 699 emigrants were recruited in Scotland with only a handful from elsewhere in the British Isles. Most of these did in fact depart from Highland districts controlled by Glengarry and Breadalbane. Johnston, *British Emigration Policy*, pp.20–3; M. McLean, '*Achd an Rhigh*: A Highland Response to the Assisted Emigration of 1815', in D.H. Akenson (ed.), *Canadian Papers in Rural History*, vol.5 (Gananoque, Ontario, 1986).

13. Reprinted in the *Glasgow Chronicle*, 15 June 1817.

14. *Scotsman*, 30 August 1817.

15. Vance, 'Emigration and Scottish Society', pp.127–8, 196–7.

16. *Hansard*, 16 December xli [1819]; *Hansard*, new series, 1 [1820] col.40–2.

17. *Scotsman*, 20 May 1820.

18. Vance, 'Emigration and Scottish Society', pp.143–4, 149–50, 153.

19. Robert Lamond to Lord Dalhousie, 27 August 1821, SRO, GD 45/3/64–85 f.217; Robert Lamond, *A Narrative of the Rise and Progress of Emigration from the Counties of Lanark and Renfrew, to the New Settlements in Upper Canada* (Glasgow, 1821). The Liverpool Ministry agreed to support 1,100 members of the emigration societies of Glasgow and Lanarkshire with a repayable loan of approximately £11,000. The government would provide the transportation from Quebec to Upper Canada but the societies would have to provide their own passage from Greenock to Quebec. A grant of 100 acres would be provided to each family along with seed corn and implements at prime cost while a further £10 would be advanced in four instalments in order to aid the settlers through their first season. In return the emigrants had to agree to clear their debt within ten years. Bathurst to Maitland, 6 May 1820, PRO, CO 43/41; *Glasgow Herald*, 8 May 1820; *Scots Magazine*, June 1820. The Colonial Office, who had not been party to the arrangement, interpreted the decision very narrowly, arbitrarily excluding petitions from Renfrewshire but eventually bowed to pressure from John Maxwell, among others, to provide assistance the following season to petitioners from Paisley in particular. Johnston, *British Emigration Policy*, pp.52–3.

20. Johnston, *British Emigration Policy*, pp.37–40.

21. Finlay had been defeated in Glasgow after holding the riding for six years but was returned for Malmesbury in 1818. G.P. Judd, *Members of Parliament* (Hamden, Conn., 1972—reprint edition), p.193.

22. Lamond, *Narrative*, p.10.

23. The same year which saw Hamilton support the idea of assisted emigration also saw his attempt to discredit the government with the Queen Caroline affair. A.W. Mitchel, *The Whigs in Opposition, 1815–30* (Oxford, 1967); J. Stevenson, 'The Queen Caroline Affair', in J. Stevenson (ed.), *London in the Age of Reform* (Oxford, 1977).

24. *Hansard*, 16 December xli [1819] col.1224; *Hansard*, 20 June, xxxvi [1817] col.1080–1; W. Hamish Fraser, *Conflict and Class* (Edinburgh, 1988), pp.104–5.

25. *Hansard*, 28 April, New Series 1[1820] col.40.

26. Robert Brown to James Hope WS., 10 October 1819, SRO, Lennoxlove Muniments, TD 89/33/1234; Admiral Fleming, of the Road Trustees, to Brown, May 1820, SRO, TD 80/100/4/1748/35.

27. R. Mitchison has explored the development of this attitude in detail. See R. Mitchison, 'Poor Law', in T.M. Devine and R. Mitchison (eds.), *People and Society in Scotland, vol.I 1760–1830* (Edinburgh, 1988) pp.252–288.

28. 'Memorial of the Noblemen, Justices of the Peace and Commissioners of Supply of the County of Lanark', 30 November 1819, SRO, TD 80/100/4/7748/3. On 15 October 1819 the Renfrewshire County Meeting resolved to make a similar request of the government, asking for a loan of £20,000 to extend the Ardrossan canal and a £30,000 donation to improve the roads with an additional request to regulate apprenticeship in the weaving trade and, finally, provide a sum to assist emigration: Robert Brown, *History of Paisley*, vol.II (Paisley, 1886), p.184.

29. *Hansard*, 16 December xli [1819] col. 1221–2.

30. Minutes of Lanark County Meeting, 22 February 1820, SRO, TD 80/100/4/1748/42–3.

31. The issue of the Scottish system of poor relief continued to be raised in debates on emigration. During the investigations of the 1826 Parliamentary

Committee on Emigration, witnesses were closely questioned on the nature of Scots Poor Law and their answers provided some of the most thorough defences of the Scottish position that can be found. In particular, the testimony of Alexander Campbell, Sheriff Substitute of Renfrewshire, P.P. 1826–7 (88) V, p.184.

32. *Hansard*, new series, 1 [1820], col.42.

33. In response to the Whig argument that the suspension of habeas corpus threatened the nation's basic liberties, Finlay stated that 'he would rather trust his majesty's ministers with the liberties of the people than he would trust those endeavouring to set the country aflame.' *Hansard*, xxxv [1817] col.1096.

34. Finlay to Lord Sidmouth, Home Secretary, 12 October 1815, SRO, RH 2/4/108 f.460, 5 February 1813, SRO, RH 2/4/100 f.51. Alexander Richmond, one of the Glasgow weavers arrested after the 1812 strike, was convinced by Finlay and James Reddie, Glasgow's Town Clerk, to become a government spy. Later critics were to claim that Richmond acted as an 'agent provocateur' who invented conspiracies in order to maintain his employment and was in fact the main instigator behind the weaver agitation in 1820. This view is no longer held to be accurate by historians, but the suggestion would prove to be a black mark on Finlay's political career. Peter MacKenzie, *Reply to the letter of Kirkman Finlay Esq. on the Spy System* (Glasgow, 1833), W.M. Roach, 'Alexander Richmond and the radical reform movements in Glasgow', *Scottish Historical Review*, 1972, pp.1–19; Fraser, *Conflict and Class*, pp.103–4, 107; Richmond put forward a vigorous defence of his own conduct in his *Narrative of the Condition of the Manufacturing Population* (London, 1824).

35. Finlay to Sidmouth, 27 December 1816, SRO, RH 2/4/112 f.762.

36. Finlay to Sidmouth, 14 September 1819, SRO, RH 2/4/126; 17 September 1819, RH 2/4/126 f.581.

37. Fraser, *Conflict and Class*, pp.101–4, 108.

38. *Glasgow Chronicle*, 22 April 1820, 10 October 1819.

39. Finlay to Henry Goulburn, Colonial Department, 21 July 1820, PRO, CO384/6 f.539.

40. *Glasgow Herald*, 12 May 1820; no evidence was presented in support of this claim.

41. The settlers were expected to provide a £10 deposit in return for free passage to the colony and the 100-acre land-grant for each adult male settler. No such deposit was required in 1815; however the 1820–1 emigrants were expected to pay their own passage. Approximately 300 individuals emigrated from the Breadalbane estate. A smaller party of fifty individuals departed from Alston, England and a further 170 left from Co. Tipperary, Ireland. Cowan, *British Emigration to North America*, pp.44–7; Johnston, *British Emigration Policy*, pp.28–30.

42. Robert McGilliewie to John Campbell, W.S., 17 January 1817, SRO, Factor's Correspondence, GD 112/41/7 p.268; Campbell to Bathurst, 11 February 1817, PRO, CO 384/1 f.141.

43. Vance, 'Emigration and Scottish Society', pp.133–4, 208–9.

44. Norman Murray, *The Scottish Hand Loom Weavers 1790–1850* (Edinburgh, 1978), pp.144–5; Fraser, *Conflict and Class*; Vance, 'Emigration and Scottish Society', pp.202–10.

45. *Scots Magazine*, June 1819, p.570; *Glasgow Chronicle*, 8 June 1819.

46. *Caledonian Mercury*, 21 June 1819.

47. *Ibid.*

48. *Scots Magazine*, September 1819, p.275.

49. *Glasgow Chronicle*, 18, 22 April 1820.

50. Vance, 'Emigration and Scottish Society', ch.7.

51. Beath's arrest is recorded in SRO, AD 14/13/8 'Weaver's Illegal Combination, 1812'; in 1820 he was arranging passage for the emigrants on board the *Prompt* with Robert Brown, SRO, TD 80/100/4/1748/50. One other name appears on both the arrest records of 1812 and in the records of the assisted emigration. A John Stewart in Wishawtown was charged with 'destroying looms' in 1812 and a John Stewart wrote to Robert Brown on 7 June 1820 from Wishawtown asking to be added to the list of emigrants departing that season—but because of the common nature of the name it is impossible to determine if it was the same individual, SRO, TD 80/100/4/1748/52.

52. Beath to Bathurst, 30 January 1821, PRO, CO 384/7 f.425.

53. J.M. [James Muir?] to a friend in Kirkfieldbank, Perth, Upper Canada, 16 October 1820, in Lamond, *Narrative*, p.87.

54. John Graham to Robert Brown, 28 April 1820, SRO, TD 80/100/4/1748/45.

55. Abercromby to Bathurst, 6 February 1821, PRO, CO 384/7 f.10.

56. James Muir, clerk of the society, to Robert Brown, 24 January 1820, SRO, TD 80/100/4/1748/10–11.

57. Baillie to Hamilton, 22 April 1820, SRO, TD 80/100/4/1748/73.

58. William Granger to Lord A. Hamilton, 4 May 1820, SRO, TD 80/100/4/1748/44.

59. *Ibid.*

60. Lamond, *Narrative*, p.104.

61. *Ibid.*, p.101.

62. P.P., 1826–27, (88), V, p.69.

63. Lamond, *Narrative*, p.78.

64. John Gemmil to Andrew Gemmil, Lanark, Upper Canada, 17 December 1827, Strathclyde Regional Archives, Gemmil Papers, TD 293/1/5.

65. Samuel Dunn, president, to Bathurst, 8 July 1819, PRO, CO 384/5 f.911.

66. John Howison, *Sketches of Upper Canada . . . for the information of Emigrants of Every Class* (Edinburgh, 1822, 2nd ed.), pp.61–2.

67. *Glasgow Chronicle*, 22 April 1820.

68. A.C. Buchanan, *Emigration Practically Considered* (London, 1828), p.90.

69. At least one 1820–1 emigrant, Ebenezer Wilson from Paisley, became a leading member of the district's reform party. Richard Reid (ed.), *The Ottawa Valley to 1855: A Collection of Documents* (Toronto, 1990), pp.cvi-cxvii, cxi; Jean S. McGill, *A Pioneer History of the County of Lanark* (Toronto, 1968), pp.150–9.

70. The emigration societies were to prove to be a permanent feature in the west of Scotland right through the mid-century. Petitions were sent to the Colonial Office annually, with their numbers reaching a peak in the early 1840s. The distribution of societies continued to be centred on Glasgow and Paisley but groups were formed as far afield as Perth and Kilmarnock. James M. Cameron, 'A Study of the Factors that Assisted and Directed Scottish Emigration to Upper Canada, 1815–55', unpublished PhD thesis, University of Glasgow, 1970, ch. 4, fig. 4.1; 'Emigration to the Colonies', *North British Daily Mail*, Friday, 17 September 1858; *Emigration to New Zealand: Report of the Speeches delivered by the Rev Dr Burns and others at the meeting in the Philosophical Hall, Paisley . . . 27th June, 1840* (Paisley, 1840).

71. Vance, 'Emigration and Scottish Society', ch. 8, 'The British Context'.

Appendix

Figures for British Emigration 1815–21

All the commentators on British emigration have relied on the 1847 Parliamentary Paper on Emigration for their figures on emigration between 1815 and 1821. These are as follows:

Year	North American Colonies	United States	Others
1815	680	1,209	192
1816	3,370	9,022	118
1817	9,979	10,280	557
1818	15,136	12,429	222
1819	23,534	10,674	579
1820	17,921	6,745	1,063
1821	12,995	4,958	384

Although customs officials in various British ports kept some independent records, it was not until after 1825 that all ports were required to keep detailed figures. However, the compilers of the 1847 report had access to earlier customs reports that are no longer extant. As a consequence the figures quoted above cannot be cross-checked with official sources.

W.F. Adams, in *Ireland and Irish Emigration to the New World from 1815 to the Famine* (New York, 1932), compared the general figures for Irish emigration with reported sailings in the Irish newspapers. He then cross-referenced these figures with newspaper reports of emigrant arrivals in British North America. He summarised his detailed enquiry with the following table:

IRISH EMIGRATION TO NORTH AMERICA, 1815–18

	United States	British North America
1815	1,000	negligible
1816	6,000	500
1817	2,500	5,000
1818	6,500	13,000

The pattern corresponds to the figures in the 1847 report. However Adam's figures suggest that the Irish constituted the majority of the emigrants departing in the post-war era.

Prior to 1815, the total number of Scots immigrants to British North America has been estimated at 15,000. By 1870 they had been joined by another 170,000 of their countrymen and another 326,000 were added to this figure by 1918. The 1871 census revealed that 20.2 per cent of the inhabitants of Ontario and 33.7 per cent of those in Nova Scotia were of Scots origin. J.M. Bumsted, *The Scots in Canada* (Ottawa, Canadian Historical Association, Booklet No.1, 1982), pp.10–11.

4

From the Southern Uplands to Southern Ontario: Nineteenth-Century Emigration from the Scottish Borders

Edward J. Cowan

'Scotland is a sad country at present . . . all is dull and still growing worse, so I think the sooner away from it the better . . . there is thousands coming over to the New World this season . . . I wish to leave this place as all is dark and gloomy about us.'[1] The year was 1832, the writer Andrew Dryden of Hawick in the Scottish Borders, addressing his son John who was en route to Dumfries Township, Upper Canada. Andrew himself was soon to emigrate to become the effective patriarch of the Canadian Drydens, dying in Galt (now Cambridge), Ontario, in 1848. Many clearly shared Dryden's views during the first three or four decades of the nineteenth century. He represented one small piece of the mosaic, part of a profound historical process which would eventually involve thousands of men, women and children who were members of a community that was truly transatlantic and which extended from Galashiels to Galt, from Hawick to Hespeler, from the Southern Uplands of Scotland all the way to the frontier of southern Ontario during the first half of the nineteenth century.

What follows is stimulated by, and is intended to represent a contribution to, the Guelph Regional Project, based at the University of Guelph.[2] Despite the stalwart efforts of several recent writers[3] the Scottish emigrant experience is still somewhat imperfectly understood because comparatively few historians have tried to trace the process across the Atlantic. In short, Scottish historians seem to lose interest when the emigrants embark while their North American counterparts deem them fit for study only when they arrive in the New World. This paper will suggest that, at least in part, Border emigrants sought the Old World in the New.

The ballad tradition had created a rich mythology of a hardy, belligerent frontier people uneasily co-existing on both sides of the Border. During Andrew Dryden's own lifetime (he was born in 1779) the Borderers and their *mentalité* were being romanticised anew in the poems, stories and collections of Sir Walter Scott and James Hogg, the Ettrick Shepherd, even though some lamented that the ballad tradition was no more.[4]

As it happens, James Hogg figures in this investigation. Dumfries Township, Ontario, the ultimate destination of the Dryden family, was founded in 1816 by William Dickson of Dumfries, Scotland. One of Dickson's associates was John Telfer, a veteran of the Hudson's Bay Company and to him William entrusted the task of recruiting people from the Border counties as settlers in the new township. At the same time advertisements were placed in Scottish newspapers. Telfer actually visited Scotland in 1820, returning with a group from Selkirkshire.[5] It may have been on that occasion, or it may have been in correspondence, that Telfer offered a farm to the literarily successful, but chronically impecunious, Ettrick Shepherd. Hogg's niece and nephew eventually settled in Galt while another group of relatives established themselves at Binghampton, New York, in the vicinity of what is now Mount Ettrick. The Galt contingent presumably established Altrive, named for their uncle's farm in Ettrick, a circumstance which probably explains the persistent local tradition that Hogg acted as an emigration agent for Dickson.[6] Corroboration of this tradition is supplied in the recent discovery of two letters (1833 and 1834) addressed by Hogg to William Dickson junior recommending individuals from Yarrow who subsequently settled in Dumfries Township.[7]

Hogg related something of his own experience of contemporary developments in his short story, 'Emigration', a piece of autobiographical fiction no less fictitious than most autobiographies, in which he related that his own brothers, sisters, nephews and nieces were all departing:

> I know of nothing in the world so distressing as the last sight of a fine industrious, independent peasantry taking the last look of their native country never to behold it more . . . It is long since emigration from the Highlands commenced . . . But never till now did the brave and intelligent Borderers rush from their native country, all with symptoms of reckless despair. It is most deplorable. The whole of our most valuable peasantry and operative manufacturers are leaving us.

He claimed that as he wrote over one hundred individuals in Hawick and its subordinate villages were 'already booked for transportation'. One of the characters in the story, an old pedlar named Sandy Ainslie, announces his intention of emigrating himself to be 'amang my countrymen about New Dumfries an' Loch Eiry', a homely and folksy reference to Lake Erie.[8]

The information on William Dickson, supplemented by Hogg's story, underlines the point—even though it was already well recognised—that Andrew Dryden was by no means unique in contemplating emigration to Dumfries Township in 1832. No less fascinating is Hogg's explicit comparison to Highland emigration. When the radical, William Cobbett, visited the western Borders in 1832 he was astonished at the numerous population: 'little Scotchies', he noted, seemed 'absolutely to swarm'. He ironically enquired—'what is to be done to prevent these Scotch women from breeding?'—only to answer his own question: 'nothing short of clearing the estates à la Sutherland'.[9] As is well known Sutherland had, by that date, experienced the worst of several sequences of Highland clearance,[10] though some of the most severe clearances were still to come. In the Borders, however, and the point has been substantially overlooked, commentators had been aware of a similar problem for over a century. The saga of the Lowland clearances is slowly unfolding but has yet to be fully told.[11]

As R.A. Dodgshon has demonstrated, the medieval monasteries had maintained great sheep ranches in the Borders. From about 1600 to 1720 sheep had to compete with subsistence agriculture. During a third phase from 1720 to 1780 or 1790 sheep began to dominate as the raising of mutton and wool became increasingly commercialised. In the process multiple tenancies were turned into large holdings and a considerable amount of arable in the Southern Uplands was transformed into pastoral for sheep; some Border villages completely disappeared with a concomitant substantial displacement of population. It is not difficult to detect an 'obvious analogy . . . with the Highland clearances—tenurial contraction was probably on a smaller scale and at a more gradual pace in the Southern Uplands, but it was still a replacement of people with sheep.'[12] While Dodgshon's arguments are convincing it is perhaps a pity that he concluded his study in 1780. As James Hogg noted there is a stronger case for suggesting a parallel with the Highland experience in the period 1780–1840, an era which we might well dub that of the 'Lowland clearances'.

The pages of the *Old Statistical Account* provide eloquent testimony on the process of transition, one which, in the Borders, rode on the broad backs of sheep. To this day there are literally hundreds of tasteless stories in circulation about Scotsmen and sheep; these must date from this period of intensified sheep-rearing in the eighteenth and early nineteenth centuries. One of the most cherished myths among people of Scottish descent in Canada is that their ancestors were transported there for sheep-stealing. This is remarkable because it is a pretty safe bet that hardly any of them ever were. As one Canadian comedian has observed it is well known that while Australia was founded by a nation of convicts, Canada was established by a bunch of people who never got caught! It would be much more accurate to argue that people found themselves in Canada—or at least that part of it under discussion—because it was the sheep who did the stealing. With the enthusiastic support of the landlords they usurped the land from the people. Be that as it may, many of those who commented on the rise of sheep husbandry detected a direct causal connection with the phenomenon of emigration.

Thus, to take a random sample, depopulation, migration and emigration were traced in the 1790s to the accumulation of small farms.[13] Population decrease was directly attributed to the conversion of arable into sheep pasture, while the small lairds who had flourished in the mid-eighteenth century had disappeared, their lands engrossed in large farms, 'their names extinguished and their mansions confounded in the dust'.[14] In 1792 the population of Crawford, Lanarkshire was said to have been halved due to sheep.[15] While some observed that the uplands were no longer cultivated and that the marks of the plough were still to be seen in many areas long under sheep pasture, others complained in the 1790s that the practice still prevailed of 'sowing great quantities of oats upon high lands which nature seems to have intended for pasture only'.[16]

In those areas sheep and crops were still clearly in competition but the overwhelming impression conveyed by these accounts is that the sheep had already won the battle. The minister of Ettrick later recalled that 'by 1796 the demand for cheviots began to increase so rapidly and still to go on so progressively, till it absolutely grew little better than the tulipo-mania that once seized the Dutch.'[17] Even where the ministers were not necessarily critical in compiling their reports, which in the present context are just as valuable whether they are impressionistic or empirical, all clearly felt themselves to be knowledgeable and expert on the subject of sheep.

The eighteenth century therefore had already experienced some emigration from the Southern Uplands. Those who did not depart found work labouring on the new farms—draining, enclosing, erecting new buildings, sheep-pens and dykes. They also found their way to the new woollen factories of such places as Hawick and Galashiels.[18] Rents rose steadily up to the end of the Napoleonic Wars in 1815, the cessation of which created a crisis in several areas of Scottish agriculture. Warning voices had sounded. Speculative farmers had been given 'an unusual opportunity of making the experiment in earnest, whether or not land can be taken too dear; several unfortunate persons have paid the forfeit of delusion'.[19] Farmers and graziers outbid one another for leases.[20] Critics, who were numerous, complained that many landlords 'impressed with the ideas that lands will always rise' (in price) insisted upon reducing the length of leases.[21] Disastrous weather compounded the problem[22] although rents remained unaffected all too often so that small farmers saw their profits drastically reduced or were, in extreme cases, forced into bankruptcy. All this, needless to say, had a spin-off effect upon the non-renting, labouring or cottar community. Even the professional classes were affected. Quite simply there was little work. In the past weavers, to take one example, had been permitted a smallholding on which they might keep an animal while growing some vegetables. As the farms grew larger the weavers' plots disappeared or were confiscated.[23]

There was, however, another dimension. Robert Douglas noted in his *General View of the Agriculture of Roxburgh* that in 1796 two-thirds of the whole county was possessed by families of only seven different surnames. For example there were ten proprietors by the name of Kerr, thirteen of Elliot and twenty-five of Scott.[24] During the period of agricultural decline many of those old proprietors were to be replaced by people with new money, men who had no ancestral ties to the community but who were thrusting capitalists wishing to maximise their returns. At the same time the more successful native proprietors distanced themselves in wealth, status and behaviour from their tenants and employees.[25] One perceptive commentator remarked that the people of Roxburghshire were no longer so attached to their lairds or masters as formerly. The point is highly significant and is worthy of expansion:

> . . . formerly the greatest respect was generally paid to family; for then almost every person considered himself of family, and was thereby led to think he had an interest therein. And his interest, in this real or supposed connection was, for the most part, not merely ideal. For, then, it was the pride of the laird or master, to have his tenants, retainers, and even domesticks of his own surname, many of them his near relations and he commonly treated them as such.

In other words the bonds of kinship had been broken and here there is an obvious and fascinating parallel to the breakdown of the clan system in the Highlands—with identical consequences. The Borderers now seemed

> more anxious how they lived than where; how they are governed than by whom; what the laws are than who are their makers; and how just and equal soever they be, are apt to consider themselves protected thereby, only so far as they have it in their power to render them efficient.[26]

The minister of Yarrow, like his above-quoted colleague at Bedrule, lamented a cosy paternalistic world that had never existed when he deplored the severance of the feudal relationship between master and servant. Significantly he linked this fracture in society with the demise of the ballad tradition brought about through the publication of Scott's *Minstrelsy*.[27] At the same time the ministers' view of the Borders past was as conditioned by the works of Scott as were their reports by the cadences of James Hogg's poetry and prose. Both of these great writers, both Borderers and both guilty of self-, and cultural, mythologisation, preserved a poetic vision of a past which had only just disappeared.[28]

That past was equally accessible to the very people who were most acutely aware of the changes transforming their world, who found their lives disrupted and themselves displaced, since, according to the ministers, most Borderers could read.[29] The minister of Linton claimed that education created wants 'for the supply of which their scanty means are incompetent and thus gives rise to discontentment and fretfulness'. A certain wistfulness for less complicated feudal days may be detected in his assertion that:

> to these sources is to be traced that very general desire of emigration to Canada which of late years the class of hinds has manifested; and the children of those whom no wordly motive could have torn from their native hills and valleys, now without a tear, nay with a sort of exultation, leave the land of their fathers.[30]

If there is little evidence of exultant emigrants perhaps those Borderers trapped between a poetic past and a painful present deserve a tear. Certain it is that any residual attachments they felt for the old ways were to be systematically, and brutally, destroyed by the neo-feudal practices of the landowning classes and the rich tenant farmers. It is perhaps in this respect that the closest parallel with the Highland clearances is to be drawn.

Several observers in the 1790s and through the 1830s stated that emigration was caused by the desire to escape oppressive laws,[31] laws which 'seemed to be the expression of an artificial land monopoly with associated political power and social prestige'.[32] People objected to thirlage, the practice whereby they were obliged to have grain or oats ground at the laird's mill; they opposed entail which was on the increase and which placed needless financial burdens upon an estate in perpetuity; they bristled at oppressive, not to say draconian, game laws.[33] Ancient rights allowing commoners to fish Border rivers were threatened; fuel sources dried up because when the common ground was divided peat was no longer accessible; the collection of firewood was forbidden.[34] Even gleaning rights at the time of harvest were withdrawn. Robert Douglas reckoned that by following the reapers a cottar could glean enough to maintain his family for six or eight weeks.[35]

Lairds and farmers deliberately destroyed or neglected cottages and dwellings so that retired farm servants would have to seek refuge in the towns.[36] Of this practice one irate minister wrote:

> it is astonishing that the aristocracy should be so blind to their own interest, not to say dead to the claims of humanity, as to incur, for the sake of a paltry economy, the hatred instead of the blessing of a class of worthy persons to whom separation from the place of their fathers' sepulchres is the greatest of calamities.[37]

On the Buccleuch estates the factor discussed measures to prevent tenants renting vacant properties to undesirables.[38]

Even the accursed sheep were requiring less attention and hence less labour, becoming more self-reliant as blackfaces were replaced with cheviots. Furthermore, as workers in the Border woollen mills know to their cost to this very day, wool manufacture was a very uncertain commodity, subject to the vagaries of the market. Also, improved technology, such as the invention of the power loom, threatened to render many of the handloom weavers redundant. William Dickson and his associates had thus chosen an auspicious time to recruit settlers for Dumfries Township, though the question arises of whether William would have found disaffected tenants, artisans and labourers, not to mention the notoriously radical weavers, conducive emigrants.

Dickson was a conservative. Like his fellow Scottish entrepreneurs in Upper Canada, all of whom he knew personally—Robert Hamilton of Queenston and his son George, founder of Hamilton, Adam Fergusson of Fergus, William Gilkison of Elora and John Galt of Guelph[39]—Dickson was primarily interested in the better sort of emigrant, preferably one possessing the wherewithal to purchase a hundred-acre lot.

In our original letter Andrew Dryden mentioned that he was reading 'Mr Fergusson's Travels'. Adam Fergusson, founder of Fergus, published two accounts of his travels in Canada; in both it is most noticeable that he attempted to appeal to the emigrant with capital. He also inadvertently reinforces the Border connection since in Eramosa Township he met men with such names as Oliver, Armstrong, Dinwoodie and Bryden, all Borderers who had done well.[40] Fergusson and other propagandists for Canada like himself appealed directly to those individuals, such as farmers or hinds, who could see their standard of living in Scotland on the slide and who could reasonably expect to better themselves in the New World. The other stream was of those with no savings but who still had a skill to sell; farming, road-building, draining, crafts and trades all acted as bait. William Dickson at Galt and John Galt at Guelph both established mills to which destitute weavers fancied they could easily transfer.[41] If such projects failed they could always fall back upon residual agricultural or labouring skills. Radical sympathies were, however, another matter.

Yet another Border emigrant provides a link with a rather intriguing radical who never left his native shores. When William Catermole published his *Advantages of Emigration to Canada* in 1831 he included a letter written from Guelph by one John Inglis to his friend in Lessudden, Roxburghshire.[42] The letter was reprinted by the *Guelph Historical Society* in 1973[43] though the editor was apparently unaware that the recipient, John Younger, shoemaker, was the author of a remarkable *Autobiography* which was completed in 1841. Lessudden was the old name for St Boswells where Andrew Dryden was born[44] he was a contemporary of John Younger who was raised at nearby Long Newton before moving into the village and whose *Autobiography* movingly catalogues the hardship and deprivation suffered by the Border community during the first forty years of the nineteenth century.

Younger was a radical and an extremely acute critic of landlords and the like, almost at times a proto-Marxist in sentiment, and one who was painfully aware of the great changes sweeping across his landscape and his lifetime. His idol was Robert Burns who 'taught me to respect myself, and in addition all human worth, under whatever garb I should meet with it'; his passion was poetry. He despised 'your toddy-noodled writers of gentle novels . . . describing the happy ignorance of the snoring peasantry without any real knowledge of such people's matters.' Younger had himself experienced the reality of poverty, starvation and rack-renting by landlords for whom he reserved his most exquisite venom. He noted that in his own lifetime 'a wonderful change had begun to take place in the world, the influence of which was extending into the very fibrous roots of society.'[45]

Inglis's letter is essentially an advertisement for emigration, detailing the experience of establishing a homestead, describing the crops and wildlife, advising the would-be emigrant of the merits of diligence and hard work by dint of which he will 'in the course of seven or eight years feel independent'.[46] He called his place Greenwells, for 'auld lang syne', such being the name of the property on which he was raised on the slopes of the Eildon Hills and where his father had worked as a forester. Younger resisted Inglis's urging to emigrate but a mutual friend of the pair, David Ovens, became a school-teacher in Hamilton before moving to Cobourg. The unfortunate Ovens represents the type of Scottish emigrant who is hardly ever discussed for he died in poverty in Montreal;[47] not all exiles enjoyed spectacular success stories.

John Younger took his radicalism to his grave but there was a view, in certain quarters, that those who shared his sentiments represented a problem that should be exported. A factor on the Buccleuch estates informed the duke that a number of 'mostly carpenters or artificers of some description who had scraped together some little means' had lately taken ship for North America—they 'were of a kind we could very well spare, being mostly discontented radicals'. The factor thought that quite a few of the duke's tenants would be happy to follow suit, suggesting that the population of Newcastleton, in particular, was 'of a character which could afford considerable emigration' since children were bred to no 'useful professions and the place itself affords them no employment—I fear also their properties and houses are going fast down.'[48] Investigations revealed in due course that a substantial number of families wished to emigrate, particularly if assistance was provided; weavers were specially interested.[49] However, better the radicals you rue that those you 'dinna ken'. The factors were concerned that most of the intending emigrants belonged to 'the better class of persons and those disposed to do well and none of them paupers at present tho eventually may become so'. Second, fears were expressed that the places of the departed would be taken by a 'much worse description of people' from neighbouring districts and the north of England who would, in time, become a drain upon poor relief.[50]

Two groups of emigrants requested financial assistance from Buccleuch, 182 from Newcastleton, Roxburghshire and 127 from Langholm, Dumfriesshire. Interestingly, the nominal lists of petitioners bear out some of the factor's earlier remarks since virtually all of those from Newcastleton are listed as labourers. Twenty-one families record the breadwinner as belonging to the latter category; the four exceptions are a shepherd, a farm servant, a cooper and a weaver, although there is a slightly wider occupation distribution amongst unmarried applicants. The Langholm sample of twenty-two families lists thirteen labourers along with two joiners, two farm servants, a mason, a shoemaker, a weaver (surprisingly not more), a blacksmith and a gamekeeper.[51] How much radical sentiment existed in these groups is, of course, impossible to tell, but the Reverend Wallace's comments on the substantial amount of emigration from the Borders—and particularly from Hawick—in the early 1830s may afford a clue:

... the border spirit, a spirit certainly more congenial with the usages of a ruder and less enlightened age than the present, is not altogether extinct. And we doubt much, if a community could be found elsewhere, more jealous than they are of what they conceive to be their own rights, more keen and indefatigable in the working out of what they reckon to be their own interests, and more determined in asserting at all hazards what they deem to be essential to their own independence. Anything like a spirit of vassalage to any man, or to any class of men, how elevated soever in rank, is what they cannot brook, and any attempt, from whatever quarter, to interfere with their ancient or established privileges is sure to be strongly and almost universally resisted. There are, moreover, few places where less attention is paid to the ordinary distinctions of rank, or where all classes are more disposed to associate together on the footing of equality. And with respect to the ordinary business of life, they exhibit a spirit of activity and enterprise and intelligence, which, setting early difficulty at defiance, is productive of most important results. In short, there are elements of character amongst them, which, if subject to the influence of religious principle and properly directed, might raise them to a very high point in the scale of moral and intellectual improvement, but which otherwise are not unlikely to carry them, as they have sometimes done in seasons of political excitement, into excesses, which no right-minded man can contemplate with any other than a feeling of unqualified condemnation.[52]

The tracing of radical sentiment in Upper Canada is no part of this paper though some of the Dumfries folk did support Mackenzie in 1837.[53] None the less, the overwhelming impression conveyed by the evidence is that when they reached the Canadian side of the Atlantic the radicals were often to demonstrate that they had suffered from what Henry Cockburn called 'sedition of the stomach',[54] during the years when 'the bowels of compassion seemed greatly to dry up in the wealthy, while the bowels of the poor dried up for mere lack of material distention.'[55] Once removed from the neo-feudal context of the homeland and given the opportunity to prosper, the so-called radicalism of the emigrants often evaporated.

William Knox, an emigrant from Lilliesleaf, the neighbouring parish to St Boswells, reported on a collection taken up for the destitute among the manufacturing classes in the west of Scotland in 1842: 'We Scots people in this distant land are not forgetful to relieve the wants of our distressed countrymen in our native land.'[56] His cousin Archie bemoaned the materialism which seemed to affect so many of his countrymen in Canada: 'From the prospect of gaining an independence people at first must be industrious from necessity but I have observed that after their land is paid and everything comfortable, that restless, insatiable desire of making money makes them as anxious as ever.' He deplored a certain 'selfishness and want of principle'.[57]

The abandonment of radical principle is well brought out in a couthy tale related by Adam Fergusson. Authors of Canadian travelogues at this period were prone to stories of worthy Scots preserving homely values—the kailyard transposed to the cornfield. Fergusson met a young Borderer named Smith who had recently purchased one hundred acres outside Galt. Upon enquiry it turned out that Smith came from a Border estate owned by a friend of Fergusson's. The Borderer said that his former landlord would 'no hae forgot Walter Smith but tell him you met the poacher, and he'll be sure to mind me'.

> I of course hinted a suspicion that some mishap attending that lawless character had accelerated his movements across the Atlantic, which, however, proved not to be the case. 'At all events,' I remarked, 'you neither need certificate nor qualification here: what do you principally shoot?' 'Indeed,' says he, 'if you'll believe me sir, I scarce ever think about it, for there's naebody here seeks to hinder us.'[58]

This is a remarkably instructive story, and it says much for the landowner—from the Woodhill estate, Perthshire—that he reported it. In Scotland poaching was a political statement; in Canada it was a redundant one.[59]

The suspicion that some minor revolution in Scotland had been averted through the process of emigration is confirmed by John M'Diarmid, editor of the *Dumfries and Galloway Courier*. His opinion is significant because virtually all of the Border emigrants sailed from western ports in the Solway Firth and north-west England. Until 1819 *Courier* editorial policy was opposed to emigration. Of those who had departed by April that year many were said to be 'doing no good' in Scotland. The paper tended to print articles dissuading people from emigrating in spite of the fact that the government had encouraged it from 1815 through assistance with transportation and free grants of land. The first hint of a change of attitude came in a report of June 1819: 'the rage, *or rather perhaps the necessity* [my italics], for emigration still continues from this quarter.'[60] The ostensible cause of such a complete reversal was the radical activity of 1819–20, the so-called Radical War.[61] Events were closely followed in the *Courier* and after a report of the unrest in Glasgow in December 1819 is appended the comment:—'emigration—extensive and well-directed—appears to be the only remedy for the evil in question.'[62] Thereafter M'Diarmid favoured the practice, his preferred metaphor being that of a field drain: 'emigration operates as a drain and it is just as useful in thinning population as extended rows of tiles are in carrying off surplus water.'[63] The *Farmer's Magazine* exemplified a similar, if less dramatic, transition in attitude by publishing an extract from Strachan's *Visit to Upper Canada*.[64] It is tempting to argue that M'Diarmid's drain served the function of syphoning off streams of social and political disaffection, thus avoiding serious upheaval in the Old Country. Unwanted radical sentiment was exported to Upper Canada.

The pages of the *Dumfries and Galloway Courier* beautifully illustrate the difficulty of tracking emigrants, a frustration shared by historians and genealogists alike. Space does not permit more than a cursory indication of the problem. In the period surveyed by this paper emigrants sailed from the following Solway ports—Dumfries, Wigtown, Kirkcudbright, Colvend, Garlieston, Newton Stewart, Glencaple and Annan. They were bound for destinations as diverse as St Johns, Pictou, Miramichi, Quebec, Montreal, Prince Edward Island, Dalhousie, Philadelphia and New York. From 1833 onwards most Border Scots sailed from Liverpool and Whitehaven in England, prior pick-ups being made at the Solway ports. In addition, agents for companies in Greenock and the Broomielaw (Glasgow) were maintained at Dumfries and Stranraer. When the *Courier* reported from time to time that a group of 'Cumberland weavers' had departed it would remark that the term might include weavers from Langholm or Annandale since the mill-owners who commissioned piece-work were based at Carlisle in Cumberland, England. Needless to say the point of disembarkation in Canada or the US often bears little or no relation to the ultimate destination of the emigrants.

What, then, of those migrants who made the long and weary journey from the Borders to the banks of the Grand River in search, we may think, of a world that had been destroyed? The population of Dumfries township in 1817 was 163; by 1834 it was 4,177.[65] Many, but of course not all, were from the Scottish Borders. One interesting collection of letters in the Scottish Record Office is that of the Scott family who emigrated from the farm of Bewliemains in the parish of Lilliesleaf to settle at Blenheimhill Farm, Dumfries Township, in 1834. The unit consisted of Charles Scott and his wife with three daughters and four sons, the most prominent of whom, John, became well known as a physician in Berlin (now Kitchener).[66] Scott's cousins, William Knox and his sister Jessie, arrived in Dumfries in 1838, naming their farm Langside after their place in Lilliesleaf. Jessie was to marry another Borderer, Robert Leitheid. When the Knoxes first arrived they visited John Gouinlock, Galt's first school-teacher, who had emigrated from Hawick along with the Scotts in 1834.[67]

Back in Lilliesleaf, folk had regarded the town of Hawick as their metropolitan, if that is not too grand a word, and in their correspondence the Knoxes and the Scotts were always sending back greetings to acquaintances, friends and relatives from 'Tiris'[68] whom they had met, or who lived close by, in Dumfries. The correspondence preserves a wonderful picture of a transatlantic Border community. William Knox chronicled his voyage to New York, by canal to Oswego, to Kingston, to Toronto, Hamilton and, eventually, Galt. He mentioned to his uncle that when he passed through New York he met 'John Stalker (Helen Smith's son) and two Melrose men, John Chisholm and R. Russell, whom I met at home', as if it was the most natural thing in the world, virtually as unremarkable as if he had run across them at the St Boswells Fair.[69] News was passed on about the migrants as casually as if they lived in the next Border glen rather than in the wilds of Upper Canada.

> I learned John Gray and his brother and sister had gone to Illinois. I gave their letters to Walter Scott and family in Hamilton . . . I saw John Fairbairn who is married to Margaret Sinton lately . . . the Turnbulls, Veitches and all your other acquaintances are well. Mary Anderson who came out along with us was married to William Watherson about a month after we came here. James who was with me is well, but I am sorry to say Walter their brother died about the time we came here. Mr Gouinlock, Mr Oliver and families are all well. Mr George and his nephew are both well . . .[70]

As was typical of so many emigrant letters Scott tried to sell his uncle, Andrew Redford, on the idea of settling in Upper Canada.[71] Scott reminds us that not all Border immigrants were radicals; he was a staunch anti-reform Tory who deplored the proposed union of Upper and Lower Canada: 'Let the ignorant, the fanatic, the misguided who cry out for liberalism and reform, come to America and witness the practical working of such things here, and if they are not disappointed with the result, I should despair of ever seeing them good subjects under any government whatsoever.'[72]

Another feature of this type of correspondence is the phenomenon of fairly regular bouts of homesickness. Archibald Knox noted how time and distance 'gives a sort of enchantment, a melancholy pleasure which words are quite unable to express . . . I can see the Eildon and Minto Hills and the surrounding country as clearly as ever and trade every stream and turn of Yill [Ale] Water for miles.' Five siblings were now married, 'all to natives of Scotland so we are not crossing the breed'. Even the rather hard-headed John Scott, the physician, could be guilty of a little nostalgia, tinted with the verbal resonance of Scott and Hogg:

> Oh what a change has come over the spirit of my dream since I used to run about Lilliesleaf, and how we forget the old familiar faces . . . After the lapse of six years my heart still warms when I think on many localities in my native land which I used to frequent, and the friend and acquaintance I have left behind.[73]

Five years later, however, he appeared reconciled, having lately talked with a number of old acquaintances who had recently been home:

> and they all tell me that they could not remain in the old country, now that they have been accustomed to American habits—I believe it to be so. We are now, of course, all Canadians . . . I should fondly yet wish again to see my old fatherland and friends there, although I could not make my home there.[74]

The greetings, the gossip, conversations and items from newspapers flowed back and forth across the Atlantic. Robert Leitheid was overfond of the bottle but 'P.S. when you write don't say anything about his drinking as it may produce a bad feeling towards us.' Canada was not a healthy country, but how could it be otherwise, 'almost froze up during the winter and another extreme during summer, people's constitution very soon gets broke up. It is a very good country for doctors.'[75] Letters were exchanged in both directions courtesy of Gideon Goodfellow 'who is coming home this winter and coming out in the Spring again'.[76] Good wishes and remembrances were sent to Mr Stourock at Midlem, Bradley Baxter–Scott the schoolmaster in Selkirk, old William Murray, Thomas Tait and Nell who used to be at Bewliemains, Mr Carrie of Linthill and dozens of others. In short the network was maintained, the transatlantic community preserved intact.

Yet, just as at home people had shown a willingness, or had been forced through financial necessity, to move from place to place, so much so that emigration can perhaps be seen as an extension of internal migration,[77] so individuals and families struck out from the original settlement very soon after it had been established. When Robert Murray emigrated to Galt in 1882 he found many Borderers there[78] but, in truth, they no longer preponderated. By the early 1840s one of Archibald Knox's brothers was a foundry superintendent while another ran a cabinet factory. John Knox, late of Bewliemains, had charge of fitting up the gas-works in Toronto (1842); his uncle of Montreal had the contract and also one for the water-works. 'John

Young late son of the gamekeeper at Riddel makes steam engines at Niagara.'[79] Further research is required to establish just how long transplanted Scottish communities such as Galt, or Fergus, or Elora, retained their identities. Despite the numerous well-intentioned, and frequently exaggerated, assertions of filopietistic local historians there is no question that the Scots enjoyed a profile in nineteenth-century Canada out of due proportion to their numbers. Indeed, it is not always realised that Scottish identity is, not infrequently, a creation of the comparatively recent past.[80] Current research would suggest that self-conscious awareness of belonging to a Scottish community seldom extended beyond a generation and many, like John Scott, 'became Canadians' much sooner than that, through a process of fragmentation and dilution.

Then, as now, of course, a political and social commitment to Canada did not preclude a cultural allegiance to the Old Country. The high profile of Scots in business, political, educational, ecclesiastical and administrative élites was reflected in the attention devoted by Canadian newspapers to 'Scottish' activities such as Burns Suppers or meetings of St Andrews societies. Caledonian Games were conspicuous as was curling, a sport so dominated by Scots wearing tam o'shanters that non-Scottish participants called themselves 'barbarians'. Curling dinners invariably featured lamentable and sentimental poems or songs in the Doric, often composed by people who had never set foot in Scotland, but who none the less felt compelled to eulogise the 'auld hame'. Such maudlin indulgence doubtless enabled participants to function as normal human beings—Canadians even—during their everyday lives. One unique experiment, apparently never repeated, was the promotion of a common riding in Galt in 1883.[81]

One aspect of the emigrant experience which is often overlooked is the pain of those left behind. A small, but highly informative, collection of letters survives which was sent by Robert and Christian Bryden of Stonedge Farm, by Hawick, to their son, Robert of Newhouse, in the Paisley Block, Guelph, in the 1830s.[82] By chance the activities of the Bryden family in Scotland overlap geographically with those of the Scotts, the Knoxes, the Drydens and John Younger and thus the letters reveal something of the local horizons of the people back home.

The Bryden correspondence is like most emanating from the Old Country: that is to say that the letters are somewhat tedious and mostly about death, market prices and the weather. Robert Bryden junior was accompanied by his sister who married one John Cleghorn. Another brother and sister remained at home. In the first letter Robert senior intimates that 'your mother and sister and brother would all come to

America, and I would be very glad to see you all myself, but I am
afraid that at my advanced age such a journey would be more than I
could accomplish.'[83] Several letters were penned on behalf of the elderly
couple by John Thorburn, Hawick, who wrote:

> your father says he has no desire to come to America if it were not
> to see you and your sister and was afraid that he would not have had
> enough of money to have brought him over to you, and such like
> excuses. I may be mistaken but it is my opinion he will never come
> to America. I believe your mother would come altho' she was ever so
> weak in body.[84]

Another letter was to be hand-delivered by a son of Robert Riddell of
nearby Chesters. 'He is a tailor and if he does not come your way he
will put it in the post.' The old folk were failing, having suffered a
bout of 'what the Doctors call influenza, or a severe cold'. More people
had died of flu than had perished in the cholera epidemic two years
previously but the senior Brydens had recovered: 'had we not been
so much reduced by that trouble we fully intended coming to America
this year.' Thorburn added his own commentary: 'your mother does
not wish to see you in Britain again because she says she would never
part with you again in this life . . . [they] will never be able to come
to America.' Robert was told that his parents wanted for nothing—the
minister of Hobkirk had recently given old Robert a pound to buy a
greatcoat, news at which junior surely winced.[85] A later letter was sent
over by the hand of Mr Oliver of Langraw, a farm only two miles
away from Stonedge.[86] The final missive in the series expresses sad
disappointment that the Guelph Brydens do not write more particularly
about their activities, nor do they give their failing parents any financial
assistance, the burden falling on the siblings at home who could ill
afford it.[87] It must be presumed that the senior Brydens never made it
to Canada. None the less when old Bryden hirpled in to Hawick market
with the aid of his stick we can imagine that he met Drydens, Scotts,
Gouinlocks, Knoxes, Veitches and the rest, all of whom had kinsfolk
on the frontier of Upper Canada.

Is it, then, permissible to write of Lowland clearances? The answer
must be in the affirmative. Historians are over-fond of distinguishing
between voluntary and forced emigration. In either case the landlords
created the preconditions for migration. Market forces did the rest.
Very few of the emigrants during the period discussed in this paper
were 'voluntary' in the true sense of the word, with the possible,
though not certain, exception of people like the Scotts who could see

a way to improve an already not unhealthy standard of living. Others, largely unchronicled and unrecorded, sailed into further despair and deprivation, while some returned home.

The label 'Lowland clearances', of course, is borrowed from the Highland experience, one with which the Borderers were perfectly familiar. Robert Bryden noted in 1837 that the people of the Highlands and Islands of Scotland were 'nearly dead through starvation [bitter cold] for want of fuel and through hunger for want of food'.[88] An acquaintance, William Brunton, had become 'a drainer of sheep land' and had ten men working under him in the northern Highlands.[89] John Younger's friend, David Ovens, worked in timber in Easter Ross to earn his stake for the New World.[90] James Hogg appropriately drew the analogy with the Highlands in his short story 'Emigration'. Most important of all was that many Borderers went to the Highlands as shepherds and remained there throughout the whole dreary cycle of the intensification of sheep-rearing and the worst of the clearances. Such experience is epitomised by the saga of the Olivers who eventually established the Homestead Farm near Galt.

Robert Oliver was born in Roxburghshire in 1786 and, upon marrying Isabel Telfer, he began work as a shepherd in Ellesden, Northumberland. From there they went to Farr in Sutherland during the first phase of the Sutherland clearances. They then moved to Cromarty in the same occupation. With eight children the couple attempted to emigrate to Canada, losing all their possessions when their ship was wrecked, though fortunately all survived. Robert returned to Cromarty to the sheep while his wife lived on the coast as a seamstress. They reunited at Kildonan, Sutherland, to produce a further eight children. When their eldest daughter, Mary, departed for Canada with her husband, the Olivers named their last-born after her. Some eight years later the whole family sailed again for Canada via New York and went on to settle for seven years in Howick, Quebec. To their delight they were reunited with Mary who lived only fifteen miles away. In 1847 the remaining Olivers—some of the children had married or deceased—sailed to Hamilton and thence to Galt. Thus at the age of sixty-one Robert Oliver settled his family in Dumfries Township, having survived not only shipwreck and poverty but having also experienced some of the most momentous phases of nineteenth-century Scottish social and economic development.[91] He was surely in the perfect position to recognise that the sentiments in the penultimate verse of the 'Canadian Boat Song' applied every bit as much to the Borders as they did to the Highlands:

When the bold kindred in the time long vanished
Conquer'd the soil and fortified the keep,
No seer fortold the children would be banished
That a degenerate lord might boast his sheep.[92]

The reflective reporter on the parish of Hutton observed in the 1830s that the consequence of agricultural distress was emigration to Canada and the United States. Attachment to the native land was losing strength with many. 'Such numbers of friends and acquaintances have preceded them, more specially to British North American possessions that they no longer consider these to be a land of strangers.'[93] The second part of this paper has attempted to stress this very point—that the network of relatives and associates served partially to remove the sting from the emigration process. What Dumfries Township illustrates is nothing less than the transposition of a Border community from Scotland to the banks of the Grand River.

William Cobbett acutely remarked in 1832 that 'absolute right to exclusive possession of land . . . is still less unjust than the doctrine which says a man has no right to be upon and have a living out of the land of his birth.'[94] The world, alas, is seldom just. Those denied a living in the land of their birth were emigrating from a place they increasingly failed to recognise, that was becoming more foreign and alien and hostile with the passing of the years thanks to the restrictive and neo-feudal practices of the landowning classes. When they decided to take their chances and settle on the frontier of Canada West, far beyond the Atlantic roar, the women and men of the Borders believed they were joining a community of compatriots whose language, customs and values they understood. It is perhaps one of the greatest ironies of both Scottish and Canadian history in the nineteenth century that through the process of emigration these people were, in a sense, returning home.

NOTES

1. Hugh Gordon, *The Dryden Family 1286–1989* (Hamilton, 1989) pp.585–6.

2. See Elizabeth Bloomfield and Gilbert A. Stelter (eds.), *Guelph and Wellington County. A Bibliography of Settlement and Development Since 1800* (Guelph, 1988), pp.1–13; see also Elizabeth Bloomfield (ed.), *Inventory of Primary and Archival Sources. Guelph and Wellington County to 1940* (Guelph, 1989). I am grateful to the project director, Gil Stelter, for many stimulating discussions on the subject of this paper.

3. C. Erickson, *Invisible Immigrants; The Adaption of English and Scottish Immigrants in Nineteenth Century America* (London, 1972); Marianne Mclean, 'Peopling Glengarry

County: The Scottish Origins of a Canadian Community', in *Canadian Historical Association Papers* (1982); '*Achd an Rhigh*: A Highland Response to the Assisted Emigration of 1815', in D.H. Akenson (Ed.), *Canadian Papers in Rural History*, vol.5 (Ontario, 1986); J.M. Bumsted, *The People's Clearance: Highland Emigration to British North America 1770–1815* (Edinburgh, 1982); Bernard Bailyn, *Voyagers to the West* (New York, 1986); Marjorie Harper, *Emigration From North-East Scotland*, 2 vols. (Aberdeen, 1988); T.M. Devine, *The Great Highland Famine: Hunger, Emigration and the Scottish Highlands in the Nineteenth Century* (Edinburgh, 1988); David Hackett Fischer, *Albion's Seed: British Folkways in North America* (Oxford, 1989).

4. N.S.A. Yarrow 58; Edgar Johnson, *Sir Walter Scott: The Great Unknown*, 2 vols. (London, 1970), I, p.192.

5. Andrew W. Taylor, *Our Todays and Yesterdays. A History of the Township of North Dumfries and the Village of Ayr* (Galt, 1970), pp.33–4.

6. James Young, *Reminiscences of the Early History of Galt and the Settlement of Dumfries* (Toronto, 1880), p.41.

7. I am indebted to Margaret Fraser of Dumfries Township who discovered the letters in the Cambridge City Archives (MG8 vol.1 A988.213.52/53). William Dickson named the main settlement in his township Galt, after John the novelist who founded the city of Guelph for the Canada Company in 1827. In the 1970s the city of Galt was incorporated, together with the neighbouring communities of Hespeler and Preston, under the uninspired and ill-chosen nomenclature of Cambridge. On Dickson see James E. Kerr 'Sketch of the Life of Hon. William Dickson', *Fourth Annual Report of the Waterloo Historical Society* (Kitchener, 1916), pp.26–32 and Edith G.K. Stirton, 'A Most Romantic Story', *The Gallovidian Annual* (Dumfries, 1931). The hazy notions which Scottish writers had of their emigrant compatriots and the country which they settled is well exemplified in the statement that 'Dumfries [Township] today includes the thriving town of Winnipeg'! James McGowan, *Distinguished Dumfriessians* (London Dumfriesshire Association, n.d.). A substantial number of Dickson's papers are preserved in the Archives of Ontario and in Cambridge City Archives.

8. James Hogg, *The Works of the Ettrick Shepherd*, 2 vols. (London, 1865), I pp.426–8.

9. William Cobbett, *Cobbett's Tour in Scotland*, ed. Daniel Green (Aberdeen, 1984), p.123.

10. James Hunter, *The Making of the Crofting Community* (Edinburgh, 1976) pp.15–33; Bumstead, *People's Clearance*, pp.27–107; Eric Richards, *A History of the Highland Clearances*, vol 1, *Agrarian Transformation and the Evictions* (London, 1982), pp.209–45.

11. Robert A. Dodgshon, 'Agricultural Change and its Social Consequences in the Southern Uplands of Scotland 1600–1780', in T.M. Devine and David Dickson (eds.) *Ireland and Scotland 1600–1850* (Edinburgh, 1983) pp.53–7; T.M. Devine, 'Social Responses to Agrarian Improvement: The Highland and Lowland Clearances to in Scotland', in R.A. Houston and I.D. Whyte (eds.) *Scottish Society 1500–1800* (Cambridge, 1989), pp.148–68; Edward J. Cowan, 'Agricultural Improvement and the Foundation of Early Agricultural Societies in Dumfries and Galloway', in *The Transactions of the Dumfriesshire and Galloway Natural History and Antiquarian Society*, LIII (1978), p.166.

12. Dodgshon, 'Agricultural Change' p.53.

13. O.S.A. Selkirk, p.707, Peebles, p.807.

14. O.S.A. Hownam, pp.467–8.

15. Robert Heron, *Observations on a Journey through the Western Counties of Scotland in the Autumn of MDCCXCII*, 2 vols. (Perth, 1792), I p.58.

16. N.S.A. Wamphray, p.150, Hutton, p.540, O.S.A. Hawick, p.449, N.S.A. Roberton, p.94.

17. N.S.A. Ettrick, p.70.

18. Norman Murray, *The Scottish Handloom Weavers* (Edinburgh, 1978), is mainly concerned with Glasgow and the west of Scotland. On the Borders see C. Gulvin, *The Tweedmakers: A History of the Scottish Fancy Woollen Industry 1600–1914* (Newton Abbot, 1973).

19. *Dumfries and Galloway Courier* 13 December 1809.

20. *Farmers Magazine* (1810), p.261.

21. Samuel Smith, *General View of the Agriculture of Galloway* (London, 1810), pp.77–8.

22. J. David Wood, 'Complicity of Climate in the 1816 Depression in Dumfriesshire', *Scottish Geographical Magazine*, 81 (1965), *passim*.

23. Murray, *Scottish Handloom Weavers*, p.173.

24. Robert Douglas, *General View of the Agriculture of the County of Roxburgh* (Edinburgh, 1813) p.17.

25. For an illuminating account of the widening gulf between farmers and labourers when the latter were not allowed beyond the kitchen, and the occupants of the 'big hoose' were regarded with a certain awe, see the first four chapters of S.R. Crockett, *Raiderland. All About Grey Galloway* (London, 1904). For a devastating fictional treatment which savagely, but effectively, dramatises Scottish rural life in the nineteenth century see James Barke, *Land of the Leal* (1939, rep. Edinburgh, 1987).

26. O.S.A. Bedrules, p.365.

27. N.S.A. Yarrow, p.58.

28. For parallel developments in the Highlands which undoubtedly influenced Border mentalities see Peter Womack, *Improvement and Romance: Constructing the Myth of the Highlands* (London, 1989).

29. N.S.A. Jedburgh, p.20, Melrose p.71, Roxburgh p.34, Yetholm p.167.

30. N.S.A. Linton, p.158.

31. E.g. Douglas, *General View . . . Roxburgh*, p.219.

32. Laurence J. Saunders, *Scottish Democracy 1815–1840. The Social and Intellectual Background* (Edinburgh, 1950), p.11.

33. Edward J. Cowan, 'The "Despotism of Law" in an Agricultural Community', *The Juridical Review*, 1980, pt.1, pp.47–60.

34. John Younger, *Autobiography of John Younger, Shoemaker, St Boswells* (Kelso, 1881), pp.200, 202.

35. Douglas, *General View . . . Roxburgh*, p.218. For interesting English parallels see Bob Bushaway, *By Rite: Custom, Ceremony and Community in England 1700–1880* (London, 1982).

36. O.S.A. Kells, p.272, N.S.A. Hownam p.198–9, St Mungo, p.211; Douglas, *General View . . . Roxburgh*, p.218

37. N.S.A. Kelso, p.322.

38. S.R.O. Buccleuch GD 224 511/20, 25 February 1843.

39. Gilbert A. Stelter, 'Combining Town and Country Planning in Upper Canada: William Gilkison and the Founding of Elora, in *Historic Guelph. The Royal City*, XXIV, *Guelph Historical Society* (1985), pp.23–27.

40. Adam Fergusson, *Practical Notes Made During a Tour in Canada* (Edinburgh, 1839), pp.412–4.

41. Opportunities for weavers in Upper Canada were outlined in William Thomson, *A Tradesman's Travels in the United States and Canada*, 2 vols. (Stonehaven, 1842).

42. William Catermole, *Advantages of Emigration to Canada* (London, 1832), pp.197–208.

43. 'A Letter from Guelph, Upper Canada 1831', *Guelph Historical Society Publications*, XIII, No.4 (1973), p.1–5. Despite claims to the contrary by the anonymous editor of Inglis's letter neither the original nor other letters by Inglis appear to be preserved in the Archives of Ontario.

44. Gordon, *Dryden Family*, p.19.

45. Younger, *Autobiography*, 118, 133, 169.

46. Catermole, *Advantages of Emigration*, p.202.

47. Younger, *Autobiography*, p.407 ff.

48. S.R.O. Buccleuch GD 224 511/20, 8 November 1842.

49. S.R.O. Buccleuch GD 224 511/20, 11 November 1842.

50. S.R.O. Buccleuch GD 224 511/20, 25 February 1843.

51. S.R.O. Buccleuch GD 224 512/20, 1834–5.

52. N.S.A. Hawick, p.388–9.

53. Young, *Reminiscences*, pp.149–70; Taylor, *Our Todays*, pp.188–92

54. Henry Cockburn, *Memorials of His Time* (Edinburgh, 1910), p.310.

55. Younger, *Autobiography*, p.128.

56. S.R.O. Scott GD 1/813/6, 14 February 1842.

57. S.R.O. Scott GD 1/813/17, n.d.

58. Fergusson, *Practical Notes*, p.131.

59. The same point is implied in Inglis's letter discussing pheasant-shooting. 'It is just fire and load as long as you please, but I very seldom ever take a shot' (*Guelph Historical Society*, 1973, p.4). Yet another example is drawn from a letter (1841) written by James Edgar of Ayr in Dumfries Township: 'We are not afraid of the Lord or Fackter. We can take a gun or fishing rod and nobody says what art thou going to do but when a man has got so much liberty he does not care so much about it . . .' James R. Barrie, '"The Hill" in North Dumfries in 1841', *Waterloo Historical Society*, 74 (1986), p.131. Incidentally, Edgar remarks that 'there is a great many people from Ayrshire settled round about' (130).

60. D.G. Courier 15 June 1819.

61. W. Hamish Fraser, 'Patterns of Protest', in T.M. Devine and Rosalind Mitchison (eds.), *People and Society in Scotland 1760–1830* (Edinburgh, 1988), pp.285–6 and refs.

62. *Dumfries and Galloway Courier* 21 December 1819.

63. *Ibid.*, 25 March 1833.

64. *Farmers Magazine* (1820), pp.321–32.

65. Kenneth McLaughlin, *Cambridge: The Making of a Canadian City* (Burlington, 1987), p.33. Dumfries Township is fortunate in having a fairly complete series of nominal censuses and assessments from 1816 onwards (University of Guelph Library CA20N RA 84652 Microfilm Reel 1). While these lists have not yet been systematically analysed they demonstrate that while Scots were in a majority they by no means monopolised settlement as they did for example on the 1820 assessment roll for the Township of Aldborough on the shores of Lake Erie in which every single

name is Scottish (mostly Highland): *The Pioneer Days in Aldborough* (Aylmer, rep. 1984), pp.92–4.

66. A.D. Campbell, 'Dr John Scott—Berlin's first Licensed Physician', in *Waterloo Historical Society Annual*, vol 72 (1984); Michael E. Vance 'Impressions of a Berlin Pioneer—the emigrant letters of Dr John Scott', in *Waterloo Historical Society Annual*, vol 78 (1990) (article wrongly attributed to William E. Vance).

67. Taylor, *Our Todays*, pp.91–2.

68. People from Hawick take their appellation of Tiris (pronounced teeries) from the song sung at the Common Riding:

> Up wi Hawick its rights and common
> Up wi a the Border bowmen
> Tiribus and Tirioden
> We are up to guard the common
>
> (N.S.A. Hawick 399)

Tiribus and Tirioden are popularly supposed to preserve the names of old Norse gods, Tyr and Odin (N.S.A. Hawick 380).

69. S.R.O. Scott GD 1/813/15, 28 October 1838.

70. *Ibid.*

71. S.R.O. Scott GD 1/813/1, 29 August 1835.

72. S.R.O. Scott GD 1/813/4, 18 September 1840.

73. *Ibid.*

74. S.R.O. Scott GD 1/813/13, 12 November 1845. Cf the Edgar letter: 'I would not like to advise any to come here for fear that they would reflect on me but I am sure if once they were here and settled they would not go back to Scotland to live again.' Barrie, 'The Hill' p.135.

75. S.R.O. GD Scott 1/813/17, n.d.

76. S.R.O. GD Scott 1/813/15, 28 October 1838.

77. Edward J. Cowan, 'Internal Migration in Nineteenth-Century Scotland', *Families*, 21, no. 4 (1982), *passim*.

78. Robert Murray, *Hawick Characters* (Hawick, 1910), pp.v–vi.

79. S.R.O. Scott GD 1/813/6, 14 February 1842.

80. Rowland Berthoff, 'Under the Kilt: Variations on the Scottish–American Ground', *Journal of American Ethnic History*, 1, no. 2 (1982); Edward J. Cowan, 'Ethnic Sports in Canada: The Scottish Contribution', *Polyphony. The Bulletin of the Multicultural History Society of Ontario*, 7, no.1 (1985).

81. The history of Scottish popular culture in Canada is the subject of a forthcoming paper by the present writer.

82. I am indebted to Mr Stuart Clarkson, Guelph, for providing copies of his ancestral letters. Copies of the Bryden letters are deposited in the University of Guelph Archives.

83. Bryden, 11 March 1835.

84. *Ibid.*, 22 March 1836.

85. *Ibid.*, 22 May 1837.

86. *Ibid.*, 3 October 1837.

87. *Ibid.*, 3 June 1845.

88. *Ibid.*, 22 May 1837.

89. *Ibid.*, 3 October 1837.

90. Younger, *Autobiography*, p.407.

91. Taylor, *Our Todays*, pp.297–8.

92. John MacQueen and Tom Scott (eds.), *The Oxford Book of Scottish Verse* (Oxford, 1966), p.422.

93. N.S.A. Hutton and Corrie, p.539.

94. Cobbett, *Tour*, p.124.

5

Landlordism and Highland Emigration

T.M. Devine

I

In the popular mind, Highland clearances and Highland emigration are inextricably linked. The depopulation of northern Scotland is seen as the direct result of the expropriation of the traditional peasantry and their forced removal from their homeland. A series of best-selling books, from Alexander Mackenzie's *A History of the Highland Clearances* (1883) to John Prebble's *The Highland Clearances* (1963), together with the impact of such theatrical works as John McGrath's *The Cheviot, the Stag and the Black, Black Oil,* have created an indelible impression on the popular interpretation of the great Highland exodus of the eighteenth and nineteenth centuries. It is seen as the inevitable consequence of landlord oppression and coercion. People left for Canada and Australasia not because they wished to but because they had to. Ironically, however, much academic writing on this subject over the last couple of decades has offered a set of explanations which are often in conflict with these perceptions. The traditional view is criticised because of its failure to acknowledge that much emigration from the western Highlands occurred in the eighteenth century during a period when landlords were entirely opposed to losing population because of the labour requirements of kelp manufacture and fishing enterprises.[1] In addition, scholars such as J.M. Bumsted have argued that this emigration was one of 'rising expectations' and a 'People's clearance' which took place in defiance of the express wishes and policies of the landlord class.[2] Other commentators, in particular Michael Flinn and Eric Richards, criticise the traditional thesis as simplistic and melodramatic. They represent that important current in academic thinking which has increasingly focused on demographic and economic forces as the root causes of the Highland movement.[3] Flinn provides a very plausible explanation of emigration increasing because rising population was pressing against the fragile economy

84

of the region, thus forcing an outflow of people. In this analysis, landlords become bit players and cease to occupy centre stage in the Highland drama. Estate policy may complicate matters at the local level but essentially the fundamental influences are those of demography and the impact of external economic constraints on the poor population of the north-west.

Perhaps only James Hunter, among recent writers, in his *The Making of the Crofting Community* (1978) has tried to provide some scholarly support for the more popular interpretation of Highland history. In Hunter's book the landlords are once again cast in their traditional role as villains, dominating and exploiting their people and systematically pursuing policies of clearance and forced emigration. But Hunter's analysis has not been generally accepted within the mainstream of historical scholarship despite its foundations in wide-ranging archival research.[4] This is partly because of the author's unwillingness to set landlord activity in its social and cultural context and his failure to combine demographic and economic analysis with an evaluation of élite behaviour. Landlordism was much more complex and more subject to powerful pressures and constraints than Hunter allows. But criticism of Hunter's position may mean that the case for a central role for landlordism in Highland emigration could go by default. This is a pity because it is the thesis of this chapter that élite influence was a vital factor in the exodus of the eighteenth and nineteenth centuries and that there has been a tendency in some recent writing to underestimate its significance.

II

'Landlordism' in this discussion encompasses the tactics and strategies of individual proprietors, the actions of estate factors and the legal structure of landlord authority. The élites of the Scottish Highlands enjoyed unusual power and it was this which gave them the capacity to influence the mobility of their people. Peasant proprietorship of land in the sense known in continental Europe did not exist. Instead, after the creation of the crofting system in the later eighteenth century, three different social groups emerged on most Highland estates.[5] The first were known as tacksmen or leaseholders, who formed a small section of the population, paid rental of £30 to £40 per annum or more and had some security of tenure with leases which gave access to land for at least seven years. The second class consisted of small tenants (on most estates the numerical majority) who possessed their small holdings only on an annual basis. Finally, there emerged through the practice of partible inheritance by tenants and natural increase in regional population, a third group, the cottars. They had no legal rights to land and as far as the law was concerned were little better than squatters. In essence, therefore, apart from the small class of tacksmen, many of whom by the nineteenth century were sheep farmers, the vast majority of the Highland population were in a profoundly insecure position and very vulnerable to the will of the landlord class. The teneurial system worked to landlord advantage.

Three factors further supported the power of the élites. First, decisions within the Scottish parliament before 1707 and the Court of Session after that date had created legal machinery which was admirably suited to enforcing mobility of population.[6] If a landlord wished to evict a tenant, either because he was in rent arrears or had refused to move after the end of a lease, a simple application to the local Sheriff Court for a 'Summons of Removal' was all that was required. This was then served on the tenant who had a specified number of days to respond or comply. Analysis of the records of the Highland courts of Portree, Stornoway and Tobermory reveals that this mechanism was employed systematically to implement clearance.[7]

Second, the social context of estate policy worked to landlord advantage. The clearances did not occur peacefully. There was certainly more dissent and protest in the Scottish Highlands than previously thought.[8] But the Highland peasantry were much less menacing than the Irish poor and few landowners were inhibited from taking action because they feared violent retaliation from the people of their estates.[9]

Third, especially after c.1820, proprietors were in an even more powerful position. Partly this was because of the collapse of the labour-intensive economy built around kelp, fishing, illicit whiskymaking and military employment and the rapid expansion after the end of the Napoleonic Wars of the capital-intensive sector of sheep-ranching. Small tenants, crofters and cottars became, in the contemporary expression, 'redundant', with limited bargaining power in relation to landowners and increasingly vulnerable to removal because of accumulating rent arrears and changes in estate priorities. At the same time, a revolution took place in Highland landownership. Between 1810 and 1860 an estimated 60 per cent of west Highland estates above 5,000 acres changed hands from the debilitated hereditary élite to a new class of merchants, lawyers, bankers, financiers and southern landowners.[10] This gave the landed class much more power to fund schemes of assisted or compulsory emigration for the poor and destitute who could not themselves afford the costs of transatlantic passage and resettlement.

The above is the essential context for understanding the central role that landlordism played in Highland emigration. To demonstrate its impact it is now intended to examine two phases of emigration in detail where sufficient data exist to distinguish the relative significance of landlord action. The first period is that of the American and Napoleonic Wars of the eighteenth century. Part of this has been explored by Bernard Bailyn, who analysed the Register of Emigrants of the early 1770s and brought a new precision to the subject.[11] The second is the assisted emigrations associated with the Highland potato famine of the 1840s and 1850s. Much information exists in landlord archives, government files and legal records which casts considerable light on this period.

III

The Seven Years' War (1756–63) seems to have been something of a watershed in Highland transatlantic emigration. Although precise figures are difficult to obtain, current estimates, based on customs records, the contemporary press and government enquiry, clearly demonstrate a quite dramatic increase in outward movement in the years between 1763 and the outbreak of the American War of Independence in 1775.[12] I.C.C. Graham, who conducted a careful survey of the existing evidence, reckons that 9,500 Highlanders left for North America between 1768 and 1775.[13] Even this total, however, is almost certainly an underestimate because Graham did not take into account the significant number of emigrants of Highland origin who left from Lowland ports. In addition, customs administration in the north was weak and patchy and an unknown number of emigrants must have escaped the surveillance of local officials.

Even given these qualifications, however, the figure is still striking. The 9,500 Highlanders represented over 60 per cent of the estimated total Scottish exodus at this time of about 16,000, although the Highland region contained less than 40 per cent of the Scottish population. Not only was Highland emigration increasing at this time, it was clearly doing so at a much faster pace than that of the rest of Scotland. Indeed, Bailyn's analysis of British emigrants to North America in 1773–6 reveals that more left from the Highlands than from any other British region with the exception of London. An astonishing 18 per cent of all British emigrants in these years came from the Highlands and Islands of Scotland, one of the most sparsely populated areas of the United Kingdom.[14]

However, it is important to note that there was no continuous or increasing volume of emigration. The great exodus of people all but ceased during the the American War. Reliable information on what happened thereafter is even more incomplete and ambiguous than before 1775 but evidence from estate papers and contemporary comment indicates that while emigration resumed it did so at a much slower pace and on a reduced scale.[15] Even the serious subsistence crisis of 1782–3 did not produce a significant renewal of emigration and when outward movement became more substantial from c.1785 it still occurred at irregular intervals with great variation between localities. After the outbreak of war in 1793 emigration slowed to a trickle until the Peace of Amiens in 1801. Between 1801 and 1803 the size of the outward movement was reminiscent of the high levels of emigration which occurred before the American War. Figures were quoted of a possible 20,000 Highlanders preparing to leave for the New World and careful enumerations by estate factors and local parish ministers suggested an actual emigration of between 3,000 and 4,000 departures from the Hebrides alone.[16] The sheer scale of the planned emigration shook both Highland landowners and government. The former were concerned about the loss of a labour force at a time when the profits of such labour-intensive activities as kelp production and fishing were high. The latter was equally sensitive to the haemorrhage of a population which had demonstrated its martial qualities in both the American and Napoleonic Wars. The immediate consequence of their dual anxieties was the passing of the Passenger Vessels Act in 1803. Its purpose was overtly humanitarian but in reality was designed to increase the costs of the transatlantic voyage and so reduce the incentives to emigrate.[17] The number of emigrants did fall drastically again after 1804 but this was mainly because of the resumption of hostilities rather than the impact of the new legislation. Nevertheless, individual parties of Highlanders continued to leave their native land. The following table summarises the rough estimates for the period 1700 to 1815.

The war was the decisive influence on this cyclical pattern of emigration. The remarkable exodus before 1775 was curtailed by the American War and that which was building up again from the early 1790s by the outbreak of conflict with revolutionary France. The chronology of Highland emigration before 1815 suggests that the internal forces making for outward movement were temporarily offset by the effects of hostilities. A clear illustration of this came in 1801 when a brief period of peace almost immediately precipitated a resurgence in high levels of emigration. War limited Highland emigration in several ways. Hostilities raised costs and interrupted sea transport. By cutting the link

TABLE 1
HIGHLAND EMIGRATION, 1700–1815

Period	Estimated Number of Highland Emigrants to North America
1700–60	Below 3,000
1760–75	c.10,000
1775–1801	2–3,000
1801–3	c.5,000
1803–15	c.3,000

with emigrant communities overseas for some years, it inevitably delayed the renewal of vital connections. One reason why emigration declined in the 1780s was that the American War severed traditional ties with North Carolina and New York and it took time to establish or renew equally close relationships with the 'new' migrant areas of Upper Canada, Prince Edward Island and Nova Scotia.[18] In addition, the Highlands made a huge contribution to the British army and navy in both the great wars of the later eighteenth century. Military service both at home and overseas became an alternative to emigration. The profits and prestige to be derived from raising family regiments from among the people of their estates encouraged some landlords to postpone the execution of the radical economic strategies which were promoting emigration. Detailed study of three different properties in mainland Inverness-shire has revealed a temporary pause in eviction and dispossession in the 1790s as landowners attempted to recruit the tenantry to their personal regiments.[19]

The main outlines of the sequence of emigration from the Highlands in this period are not in dispute. But the reasons why so many from this particular region of Scotland should seek to emigrate are far from clear.[20] Certainly a more satisfactory context for mass emigration from northern Scotland had emerged by the second half of the eighteenth century. The foundations of Highland communities in North Carolina, Georgia and New York from the 1730s created the essential basis for 'chain migration'. The commercial relationship between Scotland and North America was revolutionised by the remarkable success of Glasgow in the tobacco trade from the 1730s. The American trades helped to provide the transport infrastructure for large-scale emigration from Scotland. Most Highland communities were within relatively easy travelling distance of the Clyde ports and vessels were also often chartered from there by organised emigration parties. It was the growing trade in Canadian timber to Scotland in the early nineteenth century which helped to offset the impact of the Passenger Vessels Act of 1803 on emigration.[21] The British timber market's demand for Canadian lumber radically increased as a result of wartime needs. The timber trade required large vessels but these had low freights on the outward journey. The emigrant traffic to Upper Canada and the maritime provinces was therefore an effective means of utilising surplus capacity and cutting freight costs.

Highland society at all social levels had also become less insular by the later eighteenth century. Reference has already been made to the military service of Highlanders in the Seven Years' War, the American Wars and the French Revolutionary War. But its extraordinary scale needs to be emphasised. So extensive was it that demographers can show that marriage and fertility rates were affected in a significant way by the absence of young adult males.[22] One estimate suggested that 37,000 men were raised in the years 1793–1815, organised in forty battalions and seven militias of the Highland counties.[23] Military recruitment of this magnitude must have accustomed Highland society to greater mobility. This was even more likely when government paid off officers and men in colonial land; these military settlements then provided another point of attraction to kinsfolk at home. A key element in this Highland emigration was the leadership given to many emigrant parties by gentlemen or lesser gentry who had either obtained land in, or had become familiar with, the colonies as a result of their service within the officer class of the British army.[24]

All these influences facilitated emigration. But they could not in themselves cause it to happen. In the search for causation, contemporary commentators and later scholars have addressed both the impact of conditions in the Highlands and the opportunities emerging in North America. M.W. Flinn argues that the increasing volume of emigration reflected the pressure of rising population which led, in turn, to an outflow of 'surplus' peasants and their families.[25] This is a hypothesis which at first glance has much to commend it. Numbers did increase substantially in northern Scotland in the later eighteenth century. The Highland economy was indeed poor and underdeveloped. In the long run, when the emigration of the Highland people is examined down to the middle decades of the eighteenth century, the Malthusian explanation does have real force.[26] Population loss was inevitable because the regional economy proved utterly incapable over time of generating the necessary level of employment. However, the picture between 1760 and 1815 is considerably more complex and it is by no means certain that the demographic explanation is entirely satisfactory for that earlier period.

There are several problems. First, though numbers were increasing, economic activity was also expanding. There were indeed years of crisis, such as 1772–3, 1782–3 and 1801–2, brought about by harvest failure and they may have helped to trigger some emigration. In addition, the vast majority of the population continued to eke out an existence at, or only marginally above, subsistence level. Nevertheless, in these decades, there was a huge increase in employment opportunities, especially in the western Highlands and Islands from which most emigrants came, in kelp manufacture, fishing, illicit whisky-making, the seasonal migrant economy in the Lowlands and, above all, military service. Landlord correspondence in these years often reveals a fear of actual labour shortage on some estates, a concern which explains why most lairds were resolutely opposed to emigration from these properties.[27]

Second, detailed investigation of the emigration process does not provide confirmation of the Malthusian hypothesis. This was no flight of the very poor or of the most vulnerable in Highland society. For a start, without some assistance sea migration would have been out of the reach of the impoverished. One historian reckons that '. . . even for indigent emigrants travelling to a wilderness totally supported by charity £10 was a minimum cost per adult . . .'[28] With the majority of the landlord class firmly opposed in this period, the only evidence of substantial 'assisted' emigration was that which took place from South Uist. This was enthusiastically supported by the Catholic Church in Scotland because it feared Protestant proselytism. The venture partially explains why the Roman Catholic islands and enclaves on the western mainland tended to generate more emigrants than many other areas.[29]

The alternative for the poor and distressed was to obtain passage as indentured servants. But a remarkably small proportion of all Highland emigrants at this time travelled in this fashion. Only 150 of the nearly 3,000 Scots emigrants documented in the customs return for 1774–5 were indentured and most of these were Lowlanders.[30] The vast majority of those who left the Highlands for North America in the period did so by using their own resources. They belonged overwhelmingly to the tenant group, the middle rank in Highland society, those with some surplus above subsistence, with sufficient stocks of cattle, sheep, goats and household goods which, when sold, could raise money for passage and resettlement for themselves and their kinsfolk.[31] Examinations of passenger lists have shown that the movement was led by married tenant farmers of mature years, with their wives, children, other relatives, servants and subtenants. The emigration parties were well organised, usually had close links with established emigrant communities across the Atlantic, carried with them substantial sums of money and consisted of large numbers of related families from specific estates, communities or districts of the Highlands.[32] This was not an exodus born of desperation or the stress of hunger and destitution. Rather it was a movement which involved a degree of calculation and a careful weighing of prospects on the part of social groups who were able to exert some choice. They could exploit favourable circumstances. One reason for the sudden surge in emigration in 1802–3 was that cattle prices peaked in these years, thus yielding good returns in the sale of stock to help defray the costs of transport and resettlement.[33] At the same time, on some estates, tenants employed the threat of emigration as a means of thwarting or delaying landlord plans for the reorganisation of their holdings.[34] All this hardly suggests a people driven by the inexorable pressure of demographic forces from their native land.

J.M. Bumsted contends on the contrary that 'the Highlander chose to come to America of his own free will and usually to improve his situation rather than escape grinding depression. This emigration was one of rising expectations.'[35] The explanation recognises the lure of cheap land and freedom from feudal oppression that was clearly significant in promoting emigration. Information received by letter from earlier emigrants, the impact of chain migration, the work of emigrant agents and reports from returning soldiers had created a powerful image of the *New World* as a land of opportunity.[36] Bumsted's thesis is also consistent with our knowledge of the social composition of the emigrant parties. They were, as already seen, drawn predominantly from the 'middling' element in the society which apparently had the possibility of some freedom of choice. In addition, the argument is based on the assumption that there were no fundamental coercive or push forces which could reasonably account for emigration on this scale. He suggests that the clearance of peasant communities in order to establish large sheep farms, a pivotal factor in post-1815 emigration, was not significant in the earlier period, especially in the western Highlands and Islands from where most emigration occurred. This was then a 'People's Clearance' rather than one directly inspired by landlord action.

Bumsted is correct to an extent in his dismissal of sheep clearances as a causal factor. They were very limited before 1815 in most of the Outer and Inner Hebrides where the landed class was creating a labour-intensive economic structure based on kelp, fishing and military employment.[37] But even in this earlier period, the development of commercial pastoralism was not irrelevant to emigration. Close links have been identified between the clearances and emigration in mainland Argyll, several parishes in mainland Inverness, some parts of Sutherland and at least one estate in Skye.[38] Moreover, it is clear that the relentless march of the big sheep farmers was spreading deep alarm and anxiety throughout the western Highlands.[39] Preparation for emigration was often a prudent precaution to avoid the expected future catastrophe of complete dispossession.

The Bumsted thesis also does not fully take into account the extraordinary scale and intensity of the broader social and economic changes which were sweeping across the Highland region. Powerful forces of coercion were at work, quite apart from the familiar expansion of sheep-ranching. Long before the ill-fated Jacobite rebellion of 1745, commercialisation of the society was well under way. The cattle trade, rent-commutation, landlord 'improving' strategies, seasonal migration and exploitation of slate and timber resources were all symptoms of this process. Yet, in many ways, a military social order remained alongside these new economic tendencies. The post 'forty-five pacification accelerated the destruction of the rationale for clanship, though the old martial connection continued to be used by several chiefs to levy men for the British army from their estates. But because the state had now effectively imposed the rule of law throughout the Highlands, it had implicitly undermined the value of the clan and of military tenures as sources of protection and defence for the élite and so created a more suitable context for the rapid acceleration of commercial development. Such a process, however, was likely to cause profound social disorientation as it would be achieved in concentrated and intensive fashion over a much shorter time-scale than occurred in the Lowlands.[40]

Ironically, however, the full impact was delayed for a decade or so. Only from the later 1760s did the real magnitude of the changes become apparent because only then did southern markets for Highland produce start to expand quickly. In the next few years many landowners systematically subordinated their estates to the pursuit of profit. The methods varied from area to area but the general strategy was to extract more income from the land and to transform the traditional social structure in ways consistent with this new priority. Thus the old joint tenancy settlements or bailetoun on many Hebridean estates were dissolved and replaced by single croft holdings. This may not have been as dramatic as sheep clearances but it was nevertheless a radical attack on the delicate social hierarchy of the old order.[41] It involved both dispossession and social levelling. Often the allocation of the new crofts was designed to compel the people to depend more on the highly laborious manufacture of kelp to pay rental. Above all, the croft system was a mortal threat to the middle tenantry whose larger holdings were likely to be divided to support the larger labour force demanded for kelping and commercial fishing. Equally threatened were the tacksmen, or gentry of the clans, whose military role was now redundant and whose middleman position had no relevance in the new economic order. They contributed significantly to the leadership of many emigrant parties. Commercialisation also meant sharp increases in rental which produced acute pressures in such years of distress as 1772–3 when cattle prices were depressed but tenants needed to import more Lowland grain at higher prices. Rent inflation was characteristic of all of rural Scotland in these decades but it almost certainly caused more stress among the population of the western Highlands because of the relative poverty and hostile climate of that region. Emigration from the area before 1815 cannot then be understood without acknowledging the central role of landlord action in promoting social dislocation.

IV

From this point the discussion moves to the middle decades of the nineteenth century and to one of the greatest economic and social disasters in Highland history. In the 1840s and 1850s over 10,000 Highlanders were assisted by private landlords to move to Canada during the potato famine. Table two sets out the basic information concerning chronology and the geographical origins of the emigrant groups.

The data confirm the scale of Highland assisted emigration. One estimate suggests that about 14,000 inhabitants of the region were supported in their passage across the Atlantic in the entire period c.1800 to 1860.[42] Apparently about seventy-two per cent of this total left in the single decade 1846–56. Moreover, local and regional variation in levels of assisted emigration was very considerable. The global total of just over 10,000 conceals the great haemorrhage of people which occurred from particular districts and estates over a relatively short time-scale. Those assisted to leave Tiree, for example, in these years represented just over one-third of the population of the island.[43] Parts of Lewis, Barra and South Uist were also denuded of many families and settlements by the same process.

The coincidence between crop failure and heavy emigration seems to suggest a causal connection. Indeed, it can hardly be doubted that the great subsistence crisis did create the preconditions for a massive exodus. The duration of the potato blight was important. The meal crop tended only to fail in part and then normally for a season or two. But the potato blight endured in the Hebrides and some maritime districts of the western Highlands for virtually a decade. The poorest classes of the region, those most dependent on the potato, were also assailed

TABLE 2

ASSISTED EMIGRATION TO BRITISH NORTH AMERICA BY HIGHLAND
LANDOWNERS 1846–56

Estate	Proprietor	No. of Emigrants	Year
Mainland			
Sutherland	Duke of Sutherland	397	1847
Sutherland	Duke of Sutherland	605	1848
Sutherland	Duke of Sutherland	59	1850
Sutherland	Duke of Sutherland	24	1851
Glenelg	James Baillie	344	1839
Knoydart	Mrs Josephine Macdonnell	332	1853
Lochalsh	William Lillingston	300	1849
Glen Urquhart	Earl of Seafield	'large'	1852
	Macdonald of Lochsheil	82	1852
	Miscellaneous	256	1851
		2,399	
Islands			
Lewis	Sir James Matheson	1,554	1851
Lewis	Sir James Matheson	453	1852
Lewis	Sir James Matheson	330	1855
N Uist	Lord Macdonald	234	1849
Barra & S Uist	Col John Gordon	270	1848
Barra & S Uist	Col John Gordon	957	1849
Barra & S Uist	Col John Gordon	1,681	1851
Tiree & Ross of Mull	Duke of Argyll	1,101	1847
Tiree & Ross of Mull	Duke of Argyll	627	1849
Tiree & Ross of Mull	Duke of Argyll	533	1851
Tiree & Ross of Mull	Duke of Argyll	18	1853
		7,756	

Total, Mainland and Islands = 10,155

Sources: SRO, AD 21/25, Petition of the Inhabitants of Glenelg; *Inverness Advertiser*, 20 July 1852; *PP.*, 1854, XLVI, *Papers Relative to Emigration to the North American Colonies*, p.79; *Witness*, 3 November 1849; *Inverness Advertiser*, 4 March 1851, 20 July 1852; NLS, Sutherland Estate Papers, Dep 313/2737, p.1178; *Inverness Courier*, 26 June 1851; Ms diary of J.M. Mackenzie, 1851; *PP*, XL (1850), *Papers Relative to Emigration to North American Colonies*, pp.7,22; *Witness*, 16 and 19 August 1848; Inveraray Castle, Argyll Estate Papers, Bundles 1533, 1804, 1535; *PP*, XLVI (1854), *Papers Relative to Emigration to the North American Colonies*, p.31.

by a combination of collapse in the earnings of temporary immigrants in the Lowland economy in 1848–9, a decline in black cattle prices between 1848 and 1852 and difficulties in commercial fishing.[44] These forces produced acute social stress and in some years a desire to leave which was especially pronounced among certain social groups. The chamberlain of the Duke of Argyll's estate of Tiree reported in 1849 that 'there are many applicants [for subsistence] both among the smaller crofters and cottars, more particularly the latter, who are ready to go in hundreds if provided with the means.'[45] Petitions from the people of other estates in Lochalsh and Glenelg also indicated the desire for emigration assistance.[46] Similarly, when help towards emigration was advertised in Skye in 1852 applications were received from more than 400 families.[47]

It would be wrong, however, to conclude that the assisted emigrations of the famine period provide complete confirmation of Flinn's emphasis on demographic forces as the central influences on outward movement. The interaction between crop failure, population pressure and economic crisis was a necessary but not a sufficient cause of this exodus. Other elements, and in particular, landlord strategy, were also vital. There were several reasons for this. For a start, even in those districts where the people were keen to leave, an ephemeral and slight improvement in conditions could quickly alter attitudes from enthusiasm for emigration assistance to determined opposition. Such responses were noted on the Macleod property in Skye in 1855 and on the Duke of Sutherland's lands in 1848.[48] In addition, there was considerable variation between districts in social attitudes to emigration, even in the depth of the crisis. Throughout the famine there was great reluctance to emigrate on Lord Macdonald's estate of North Uist, the Macdonnell property in Knoydart and Sir James Matheson's lands on Lewis.[49] The most remarkable instance of opposition came from the island of Lewis itself. Matheson's chamberlain, John Munro Mackenzie, surveyed the population in 1851 and selected c.2,500 for emigration assistance. Only seventeen per cent of the total agreed to accept. The fact, however, that over 2,200 were eventually 'emigrated' by the estate demonstrates how landlord strategy and coercion could effectively change attitudes even among those who were resolutely opposed to going.[50] The most reluctant were the poorest classes who were most dependent on relief. Yet, as will be seen in more detail below, it was precisely this group which most landowners were eager to expel.

Finally, as Table three demonstrates, there was little correlation between demographic crisis and the detailed chronology of assisted emigration. The years of most acute difficulty were 1846–7. But of the total number of assisted emigrants over the entire period of the famine, only fifteen per cent departed in this initial phase. Yet between 1849 to 1851 emigration accelerated and over sixty-five per cent of assisted parties left. This was the particular time when, as will be clarified below, landlords had a vested interest in promoting movement as policy moved from the provision of relief to expulsion of people. Between 1846

TABLE 3
TOTAL EMIGRANTS ASSISTED BY LANDOWNERS (AREA AND YEAR)
1846–56

Year	Mainland Emigrants	Island Emigrants	Total	As annual % of 1847–1855
1846	–	–	–	–
1847	397	1,101	1,498	15
1848	605	270	875	9
1849	644	1,816	2,460	24
1850	59	–	59	1
1851	280	3,768	4,048	40
1852	82	453	535	5
1853	332	18	350	3
1854	–	–	–	–
1855	–	330	330	3
Total	2,399	7,756	10,155	
% of Total	24	76	–	100

Sources: As for Table 2 above.

and 1856, therefore, the correlation was not so much with demographic disaster as with landlord pressure.

Highland proprietors had significant incentives to support extensive emigration in these years. The eighteenth-century hostility to loss of population crumbled in the years of economic crisis and continued growth in population after 1815. During the 1820s and especially during the harvest failures of 1836–7 several proprietors established schemes of assisted emigration.[51] But in the 1840s these early initiatives expanded on an unprecedented scale. As already indicated, in 1846–7 most landowners sought to provide relief for the distressed inhabitants of their estates. This benevolence, however, was ephemeral and from 1849 the strategy switched to one designed to export the poor and the destitute. The fear was that the entire burden of maintaining the stricken population would fall on the proprietors. Partly this was because the main organisation for famine relief, the Central Board of Management for Highland Destitution, intimated its intention to terminate its activities in 1850.[52] But it was also due to the rumours, widely circulating in the region, that the government was contemplating the introduction of 'an able-bodied Poor Law' as the best means of averting the persistent threat of starvation in the Highlands.[53] This would give the destitute, who formed the majority on most Highland properties, the legal right to claim relief. It would also establish the principle of compulsory rating and so threaten many proprietors with financial ruin. The mere suggestion of such legislation was enough to send tremors of alarm through the ranks of the landed classes. One observer noted in 1849 that it was 'being talked of in high quarters as a remedy for the grievances' of the Highlands.[54] Others suspected that Sir John McNeill, chairman of the Board of Supervision of the Scottish Poor Law, who was conducting an enquiry into Highland destitution in 1851, was likely to report in favour of such a measure.[55] In the event, however, he advised a programme of assisted emigration as the solution to the problems of the region. But before government came to a decision on his report, several landlords had concluded that they were likely to be left with the final responsibility for maintaining the poor on their properties, whether through direct famine relief or through the indirect cost of contributing to a massive extension of the Poor Law. Their eagerness to support emigration derived ultimately from the fact that the costs of assisted passages were in the long run much lower than either of these alternatives.[56]

This was the background to the assisted emigration schemes outlined in Table four. But the term 'assisted' gives a false impression of philanthropic motivation. Certainly most proprietors cancelled the rent arrears of those who emigrated, took their stock and other possessions at valuation, covered costs of passage to Canada and sometimes provided cash and meal for those who had to travel inland to their final destination. But several contemporary critics asserted that many schemes involved much pressure and that there

TABLE 4
TOTAL EMIGRANTS ASSISTED BY INDIVIDUAL PROPRIETORS, 1846–56

Proprietor	Total Assisted	Percentage of Total
John Gordon of Cluny	2,906	29
Sir James Matheson	2,279	22
Duke of Argyll	2,337	23
Duke of Sutherland	1,085	11
James Baillie	344	3
Mrs Josephine Macdonnell	332	3
William Lillingston	300	3
Lord Macdonald	234	2
Macdonald of Lochshiel	82	1
Miscellaneous	256	3
Total	10,155	100

Sources: As for Table 2 above.

was a good deal of 'compulsory emigration' or 'enforced expatriation' involved.[57]

A scrutiny of estate and legal papers associated with the landowners listed above confirms that coercion was indeed very widespread. It occurred on a significant scale on the lands of those proprietors who assisted 80 per cent of the emigrants in Table 3.[58] The most popular strategy was the serving of summonses or removal and presenting the bleak choice of eviction *or* loss of land and emigration assistance. After 1848 the volume of summonses of removal granted to landlords in west Highland Sheriff Courts dramatically increased. One hundred and eighty-seven writs of removal were issued to the Matheson estate in Lewis alone between 1846 and 1848 and in the following three years this multiplied sixfold to 1,180.[59] Yet it is important to note that clearance, or the threat of it, was only one of several weapons employed with great vigour to induce movement. These included the threat of confiscation of cattle stocks for those in rent arrears, prohibition of the right to cut peat supplies during the summer months for winter use and refusal to grant famine relief to those in distress.[60] Such techniques were applied with clinical care. Only the most destitute were normally offered support. As the Duke of Argyll noted in May 1851: 'I wish to send out those whom we would be obliged to feed if they stayed at home; to get rid of that class is *the object*' (underlined in letter).[61] Thus, on Tiree, great discrimination was employed in order to remove 'all the poorest and those most likely to be a burden on the property'.[62] Much of the strategy was designed to rid estates of that 'redundant' population which now languished in destitution as a result of the decline in kelp manufacture. This explains why on arrival in Canada many were compared to the Irish because of their ragged appearance. A detailed study of estate policy on the island of Lewis reveals that the administration tried to clear crofting townships in the west which had relied on kelp production while, at the same time, maintaining and consolidating fishing communities on the east coast which had a good record of regular rent payment.[64] Such selective use of emigration assistance ultimately depended on the application of threats, pressure and coercion.

V

This survey of two contrasting periods in Highland history suggests that landlordism has been underestimated as a force in emigration in some recent writing. Until the later nineteenth century, the western Highlands and Islands contributed disproportionately to Scottish emigration.[64] This chapter has argued that this was not simply the result of poverty, demographic stresses or economic weaknesses of the region but was also related to the changing priorities and aims of landlord policy. The creation of the croft system in the later eighteenth century produced more strain and induced more mobility among the middling social groups of the north-west than is sometimes assumed. The assisted emigrations of the middle decades of the nineteenth century resulted in an unprecedented movement of the very poor, the class which traditionally in the Highlands had been most reluctant to leave. That they did so in large numbers in these years was not simply because of the stress of hunger. It was also a consequence of estate strategy. In an important sense, these emigrations were the ultimate manifestations of the power of Highland landlordism.

NOTES

1. J.M. Bumsted, *The People's Clearance: Highland Emigration to British North America, 1770–1815* (Edinburgh, 1982).

2. *Ibid.*, p.63.

3. M.W. Flinn (ed.), *Scottish Population History from the Seventeenth Cenutury to the 1930s* (Cambridge, 1977), pp.443–6; M.W. Flinn 'Malthus Emigration and Potatoes in the Scottish North-West, 1770–1870', in L.M. Cullen and T.C. Smout (eds.), *Comparative Aspects of Irish and Scottish Economic and Social History* (Edinburgh, 1977); E. Richards, *A History of the Highland Clearances, vol. 2, Emigration, Protest, Reasons* (London, 1985).

4. See, for example, Allan I. Macinnes, 'Scottish Gaeldom: The First Phase of Clearance', in T.M. Devine and Rosalind Mitchison (eds.), *People and Society in Scotland, I, 1760–1830* (Edinburgh, 1988), pp.72–3; T.M. Devine, *The Great Highland Famine: Hunger, Emigration and the Scottish Highlands in the Nineteenth Century* (Edinburgh, 1988), pp.88–91.

5. These social groups are analysed in more detail in Devine, *Great Highland Famine*, ch.1.

6. *Ibid.*, p.185.

7. SRO, SC59/2/4–14, Sheriff Court Processes, Tobermory; SC32/5/1–2 Sheriff Court Processes, Portree; SC33/17/24–34, Stornoway.

8. E. Richards, 'How tame were the Highlanders during the Clearances?', *Scottish Studies*, xvii (1973).

9. T.M. Devine, 'Social Responses to Agrarian "Improvement": the Highland and Lowland Clearances in Scotland', in R.A. Houston and I.D. Whyte (eds.), *Scottish Society 1500–1800* (Cambridge, 1989), pp.148–68.

10. T.M. Devine, 'The Emergence of the New Elite in Scottish Highlands, 1790–1860' in T.M. Devine (ed.), *Improvement and Enlightenment* (Edinburgh, 1989).

11. B. Bailyn, *Voyagers to the West* (London, 1986).

12. This pre-1775 emigration can be examined in Bumsted, *The People's Clearance*, pp.1–82; Flinn, *Scottish Population History*, pp.443–6; I.C.C. Graham, *Colonists from Scotland: Emigration to North America 1707–1783*, (Ithaca, 1954).

13. Graham, *Colonists from Scotland*, p.114.

14. Bailyn, *Voyagers to the West*, p.111.

15. The pattern described below has been built up from an examination of correspondence in the following sets of estate papers in the Scottish Record Office, Edinburgh: GD201, Clananald Papers; GD221, Lord Macdonald Papers; GD46, Seaforth Muniments. In addition, material has been gathered from contemporary newspapers and periodical literature.

16. *Transactions of the Highland and Agricultural Society*, ii (1803), vii–xi; *Parliamentary Papers, Survey and Report on the Coasts and Central Highlands of Scotland*, pp.iv (1802–3), pp.9–10; Anon, *Remarks on the Earl of Selkirk's Observations on the Highlands* (Edinburgh, 1806), pp.288–9.

17. Hunter, *Making of the Crofting Community*, pp.24–6.

18. Marianne Maclean, 'In the New Land a New Glengarry: Migration from the Scottish Highlands to Upper Canada, 1750–1820', unpublished PhD thesis, University of Edinburgh, 1982, p.162.

19. *Ibid.*, p.219.

20. As long ago as the 1920s Margaret Adam was addressing some of these issues in a series of pioneering essays. See M. Adam 'The Highland Emigration of 1770', *Scott. Hist. Rev.*, xvi (1919); 'The Causes of the Highland Emigrations of 1783–1803', *Scott. Hist. Rev.*, xviii (1920); 'Eighteenth Century Highland Landlords and the Poverty Problem', *Scott. Hist. Rev.*, xix (1921–2).

21. Bumsted, *People's Clearances*, pp.191–2.

22. Flinn, *Scottish Population History*, p.14.

23. Eric Richards, *A History of the Highland Clearances* (London, 1982), I, p.148.

24. Maclean, 'In the New Land', *passim*.

25. Flinn, 'Malthus, Emigration and Potatoes in the Scottish North-West'.

26. Devine, *The Great Highland Famine*, *passim*.

27. Richard R. Berry, 'The Role of Hebridean Landlords in Early Nineteenth-Century Emigration', BA dissertation, Department of History, University of Strathclyde, 1979.

28. Bumsted, *People's Clearance*, p.12.

29. J.M. Bumsted, 'Highland Emigration to the Island of St John and the Scottish Catholic Church, 1769–1774', *Dalhousie Review*, 58 (1978), pp.511–27.

30. Bailyn, *Voyagers to the West*, p.165.

31. All detailed studies confirm this point. See Berry, 'Hebridean Landlords', pp.27–8; Bailyn, *Voyagers to the West*, pp.165, 515–16; Bumsted, *People's Clearance*, pp.74, 99; Maclean, 'In the New Land', pp.21, 368.

32. *Ibid.*

33. Thomas Douglas (Lord Selkirk), *Observations on the present state of the Highlands of Scotland* (London, 1805), p.79.

34. Scottish Record Office, Lord Macdonald Papers, GD 221/15, Minutes of Commissioners of Lord Macdonald, 7 November 1802.

35. Bumsted, *People's Clearance*, p.63.

36. Murdoch, 'Emigration to North Carolina in 1772', pp.438–49.

37. Devine, *Great Highland Famine*, ch.1.

38. Hunter, 'Crofting Community', p.27; Maclean, 'In the New Land', *passim*; Berry, 'Hebridean Landlords', p.8.

39. Selkirk, *Observations*, p.110.

40. The social impact is assessed in Devine, 'Social Responses to Agrarian "Improvement": the Highland and Lowland Clearances in Scotland', pp.148–68.

41. Macinnes, 'Scottish Gaeldom', pp.70–90.

42. James A. Cameron, 'A Study of the Factors That Assisted and Directed Scottish Emigration to Upper Canada, 1815–55', unpublished PhD thesis, University of Glasgow, 1970.

43. Inveraray Castle, [thereafter IC], Argyll Estate Papers, Bundle 1529, Lists of Families, Tiree and Ross of Mull, 1841 and 1849.

44. Free Church Destitution Committee, *Statements and Reports* (Edinburgh, 1847), Second Statement, pp.6–13; pp, 1851, xxvi, *Report to the Board of Supervision by Sir John McNeill on the Western Highlands and Islands*, appendix A, p.75.

45. IC, Argyll Estate Papers, Bundle 1805, John Campbell to Duke of Argyll, 17 May 1851.

46. SRO, HD 21/25, Petition of the inhabitants of Glenelg; *Inverness Advertiser*, 3 July 1849; *Witness*, 3 November 1849; IC, Argyll Estate Papers, John Campbell to Duke of Argyll, 17 May 1851.

47. *Report of the Highland Emigration Society* (London, 1853), p.10. See also Dunvegan Castle, Skye, Macleod Muniments 659/7/73, Ferguson to Madam Macleod 25 June 1852.

48. SRO HD 4/4, J. Chant to H. Rollo, 30 April 1848; Mitchell Library, Glasgow, MS 21506, Sir John McNeill to Sir Charles Trevelyan, 23 June and 21 August 1852; National Library of Scotland, Sutherland Estate Papers, Dep. 3B/2811, R. Horsburgh to E. Maciver, 2 June 1848.

49. PP., 1854–5, xxiv, *Ninth Annual Report of the Board of Supervision of Relief of the Poor in Scotland*, appendix A, no.1; P. Cooper, *An Old Story Retold* (Aberdeen, 1881); MS diary of J.M. Mackenzie, Chamberlain of the Lews, 1851.

50. MS diary of J.M. Mackenzie, 1851.

51. Cameron, 'Scottish Emigration to Upper Canada', *passim*.

52. Landlord motivation is surveyed in more detail in T.M. Devine, 'Highland Landowners and the Highland Potato Famine' in L. Leneman (ed.), *Perspectives in Scottish Social History* (Aberdeen, 1988).

53. *Witness*, 16 April 1851; National Library of Scotland, Sutherland Estate Papers, Dep.313/1176, J. Loch to Duke of Sutherland, 26 June 1848; SRO, HD 7/47, W. Skere to C. Trevelyan, 21 February 1848.

54. Anon, *The Depopulation System in the Highlands* (Edinburgh, 1849), p.23.

55. *Witness*, 16 April 1851.

56. See, for example, the very revealing letter written by Lord Macdonald in 1852 where he describes in detail the financial advantages of getting rid of 'our surplus population' through assisted emigration. Mitchell Library, Glasgow, MS 21506, Lord Macdonald to Sir John McNeil, 9 June 1852.

57. See, for example, Thomas Mulock, *The Western Highlands and Islands of Scotland Socially Considered* (Edinburgh, 1850).

58. This conclusion is based on a scrutiny of the estate papers and other documentation listed after Table 1 above.

59. SRO, Sheriff Court Processes, Stornoway, SC 33/17/26–33.

60. Devine, 'Highland Landlords', *passim*.

61. IC, Argyll Estate Papers, Bundle 1558, Duke of Argyll to ?, 5 May 1851.

62. *Ibid.*, Bundle 1805, John Campbell to Duke of Argyll, 17 May 1851.

63. PP, xxxiii (1852), *Papers relative to Emigration to the North American colonies*, p.567.

64. Devine, *Great Highland Famine*, pp.212–25.

65. I. Levitt and C. Smout, *The State of the Scottish Working Class in 1843* (Edinburgh, 1979), pp.236–58.

6

The Importance of Emigration in Scottish Regional Population Movement, 1861–1911[1]

Jeanette M. Brock

In the period 1861 to 1911 between 10 per cent and 47 per cent of the natural population increase of Scotland left the country each decade.[2] As the introduction to this volume indicated, in relation to European overseas emigration in this period, Scotland ranks very high, exceeded in the proportion of losses only by Ireland and Norway.[3] Although some studies of Scottish movement have been made, no national analysis of the geographical origins of emigrants has been attempted, and even now it is still not clearly established if this was a predominantly urban or rural movement.

The author Robert Louis Stevenson travelled on an emigrant ship from Glasgow and noted the urban origins of many emigrants,[4] a finding that has been supported by Erickson using passenger lists of British emigrants to the United States.[5] However, Brinley Thomas has suggested that the emigrant population was predominantly rural-born[6] and Flinn has argued that many of the large majority of urban emigrants identified by Erickson may have previously migrated from rural areas.[7] This hypothesis implies a relationship between emigration and migration and indeed in England and Wales Brinley Thomas identified an inverse relationship between these two forms of mobility.[8] In decades of low emigration migration was high and vice versa. More recent work suggests that the origins of emigrants reflected the increasingly urban character of Scotland, and that there was indeed a 'preponderance of urban emigrants'.[9] Even so, it is still possible that in proportional terms emigration was greater among the rural-born than among those of urban origin. Clearly, this considerable degree of uncertainty over the origins and nature of emigrants can only be resolved if quantitative estimates of Scottish emigration are available.

The aim of this study is to quantify outmovement from Scotland at the regional level, using a modification of the method devised by Baines for work in England and Wales.[10] The technique involved use of the county-of-residence by county-of-birth enumeration tabulated in the census, adding births and deducting deaths for every county over a given period and comparing the results of these calculations with the figures in the subsequent census.[11] The difference between the calculated and the actual figures represents Scots who were missing and were assumed to have emigrated. Emigration therefore includes all movement from Scotland including that into other parts of Britain. However, this simple model is complicated by internal migration, and it therefore became necessary to calculate current migration. This measures the first move of individuals from one Scottish county to another; subsequent moves cannot be identified. Emigration and migration represent two interrelated aspects of mobility and therefore need to be considered together when discussing regional outmovement.

The accuracy of estimates of emigration is limited by the data available. The census is only produced every ten years and this is not necessarily the best framework by which to measure movement. Adjustments had to be made to the original data because of changes in the county boundaries, which created 'spurious migration' and other computational problems.[12]

This chapter will begin by considering emigration nationally. It will then analyse and compare movement from the various regions and discuss the issues that arise. The final part will explore the relationship between emigration overseas and that within Britain, but outside Scotland. It will also speculate on how emigration and migration might interact as population movements.

1. Emigration From Scotland

Table 1[13] shows that Scottish emigration losses created a pattern of three peaks interspersed by two troughs. Irrespective of these fluctuations, there were always far more male emigrants than female, both as a proportion of the population and also in actual numbers. The largest volume of emigrants left Scotland in the final decade (1900–11), which is to be expected because the Scottish-born population was increasing.[14] However, in proportional terms the highest emigration of the male population was in the decade 1881–91, although for females the decade 1901–11 was higher. Thus although Baines has suggested that the emigration rate in the decade before the First World War was higher than in all previous decades,[15] this evidence for Scotland suggests that 1881–91 was equally significant. Furthermore, it must be remembered that measurement of emigration is always net of returns. This means

TABLE 1
SCOTTISH CURRENT EMIGRANTS IN EACH DECADE, 1861–1911

Decade	Current Emigrants*		Proportion of the Total Scots-Born Population**†		Male: Female Ratio
	Male	Female	Male	Female	
1861–71	115,745	81,619	7.4	4.8	1.4
1871–81	116,853	89,351	6.7	4.8	1.3
1881–91	162,892	114,226	8.5	5.6	1.4
1891–1901	103,085	62,837	5.0	2.9	1.6
1901–11	188,014	137,286	8.2	5.7	1.4

* Tolerance level: male +0.4% −0.9%; female +0.2% −0.5%.
† The proportion is calculated as current emigrants over the total population born in Scotland in the subsequent census plus current emigrants (that is the total population at the end of the decade if nobody had moved out).

that each returning emigrant will cancel out an outward emigrant of the same age and sex in the same decade. It cannot therefore automatically be assumed that a decade with a low proportion of emigrants such as 1891–1901 reflects low emigration, as it may indicate a high rate of return.

There is some controversy over the age of emigrants. Stevenson was surprised to find many relatively old emigrants 'encumbered with families',[16] whereas Anderson and Morse have suggested that most emigrants were much younger, aged about 15–25 years.[17] In the present study, although the tolerance levels on estimates of the age of departure of emigrants were far broader than those for the calculation of volume lost,[18] the data suggest that at least forty per cent of all emigrants were under twenty years. The fact that the majority of these young people were less than ten years supports Stevenson's impression of some family movement, rather than just young adults. Although a relatively higher proportion of the female emigrant population fell within the 0–9 years age group, this was due to the smaller numbers of older female emigrants, and in actual volume, young boys exceeded girls in every decade. In the decades of very high emigration (1881–91 and 1901–11) there were proportionally fewer children. Peak adult movement was found in the age band 20–9 years, although for females the subsequent age band (30–9 years) was also important. As has already been noted the estimates are net of returns, which has the effect of making both movements appear to be composed almost entirely of young people. Scots returning were inevitably older on average than those leaving, which means that the effect of return movement is disproportionately concentrated on the older age bands, and disguises the outward movement of older people.

This indicates that the proportion of young emigrants is not necessarily as great as the data might suggest and that the older emigrants described by Stevenson undoubtedly formed a significant part of the emigrant population.

2. Regional Movement

The preceding discussion of the proportions of the Scottish population which emigrated, whether in total or by age and sex, provides national averages for these parameters. This section will now discuss the extent to which the national estimates disguise variations in different parts of the country. For this purpose Scotland has been divided into four population regions. These comprise groups of counties classified essentially according to their demographic characteristics: that is the degree to which the county-of-residence population increased or declined during the study period. This means that these regions (which are listed in Table 2) do not necessarily correspond to contiguous geographical areas.

Two regions experienced population decline. In the north, the region referred to as the Highlands embraced more than just the traditional Highland counties, as it included Caithness, Kinross, Orkney and Shetland, but omitted Bute. Further south there was a second region with population decline, which has been described as the Borders. This region included all the counties that adjoin either England or the Solway Firth. The third region, which experienced modest population rise, has been called simply the growth region, as this is the most heterogeneous of the four. It includes the counties which normally comprise the north-east, and also six other counties which fringe the Central Lowlands, namely Ayr, Bute, Clackmannan, Angus, East Lothian and Peebles. The final region, in which there was considerable population increase, is the Central Lowlands. This comprises the majority of the counties in the Central Belt, plus Selkirk. Throughout this discussion it must be remembered that emigration is recorded from the county of birth, and that an emigrant did not necessarily move directly from this county, but could have spent an interim period anywhere in Scotland. It should also be noted that while counties were assigned to these regions according to their county-of-residence population, outmovement is measured from the county-of-birth.

The proportions of emigrants lost from each region is shown in Table 3 and can be compared with the aggregate figures shown in Table 1. Each region will be considered separately, and will be introduced by

TABLE 2

THE DISTRIBUTION OF COUNTIES INTO REGION* ACCORDING TO
POPULATION GROWTH OR DECLINE, 1861–1911

Region	Civil County	% Population Growth or Decline
Highlands		
	Argyll	−11.1
	Caithness	−22.1
	Inverness	−1.8
	Kinross	−5.6
	Orkney	−20.1
	Perth	−6.9
	Ross & Cromarty†	−6.1
	Shetland	−11.9
	Sutherland	−20.1
Borders		
	Berwick	−19.5
	Dumfries	−4.0
	Kirkcudbright	−9.7
	Roxburgh†	−10.4
	Wigtown	−24.0
Growth		
	Aberdeen	+40.9
	Ayr	+34.9
	Banff	+3.7
	Bute	+11.4
	Clackmannan	+45.1
	Moray	+1.7
	Angus	+37.7
	East Lothian	+14.9
	Kincardine	+19.0
	Nairn†	+2.7
	Peebles	+33.8
Central Lowlands		
	Dunbarton	+168.7
	Midlothian	+82.3
	Fife	+73.0
	Lanark & Renfrew	+117.7
	West Lothian	+107.4
	Selkirk†	+147.3
	Stirling	+75.1

* Region and not homogeneous clusters but counties with similar population growth
patterns.
† Calculation based on modified civil county. See Brock, 'Scottish Emigration', vol.II,
appendix I.

TABLE 3

SCOTTISH CURRENT EMIGRATION AND MIGRATION BY REGION IN EACH
DECADE, 1861–1911

Decade	Current Emigrants*		Proportion of Emigrants in the Total Scots-born Population†		Male: Female Ratio Emigrants	Current Migrants		Male: Female Ratio Migrants
	Male	Female	Male	Female		Male	Female	
Highlands								
1861–71	19,219	11,811	6.6	3.6	1.6	20,613	24,565	0.8
1871–81	16,653	11,596	5.8	3.6	1.4	18,287	22,487	0.8
1881–91	21,124	13,238	7.4	4.2	1.6	17,352	18,873	0.9
1891–1901	13,677	8,376	4.9	2.7	1.6	18,684	21,199	0.9
1901–11	23,424	14,754	8.6	4.9	1.6	9,018	13,080	0.7
Borders								
1861–71	12,576	10,094	9.5	7.0	1.2	9,531	9,874	1.0
1871–81	10,965	10,805	8.2	7.4	1.0	10,486	11,030	1.0
1881–91	11,319	9,575	8.4	6.6	1.2	10,905	10,362	1.1
1891–1901	10,086	8,120	7.7	5.8	1.2	11,001	11,316	1.0
1901–11	9,172	8,494	7.2	6.3	1.1	7,219	7,811	1.0
Growth								
1861–71	30,682	19,056	6.6	3.8	1.6	31,573	33,611	0.9
1871–81	29,224	21,018	5.8	3.9	1.4	35,779	37,787	0.9
1881–91	47,695	32,216	8.6	5.5	1.5	32,369	33,285	1.0
1891–1901	25,978	13,964	4.5	2.3	1.9	44,011	43,023	1.0
1901–11	57,773	38,830	9.4	6.0	1.5	28,345	32,908	0.9
Central Lowlands								
1861–71	53,267	40,658	7.9	5.6	1.3	33,592	36,850	0.9
1871–81	60,012	45,931	7.4	5.4	1.3	43,170	47,819	0.9
1881–91	82,754	59,197	8.7	6.0	1.4	39,199	44,552	0.9
1891–1901	53,344	32,376	4.9	2.9	1.6	46,559	52,837	0.9
1901–11	97,645	75,208	7.7	5.7	1.3	48,536	56,681	0.9

* Tolerance level: male +1.3% −3.6%; female +17.1% −5.6%.
† The proportion is calculated as current emigrants over the total population born in
Scotland in the subsequent census plus current emigrants (that is the total population at the
end of the decade if nobody had moved out).

a brief summary of possible push-pull factors prior to examining in
detail the pattern of emigration. This movement will be compared
with that of migration within Scotland[19] in order that total regional
mobility can be analysed. It should be noted that this last calculation
is a somewhat artificial measurement because whereas migration is by
definition directly from the county-of-birth, an emigrant could, as
already mentioned, have left Scotland after having made an interim
move to anywhere else in the country. In such cases it is therefore quite

possible that factors in the county of residence rather than the county of birth determined a final decision to emigrate. For example, consider a person from Argyll who moved to Glasgow (Lanark) and later emigrated. In this study the framework of measurement assumes that the emigrant was influenced by factors in Argyll (the county of birth), whereas the decision may have been made subsequently because of entirely different circumstances in Lanark, the county of residence prior to emigration. Furthermore, emigration by definition involves loss of native population from the region in question, whereas migration includes not only those who left the region but also outmovement between the counties within the region. Thus the losses through migration in Table 3 do not necessarily represent actual losses from the region, and are intended to act as an indication of total population movement within any given decade.[20] Finally, it should be noted that Table 3 shows that the inverse relationship between emigration and migration identified in England and Wales by Thomas is also apparent in Scotland.[21]

Movement from the Highlands

Between 1861 and 1911 the proportion of the Scottish population resident in the Highlands declined from over 18 per cent to little more than 10 per cent.[22] The counties were generally very large,[23] and all were very thinly populated, particularly Sutherland. Orkney had the highest density, although even this was relatively low when compared with other regions.[24] The Highlands was an overwhelmingly rural area with only a few towns.

In the 1860s and 1870s the crofting communities of the north-west experienced two decades of relative stability. Richards has argued that this raised expectations of greater prosperity which were not thereafter fulfilled.[25] Crofters were frequently not self-sufficient. Local casual work was sometimes available,[26] but a crofter's income was mainly supplemented by temporary migration.[27] This introduced crofters to Lowland life and may have encouraged permanent movement. Moreover, Devine has shown that other push factors, such as coercion through a strictly enforced estate policy over the control of subdivision of holdings, could in the long term cause substantial outmovement.[28] In some areas crofters were being deprived of their hill pasture for animals as it was fenced for deer forests.[29] This pattern continued until 1886 when the Crofters Holdings (Scotland) Act curbed the power of the landlords by giving crofters security of tenure. Nevertheless, the fundamental economic problems of the Highlands remained and may have been made worse by 'the freezing of the availability of land and so the structure of Highland society and economy'.[30] The 'subsistence economy continued to decay and the region remained a rural slum into the twentieth century.'[31]

Although there is less information available on the southern and eastern parts of counties in the Highlands region[32] which more as-similated Lowland life,[33] changes in the rural environment were clearly under way. In the central Highlands sporting estates were replacing sheep,[34] although many sheep farms remained and the impact of this process on population movement may not have been significant. In these areas the population had already been thinned by estate policies of clearance, the consolidation of farms, and the banning of partible inheritance. Parishes were becoming depopulated well before 1860 and thereafter the trend continued.[35] In the east there were smaller but still substantial arable farms. There the majority of the population were wage labourers, but new technology was reducing the demand for seasonal labour.[36] Elsewhere smaller farms prevailed and some crofting survived on marginal land. Fishing was the only important labour-intensive industry, but this was confined to the north and east coasts and Argyll. The Highlands was a low-wage area; indeed in 1907 labourers in Caithness, Orkney and Shetland were the worst paid in Britain.[37] Throughout the Highlands region there was a deliberate policy by landowners to rid the area of surplus population, but once this pattern of outmovement was established it became self-perpetuating with districts becoming linked to specific overseas destinations[38] or towns in Scotland.[39]

Table 3 shows three peaks in Highland emigration which conform to the national pattern. These peaks reveal an increasing volume of emigration from the Highlands and this should be considered in relation to the region's declining population. Although the proportion of emigrants was growing, it nevertheless generally remained below the national average[40]. The ratio of male to female emigrants was usually the highest of any region in Scotland, and it was only in the decade 1871–81, which had a lower proportion of emigrants, that female emigration exceeded 40 per cent of the total. Relatively few children emigrated from the Highlands. The peak age band of adult emigration was probably sex specific, this being 20–9 years for males, but 30–9 years for females, for whom emigration was far more concentrated into a narrow age range.

In contrast to emigration, migration from the Highlands was high,[41] and almost invariably above the national average.[42] However, current migration was declining over time in volume, although not as a proportion of the population. Furthermore, the volume of female migrants invariably exceeded that of males. This means that the sex ratio of total population losses was more balanced than the separate consideration of emigration or migration would indicate. Nevertheless, as Table 3 shows, more males did leave their county of birth than females.

During the study period this region was experiencing a declining native population, and despite increasing emigration, the proportion of the population leaving through a combination of emigration and migration was also decreasing.[43] This pattern of below-average emigration and above average migration is in complete contrast to those earlier periods studied by Devine,[44] Flinn,[45] and by Levitt and Smout,[46] in which most of the population losses were due to emigration. This suggests that the entire nature of outmovement from the Highlands had recently changed, possibly after the clearances and emigrations of the famine period 1846–55,[47] and that peak outmovement may actually have occurred shortly before 1860.

Movement from the Borders
The Borders had by far the smallest total population of the four regions considered. In 1861 the proportion of the Scottish-born population living in the Borders was only 8 per cent and by 1911 it had declined to 4.5 per cent.[48] The counties were generally small in area and their population densities low, although markedly higher than in the Highlands.[49]

The Borders was a rural area, albeit with some towns, and the nature of rural work was changing over time. In the dairy farming counties of the south-west,[50] both male and female employment in agriculture generally fell more heavily than in Scotland as a whole.[51] Further east in Berwick and Roxburgh mixed farming prevailed, but here too social changes were under way. Although a high proportion of farm servants were female, they became increasingly unwilling to do regular agricultural work.[52] Moreover, the increasing use of machinery reduced the need for farm servants and seasonal workers.[53] Farm service in the Borders, and indeed in other Lowland regions, represented a stage in many people's lives, as regular work for married servants was limited. Agricultural wages in the Borders were high and this was the staple economic activity.[54] Nevertheless, while high rural wages may have encouraged young adults to remain in the area, marriage forced many to seek non-agricultural work and made outmovement inevitable.

Unlike the Highlands, the proportion of emigrants in the Borders was almost invariably above the national average,[55] although the age profile of the emigrant population was similar apart from a higher proportion of children. However, the emigration pattern in the Borders was quite distinctive in three ways. First, although the sexes peaked in different decades, losses through emigration, both in absolute numbers and as a proportion of the population, were highest at the start of the study in 1861–81 and experienced a relatively steady fall thereafter. This was in marked contrast to other regions, which recorded their greatest volume and highest emigration rates much later. Second, unlike the other regions, there were only slight fluctuations between decades in the proportion of the population lost through emigration. Third, although male emigrants still predominated, the male to female ratio was much closer to unity than in the other regions.

How can this distinctive pattern of emigration be accounted for? The counties which comprise the Borders region are all close to England, and as already noted, in this study movement into England is defined as emigration. Table 4 shows the counties of birth of the Scottish life-time population in England and Wales in 1911[56] and reveals that all the counties from which more than 10 per cent of the population had moved to England and Wales were in the Borders region.[57] Thus the abnormal emigration pattern may well reflect a long-standing[58] pattern in a region in which emigration (as defined in this study) was as easy as migration. Indeed the more equal numbers of males and females suggests that emigrant movement from the Borders was really a combination of both migrant and emigrant types of movement,[59] because the Borders migrant population ratio was also unity. This is not to argue that there was no overseas emigration from this region, but rather that it was obscured by emigration to England, which had the characteristics of migration rather than emigration. It has already been noted that in Scotland as a whole, the proportions of emigrants and migrants were inversely related. The fact that this region recorded a consistently high proportion of emigrants while other regions experienced decades of relatively low emigration strengthens this argument that much of the emigration was into England.

There were excellent reasons for emigrating only a fairly short distance south. Although the Borders had relatively high agricultural wages, they were even higher in the four closest English counties.[60] Indeed, according to Hunt wages in the north-east of England were generally 'amongst the highest in Britain'.[61]

Despite the fact that much of the migration-type movement from the Borders is classified as emigration, the proportion of migrants in this region consistently exceeded the national average, and was generally higher than for any other population region. It is therefore not surprising that the total proportion of the population lost was almost

TABLE 4

THE SCOTTISH COUNTIES WHICH LOST MOST NATIVES TO ENGLAND
AND WALES IN 1911 IN RANK ORDER

Males County of Birth	*% of Total Born* *in County*★	*Females* County of Birth	*% of Total Born* *in County*★
Dumfries	17.0	Dumfries	17.5
Berwick	16.4	Berwick	16.0
Roxburgh	15.1	Kirkcudbright	14.6
Kirkcudbright	14.3	Roxburgh	12.8
Wigtown	11.0	Wigtown	12.0
Midlothian	8.3	Midlothian	9.9
Aberdeen	7.9	Nairn	8.7
Selkirk	7.8	Moray	7.8
Shetland	7.7	Aberdeen	7.4
Angus	7.5	East Lothian	7.0
Moray	7.3	Peebles	7.0
Nairn	7.2	Inverness	6.7
Perth	7.2	Selkirk	6.6
Peebles	7.2	Perth	6.5
Bute	6.9	Bute	6.3
Inverness	6.6	Sutherland	6.0
East Lothian	6.5	Caithness	5.8
Caithness	6.5	Angus	5.7
Kinross	6.1	Banff	5.5
Renfrew	6.0	Kincardine	5.4
Lanark	5.8	Orkney	5.3
Kincardine	5.7	Ross and Cromarty	5.3
Orkney	5.6	Lanark	5.2
Banff	5.6	Renfrew	5.2
Ayr	5.4	Shetland	5.1
Fife	5.2	Argyll	4.8
Argyll	5.1	Stirling	4.7
Sutherland	5.0	Ayr	4.6
Stirling	5.0	Fife	4.4
Ross and Cromarty	4.9	Kinross	4.4
Dunbarton	4.8	Dunbarton	4.3
Clackmannan	4.7	Clackmannan	4.1
West Lothian	3.8	West Lothian	3.6

★ The total born refers to those Scots living in England, Scotland and Wales.
Source: taken from the *1911 Census (England & Wales)*, vol.IX, p.242 and the *1911 Census of Scotland*, vol.X, pp.502–23.

invariably higher than from any other region.[62] As with emigration total losses were highest at the start of the study, between 1861 and 1881.[63] Thereafter there was a gradual decrease in total mobility for both sexes, although losses remained well above the national average. These high losses were thus exacerbating the steady population decline, and the Border counties were in consequence experiencing a massive haemorrhage of their native population throughout the entire period.

Movement from the growth region
Overall the population of this heterogeneous group of counties increased between 1861 and 1911, albeit by less than 50 per cent, and some counties within the region may have experienced periods of decline. Nevertheless, as with the preceding regions, the proportion of the total Scottish-born population resident in the counties of the growth region showed a decline, from 29 per cent in 1861 to 24 per cent in 1911.[64] These counties had a very varied population density; at one extreme Clackmannan was as populous as many Central Lowlands counties, while Nairn and Peebles had very low densities.[65] Several of the growth region counties had considerable urban development and indeed Angus, Ayr and Clackmannan all had less than 16 per cent of males employed in agriculture in 1881, which constitutes the definition of an urban population in this study.[66]

As the growth region counties were very dispersed, it is difficult to generalise on possible push factors. Agricultural wages were below the British average in 1867–70, but improved over time and were above the British average by 1898.[67] Carter estimates that in the north-east real wages rose by 30 per cent over the period.[68] This was because farm labour was in short supply, due to a decline in crofting, which was the traditional source of additional farm workers in the district. There was also reduced access to land in the north-east through the enlargement of farms, and Harper has shown that this encouraged farmers to emigrate.[69] Further south, the pattern of farm service was similar to that found in the Borders and described in the preceding section.

The wage levels in individual industries varied. Campbell has shown that in 1886 wages in the Aberdeen granite industry were high, whereas in the jute industry in Angus they were low.[70] In coal mining, a major industry, some mines in Ayr and Clackmannan were becoming difficult to work.[71] Workers in the industrial counties, both in this region and also the Central Lowlands, were very vulnerable to cyclical and seasonal unemployment. Treble has shown that in the building industry demand for workers could vary enormously.[72] Thus although there were more opportunities than in the regions previously considered, there were also problems that could encourage outmovement.

Table 3 shows that this region generally had a lower proportion of emigrants than the national average, except in 1901–11 and for males in 1881–91. These peaks in emigration correspond to the national pattern.

Although demographic growth in this region was less than 50 per cent, the volume of emigration virtually doubled for both sexes between the first and last decades. Child emigration was higher than in the regions considered previously, but adult emigration maintained the same pattern in that peak male emigration occurred one age band younger than for females.

In the growth region population movement changed over time. It was well below the national average in the first two decades (1861–81), but thereafter exceeded it.[73] The fluctuations in the proportions leaving were pronounced, and for both sexes the pattern of total movement closely followed that of emigration. There was thus a marked fall in total mobility in the decade 1891–1901 due to a decrease in emigration. Overall far more males were involved in outmovements than females despite the fact that the latter were more numerous as migrants. Thus, although this region comprised counties with some population growth, there was increasing mobility over time in relation to the national average.

Movement from the central Lowlands
This region experienced the greatest demographic growth in Scotland, and all the counties accomplished population increase in excess of seventy per cent over the fifty-year period. All the counties in the Central Lowlands except Selkirk had fairly high densities of population. The proportion of the total Scottish-born population in the Central Lowlands increased from 44 per cent in 1861 in 1911,[74] and as early as 1881 this predominantly urban region contained the majority of the Scottish-born population.[75]

Wages in the Central Lowlands[76] in both agriculture and industry improved, so that 'by the early twentieth century it was one of the four highest-wage regions in Britain'.[77] Clearly for natives of this region nowhere else in Scotland was able to offer better prospects, while at the same time it was extremely attractive to inmigrants. As Hunt has noted, the 'long-term demand for labour was buoyant and wages were characterised by long-term improvement relative to other parts of Britain.'[78] Nevertheless, there was contraction in some manufactures, for example textiles, though this was balanced by expansion in others such as heavy engineering and mining. An important point to note is that once a Scot was within the Central Lowlands, he was part of a contiguous belt of counties, each of which was experiencing a variable degree of industrial growth. Consequently, inter-urban migration within this region was common. Despite this economic growth, Lee has found that only in the Lothians was service provision comparable to that in the south-east of England, and the professional classes were under-represented in Dunbarton, Fife, Lanark, Renfrew, and Stirling. Thus the counties that comprised the Central Lowlands did not necessarily offer good employment prospects for all classes, and for some better prospects were available elsewhere in Britain or abroad.[79]

Despite the prosperity of the Central Lowlands and its attractiveness to inmigrants, Table 3 shows that the emigration of natives from this region was generally above the national average.[80] It is probable that potential emigrants had skills that were in demand abroad and were more likely to be aware of the opportunities available.[81] This high level of emigration, together with the fact that the Central Lowlands contained around half the population of Scotland, strongly supports the suggestion that the Scottish emigrant population was mainly of urban origin[82] and not, as Thomas suggested, a mobile rural population.[83]

The age profile of emigrants from the Central Lowlands was quite different from that found in all the other regions. There were far more child emigrants; indeed in all the decades up to 1901, emigrants less than five years old exceeded in volume those in any other age band. However, there was a second peak in emigration at 20–9 years.[84] In the older age bands, male movement remained more important than female, although there was evidence of movement in both sexes.

There are two possible reasons why child emigrants from the Central Lowlands were so numerous. First, some of the emigrant children (born in the Central Lowlands), were undoubtedly travelling with parents who were born (and therefore recorded as emigrating from) elsewhere in Scotland, the parents having migrated to the Central Lowlands at an earlier date. This may account for the relative lack of child emigrants from the Highlands. Emigration of females born in the Highlands region was concentrated in the 30–9 year age band, an age when one might have expected accompanying children. Taken together these findings suggest a pattern in which Highlanders first migrated to the Central Lowlands, where they had children and then emigrated. This pattern could to some extent contribute to emigration from the other regions.

Second, it is possible that some of the Scots-born child emigrants were travelling with English- or Irish-born parents. Certainly there were large concentrations of immigrants in the counties that comprise the Central Lowlands.[85] Irish immigration in particular appeared to fluctuate in volume, following a pattern that complements the peaks and troughs of the Scottish national emigration.[86] It is possible that many young adult Irish who arrived in Scotland had children and then emigrated when there was an upturn in emigration from Scotland. This would have had the effect of increasing the volume of Scottish-born child emigrants without any corresponding increase in Scots-born adults, and would also cause an apparent reduction in immigration from Ireland in years of high outmovement, due to what is essentially a reversal of the return emigration effect.[87]

If one now examines total mobility in the Central Lowlands, it is found that the proportion of the regional population leaving was never above the national average. This was because although the proportion of emigrants lost was, as expected, almost invariably high, migration was relatively low, since as discussed above, nowhere else in Scotland offered better opportunities.

To conclude this section, it is evident that the four regions had markedly different patterns of outmovement, and only in the Borders were both emigration and migration equally high. The Central Lowlands had consistently high proportions of emigrants, whereas the Highlands and growth region had rates of emigration that were generally below the national average, although these two regions had an above average proportion of migrants.

3. The Emigrant Population

The regional analysis of emigration has shown that not only did the volume of emigration vary considerably both according to decade and from one part of Scotland to another, but that there were also important differences in age and gender. These issues, together with the impact of temporary emigration, will now be considered in more detail.

Child emigration

The proportion of child emigrants varied markedly according to the region, it being relatively unimportant in the Highlands and the dominant movement in the Central Lowlands. Possible reasons for this have already been considered in the preceding regional discussion. It should be noted that there was some assisted emigration of children from Scotland,[88] but it only accounted for a very small proportion of child emigration.

The adult emigrant population

Far more adult males emigrated than females, and males tended to emigrate at a younger age than females. It is interesting to consider why these differences between the adult male and female emigrant age structures may have arisen. If emigrants were predominantly married men leaving with their wives, the ages of male and female emigrants would have been fairly similar. Erickson studied British emigration to the United States,[89] which was the most popular overseas destination for Scots,[90] and found that in fact single men always outnumbered married men. In the 1880s, a decade of high emigration, the ratio was as high as 8:1.[91] Although the Scottish ratio may differ from Britain as a whole, the average age of marriage for males in Scotland[92] was higher than the age band for peak adult male emigration, and so it is probable that most Scottish male emigrants were also unmarried. As peak female emigration frequently occurred one age band higher than for males, it seems likely that many men went abroad alone first and were later joined by their wives or fiancées.

It thus appears that female emigration was largely a response to earlier emigration by males. However, there was some independent emigration of females. Harper has analysed organised female emigration from the north-east and found that domestic servants were particularly in demand.[93] Although the numbers involved are probably not significant in national terms[94] it might begin to account for the fact that the peak age for female emigrants in the smaller north-east counties was lower than elsewhere. Finally, it is possible that some older single or widowed females were emigrating in order to find marriage partners.

There was an interesting cyclical pattern in the emigrant age profiles. It has been shown that in years of low emigration there were proportionally more emigrants from the trades and professions because they were 'relatively insensitive to the short-term forces governing' semi-skilled and unskilled, emigration and their numbers therefore remained fairly constant.[95] Thus the 'trough' decades probably reflect a minimum number of emigrants who had decided to leave whatever the circumstances, or for whom economic considerations were not the primary motivation. In contrast, opportunities for the semi-skilled and unskilled were greater in the 'peak' decades.[96] Although the biggest increases were of young adults, it was not just the young who were unskilled, and increases were also found over a wide range of adult age bands. The ratios of married to unmarried male emigrants calculated by Erickson and mentioned earlier all referred to years of exceptionally high emigration, and may well have been lower in decades of low emigration.[97]

Older emigrants

It has already been noted that older emigrants are underestimated by the method used in this study because of return movement. Nevertheless, there was clear evidence of some emigration amongst the elderly. The process of men going abroad first, to be followed later by wives or fiancées may have extended to subsequent movement of other members of the family such as parents, who could join the younger members of their family once they had become established abroad.[98]

Temporary emigration

Return emigration has already been briefly referred to. Some emigrants probably went abroad intending to stay but later changed their mind, while others may have gone with the intention of only staying a short time (these are referred to as transient or temporary emigrants). The method used in this study cannot distinguish between the two types of return movement, both of which create return emigration. Although this study cannot measure temporary emigration, it can provide evidence of its significance through population samples.

Temporary emigration probably increased rapidly during the second half of the nineteenth century. Anderson and Morse have estimated that a third of Scottish emigrants returned.[99] The development of steam shipping in the late 1860s altered attitudes to emigration by reducing the financial and emotional costs to emigrants. The steamship meant that emigrants wasted far less time travelling,[100] thus greatly reducing the costs in terms of lost income while on the journey. For the first time a return was feasible,[101] and temporary emigration abroad became practicable.[102]

In the 1880s Erickson found transient movement to the United States among professional and commercial occupations and also for workers in building, iron, steel and engineering.[103] Harper has also described temporary emigration to the USA of Aberdeen granite masons.[104] Transient emigrants could also involve civil servants, merchants or others working in the colonies. Many of these people had their families with them but ultimately intended to retire to Britain.[105] In the present study evidence of return emigration has been found by examination of the Scottish census enumerator's books. For example, in 1891 nearly a quarter of the return emigrants identified were miners,[106] and this was the most numerous occupation recorded.[107] Finally some people who were merely visiting overseas would have been picked up within the data, and Stevenson found visitors to the United States even amongst the poorer steerage passengers.[108]

So far the discussion of temporary emigrants has considered only those who went abroad. However, temporary migration to other parts of Britain must have also occurred. Fewster identified temporary migrants in the Yarmouth fishing industry, there being about 38,000 Scots employed for the fishing season in 1913 of whom nearly 13,000 were female gutters.[109]

Although return emigrants must overall be older than out emigrants, there is evidence from birthplace information in the enumeration books of return emigration even amongst the very young. For example, a family from the Borders was found to have emigrated to Australia with two children and returned with four. The younger of the two Scots-born children was no more than seven years old when the family returned and she thus became a seven-year-old return emigrant. This flow of returning emigrants would have had important repercussions in Scotland, because they would have been a useful source of information to potential future emigrants. Those Scots who returned were not necessarily less prosperous than those who remained abroad; indeed those who failed abroad probably could not afford to return.

4. Emigration as an Aspect of Population Movement

At the beginning of this chapter the relationship between emigration and migration was briefly mentioned. Moreover, it is now apparent that emigration itself could now be subdivided into emigration overseas and emigration to other parts of Britain, which tended to have some of the characteristics of migration. The relative importance of these three types of movement (emigration within Britain, emigration overseas and migration) in total population mobility and their interrelationships will now be discussed in more detail.

The relative importance of emigration overseas and to other parts of Britain

As already noted not all emigration in this study was to overseas destinations, because Scottish movement into England and Wales has also been defined as emigration.[110] Although every Scottish county was involved in emigration to the rest of Britain, the greatest proportion came from the Borders, as can be seen in Table 4. Baines has made estimates of Scottish immigration into England and Wales[111] and if his figures are deducted from those for total emigration from Scotland produced in this study, the number of emigrants moving overseas can be calculated. Table 5 shows the proportions of the total Scottish population that went either to England and Wales or overseas. In this context overseas destinations include Ireland, but the life-time[112] Scottish immigrant population in Ireland was only about 10 per cent or less that in England and Wales.[113]

In almost every decade[114] overseas emigration exceeded that within Britain.[115] Male emigration overseas was markedly higher, but for

TABLE 5

THE PROPORTION OF THE SCOTTISH POPULATION WHO EMIGRATED TO
OVERSEAS DESTINATIONS AND TO ENGLAND AND WALES*

Decade†	Overseas Destinations‡			England and Wales§		
	Proportion of the Total Scots-Born Population**		Male:Female Ratio	Proportion of the Total Scots-Born Population**		Male:Female Ratio
	Male	Female		Male	Female	
1861–71	4.7	2.5	1.7	2.7	2.3	1.1
1871–81	4.3	2.6	1.5	2.5	2.2	1.0
1881–91	6.6	3.8	1.6	1.9	1.8	1.0
1891–1901	2.9	1.2	2.4	2.1	1.7	1.2

* Baines, *Migration in a Mature Economy*, table 4.5. p.115. Baines's estimates are lower than those of Flinn, *Scottish Population History*, table 6.1.2. p.442.
† Baines did not estimate data for 1901–11.
‡ The proportion of Scots-born population emigrating abroad has been calculated by deducting Baines's estimate of Scottish movement into England and Wales from the total emigrant population estimated in this study.
§ Calculated by Baines.
** The proportion is calculated as current emigrants over the total population born in Scotland in the subsequent decade plus total current emigration (that is the total population at the end of the decade if nobody had moved out).

females movement was more equally spread between the two destinations and only in 1881–91, the decade of exceptionally high emigration, was the proportion of female emigrants going overseas markedly higher than to the rest of Britain.

The cycle of peaks and troughs in emigration has already been mentioned, and it is now useful to consider how this relates to the distribution of emigrants to destinations within Britain or abroad. From 1861 to 1881 the relative proportions emigrating to England and Wales or overseas remained approximately constant, but in the subsequent decade of high emigration far more emigrants of both sexes went abroad. There followed a decade of low emigration, 1891–1901, when the proportion of males going to England and Wales only increased slightly. Unfortunately, Baines's study ended in 1900 and it is impossible to assess emigration to England and Wales in the final decade,[116] but Flinn has also estimated emigration to the rest of the United Kingdom,[117] and his calculations suggest that there was a marked decline in the volume emigrating south in 1901–11, despite the fact this was a decade of high emigration.[118] Taken together, these findings suggest that emigration to the rest of Britain became progressively less popular over the period of this study and movement overseas, while fluctuating, was increasing.

It is also evident that emigration to other parts of Britain was generally higher in the years of lower overseas emigration,[119] and therefore the largest flows south were in the years of high migration. However, the strength of these flows was decreasing. It has already been mentioned that wages within the Central Lowlands were high, and they improved over time relative to other parts of Britain. Thus by 1891–1901, when overseas emigration was low, there was less comparative advantage in moving to England or Wales and the prospects abroad were better in the subsequent decade.

For some Scots outmovement to England and Wales was probably performing a compensating function to overseas emigration similar to migration within Scotland in decades of low overseas emiration. For other emigrants, movement into England and Wales may have reflected stage emigration, with movement south occurring when the economic situation abroad was poor, to be followed by movement overseas later when the situation there improved. As these estimates are net, a Scot going abroad, who had previously been resident in England would cancel out a new arrival in England, whether he came directly from Scotland or returned from overseas.[120] Indeed it is possible that the overseas emigration of Scots from England disguised new inmigration into England in the final decade.

The relationship between emigration and migration
Thomas has linked the fluctuating levels of overseas emigration to urban growth, and to building and investment booms on both sides of the Atlantic. In certain decades British urban expansion could absorb rural migration which therefore increased, while in others the mobile population emigrated overseas.[121] This theory assumes that there was a potentially mobile rural-born population that moved either within Britain or abroad according to the economic climate. This hypothesis has been criticised by Baines with regard to England and Wales, as he was unable to find any evidence of a mobile rural population that was willing to migrate or emigrate according to the trade cycle.[122] Thomas's theory does, however, provide a useful framework within which to consider Scottish emigration, and this discussion will attempt to determine whether indeed there was essentially one mobile population. Both forms of movement had fluctuations which showed an inverse relationship, but whereas the proportion of emigrants in the peak decades increased over time, migration fell and total mobility also declined. Thus over time increased emigration failed

to compensate for decreased migration, and the highest proportion of total movement in every population region was in or before the decade 1881–91.

If emigration and migration involved the same mobile population, the proportions of the total population moving from each region should remain fairly constant regardless of whether movement consisted predominantly of emigration or migration, even allowing for the different bases on which each was calculated.[123] This was not the case, as can be seen by adding both forms of rural outmovement from the Highlands (Table 3), and shows that migration was not necessarily a substitute for emigration. The same was also true in the urban context, though the reasons were probably different. If one compares outmigration from the growth region with that from the Central Lowlands in the decade 1891–1901 it can be thus seen in the growth region, outmigration increased, as the mobile population had the option of moving to the more prosperous Central Lowlands as an alternative to emigration. In contrast, for those already in the Central Lowlands such an option was clearly not available, and total mobility was therefore reduced by a greater proportion.

All in all, the evidence suggests that there were several interacting mobile populations. Baines has argued that in the later nineteenth century emigrants were generally 'not fleeing from problems at home, nor were they going blindly overseas,'[124] but would 'have been going to parts of the world which they knew something about.'[125] If emigration was a planned event, it seems unlikely that many potential emigrants would consider migration an adequate alternative to emigration, unless, forced to leave their county of birth. Indeed many of the return emigrants sampled from the census books had returned to their county of birth, which suggests that for these people migration was not an alternative. It was therefore probably only the most mobile element of the population that would migrate if emigration was unattractive. It is this element which probably accounts for the fact that all population regions showed some increase in migration in decades of low emigration, but the proportions never fully compensated the reduced losses due to a decrease in emigration.

It has already been established that the majority of the Scottish population lived in the urban counties of the Central Lowlands, and several urban counties also existed in the growth region. Therefore, if one is looking for rural–urban movement it can only be found in the Highlands, Borders and in parts of the growth region such as the north-east and a few counties fringing the Central Lowlands,[126] all of which together held only a minority of the Scottish population. These rural areas may have provided a considerable source of migrants, but with the exception of the numerically insignificant Borders region they did not experience high levels of emigration. Moreover, emigration from the Borders included a large component that involved movement to other parts of Britain, not overseas.

The effects of mobility on the Scottish population

As already noted children comprised a large proportion of the aggregate Scottish mobility, but as a proportion of the total native population in the relevant age bands they were relatively unimportant. Nevertheless, it was still sufficient to cause a steady erosion of the potential adult native population, particularly in certain areas. Thus in counties attracting inmigration, such as Dunbarton and West Lothian, outmovement of native children had no significant effect as there was a compensating flow of migrants from elsewhere, but in counties that failed to attract migrants it was very important. In these counties, when adult movement increased, the majority of losses were from age bands that were already severely depleted, and they were thus losing their most economically active age groups.

Superficially it might seem that the high proportion of emigrants from urban areas may have created labour shortages that permitted the easy assimilation of in migrants to the Central Lowlands. However, the decades of highest inmigration were also the decades of low emigration, and moreover migrants were predominantly female and emigrants male. This simple pattern therefore appears not to apply and needs further investigation. A complicating factor is that migrants from other parts of Scotland were not the only source of replacement of labour: a second important source existed in the form of immigrants from other parts of Britain[127] and Ireland and in lesser numbers abroad.[128] Scotland was losing more males than females, and although the sex ratio of English and Welsh immigrants was almost unity, the majority of Irish and foreign immigrants were generally male,[129] which helped to redress the sex ratio. Moreover, Collins has shown that Irish immigrants were mainly young adults, and that they concentrated in the urban counties,[130] from which many of the economically active Scots of the same age group were leaving.[131] Thus in terms of both age and sex Irish immigration partly compensated for the loss of economically active Scots.

Nevertheless, there was an imbalance here too in that immigration into Scotland from Ireland was highest in decades of low Scottish emigration.

This can be explained by the fact that most Scots emigrated when the American economy was buoyant and the British weak, so demand to replace workers may not have existed. In contrast both in migration and immigration were greatest in decades when the British economy was thriving, as it was at this stage in the cycle that the workforce needed replacing or expanding.

Conclusion

This chapter has argued that Scottish emigration was predominantly from urban and industrialised counties. Indeed Scotland appears to have a more urban bias to emigration losses than England and Wales.[132] Not only did the majority of the Scottish population live in urbanising counties, but overseas emigration from these counties was disproportionately high. Emigrants came mainly from the Central Lowlands, a high-wage region which attracted considerable immigration as well as in migration. The explanation for this mainly urban overseas emigration is not immediately obvious although it is argued that emigrants were not fleeing from problems within Scotland. Instead, as argued in Chapter 1, it is more likely that emigrants with appropriate skills, and experience of a technically advanced urban and industrial environment, considered that they could benefit from emigrating, perhaps perceiving that the opportunities for further advancement at home were severely curtailed.

It may be that emigration was less attractive to the rural population in this later period because the enlargement of farms in Scotland had not only restricted the access to land, but also reduced the opportunities for acquiring the capital to buy land abroad. It was only in the north-east that farmers with sufficient capital to emigrate were still being evicted.[133] The agricultural labourer was therefore less likely to be able to benefit from emigration, except in the Borders where movement into England was easy. Elsewhere rural–urban migration offered advantages without the expense of emigration.

In conclusion, Scotland's population loss through emigration was distinctive in European terms in that it experienced some of the highest losses ever recorded in proportion to its population. However, these other countries were overwhelmingly rural economies, and the high Scottish losses were unique in that they were from a predominantly urban population.[134] These urban emigrants had benefited from improving standards of living, and their outmovement was not a response to destitution but rather a reflection of economic choice.

NOTES

1. This chapter is based on the author's unpublished PhD thesis 'Scottish Emigration and Migration 1861–1911', University of Strathclyde, 1990. I would like to thank my supervisor Professor T.M.Devine, Dept. of History, for his help and encouragement, and Dr S.K.Tagg, Dept. of Marketing, for his advice on matters of computing.

2. M.Flinn (ed.), *Scottish Population History from the Seventeenth Century to the 1930s* (Cambridge, 1977), Table 6.1.1., p.441.

3. D.Baines, *Migration in a Mature Economy: Emigration and Internal Migration in England and Wales, 1861–1900* (Cambridge, 1985), Table 2.1. p.10.

4. R.L.Stevenson, *The Amateur Emigrant* (Edinburgh, 1895, reprinted London, 1984), p.17.

5. C.J.Erickson, 'Who Were the English and Scots Emigrants in the Late Nineteenth Century?' in D.V.Glass, and R.Revelle (eds.), *Population and Social Change* (London, 1972), pp.345–81.

6. B.Thomas, *Migration and Economic Growth: A Study of Great Britain and the Atlantic Economy* (Cambridge, 2nd. ed., 1974), pp.124–6.

7. Flinn, *Scottish Population History*, p.454.

8. See n.6.

9. R.H.Campbell, 'Scotland', in R.A.Cage (ed.), *The Scots Abroad: Labour, Capital, Enterprise, 1750–1914* (London, 1985), p.15. See also M.Gray, *Scots on the Move: Scots Migrants 1750–1914* (Dundee, 1990), pp.35–6 and E. Richards, 'Varieties of Scottish Emigration in the Nineteenth Century', *Historical Studies*, 85, 1985, pp.479–80.

10. Baines, *Migration in a Mature Economy*, pp.90–125.

11. See J.M.Brock, and S.K.Tagg, 'Using SPSS-X to create a suitable Database for estimating Scottish Population Movement, 1861–1911', *History and Computing*, 2 (1), 1990, pp.17–23; S.K.Tagg and J.M.Brock, 'The Scottish Census 1861–1911', Assess SPSS User Group Conference Proceedings, Glasgow, 1990; J.M.Brock, 'Scottish Emigration', vol.I, pp.98–150 and vol.II, appendix XI, pp.101–26.

12. J.M.Brock, 'Spurious Migration in the Scottish Census', *Scottish Economic and Social History*, 9, 1989, pp.80–7.

13. Tables have the tolerance levels expressed. This has been calculated by incorporating two standard errors (plus or minus) to the migrant age profile (the only data derived by sampling). This represents the worst case situation and has made the test a very rigorous one. See Brock, 'Scottish Emigration', vol.II, appendix XII, pp.126–9.

14. The Scottish-born population resident in Scotland rose from 2,785,800 in 1861 to 4,362,473 in 1911.

15. Baines, *Migration in a Mature Economy*, p.95.

16. Stevenson, *Amateur Emigrant*, p.14.

17. M.Anderson and D.J.Morse, 'The People', in W.H.Fraser and R.J.Morris (eds.), *People and Society in Scotland*, vol.II, *1830–1914* (Edinburgh, 1990), p.22.

18. See n.13.

19. In this study regional migration measures first movement from the county of birth. Movement out of the county of birth but within the same region has been calculated as a regional movement. This calculation is intended to give a flavour of the total mobility of the region and not just interregional movement as for example is found in Flinn, *Scottish Population History*, Table 6.3.1, p.463.

20. Clearly, losses through migration from many of the growth region counties was genuine outmovement from the region because the southern, growth region

counties were so dispersed. The two regions (Highlands and Borders) that experienced population decline were both more geographical units, but their decline indicates that many migrants did move outwith the region and this is confirmed by birthplace data in the Scottish census.

21. See n.6.

22. The proportion of the Scottish-born population in the Highlands region.

Year	Male	Female
1861	18.3	18.5
1911	10.3	10.5

23. The only small counties in Highlands region were Kinross, Orkney and Shetland.

24. The counties in the Highlands region with extremes in population densities (inhabitants per sq. mile) in 1891 were:

Orkney	80.9
Sutherland	10.8

25. E.Richards, *A History of the Highland Clearances*, vol.II, *Emigration, Protest, Reasons* (London, 1985), p.489.

26. T.M.Devine, *The Great Highland Famine: Hunger, Emigration and the Scottish Highlands in the Nineteenth Century* (Edinburgh, 1988), p.287.

27. T.M.Devine, 'Temporary Migration and the Scottish Highlands in the Nineteenth Century', *Economic History Review*, 32 (3), 1979, pp.334–59.

28. Devine cites four ways in which estate policy could encourage outmigration: by preventing the subdivision of plots; consolidating plots when tenants died, emigrated or where insolvent; creating small farms out of unified crofts and finally, whilst encouraging this removal, apply substantial investment in improvement to the land. Devine, *Great Highland Famine*, pp.239–40.

29. W.Orr, *Deer Forests Landlords and Crofters: The Western Highlands in the Victorian and Edwardian Times* (Edinburgh, 1982), pp.119–23 and 131–2.

30. R.H.Campbell, and T.M.Devine, 'The Rural Experience', in Fraser and Morris, *People and Society in Scotland*, vol.II, p.51.

31. E.Richards, *A History of the Highland Clearances. Agrarian Transformation and the Evictions 1746–1886* (London, 1982), p.459.

32. The south and east Highlands refers to Argyll, Caithness, central and eastern Inverness, Perth, central and eastern Ross and Cromarty and eastern Sutherland.

33. Most of this paragraph is taken from M.Gray, *The Highland Economy 1750–1850* (Westport, Connecticut, 1976), pp.223–36.

34. A.Bil, *The Shieling 1600–1840: The Case of the Central Scottish Highlands* (Edinburgh, 1990), pp.333–5.

35. *Ibid.*, pp.53–6.

36. I.R.M.Mowat, *Easter Ross 1750–1850: the Double Frontier* (Edinburgh, 1981), p.47.

37. E.H.Hunt, *Regional Wage Variations in Britain 1850–1914* (Oxford, 1973), pp.53–6.

38. Devine found evidence of chain emigration with long-term connections between localities in host and source countries in the Great Famine. Devine, *Great Highland Famine*, pp.239–40.

39. Highland Perth was the main exporter of population to Dundee in the early nineteenth century, but by the second half of the century the influence of Dundee

had expanded and Ross and Cromarty had exceeded Perth in importance. C.Withers, 'Highland Migration to Dundee, Perth and Stirling 1753–1891', *Journal of Historical Geography*, vol.II (1985), p.401.

40. Only for males in 1901–11 was emigration was above the national average.

41. Outmigration was high despite the fact that the Highland counties were generally much larger than those elsewhere, and several counties straddled Scotland. Thus in this study many long-distance migrations, for example from Harris (Outer Hebrides) to Inverness, were not recorded because the migrant never left their county of birth.

42. Migration was not above the national average for Highland males in 1901–11; however in that decade emigration was high.

43. The proportion of males leaving fluctuated, but if the three decades of greatest loss are considered (1861–71, 1881–91 and 1901–11), the proportion lost decreased over time.

44. T.M.Devine, 'The Highland Clearances', *Refresh*, Spring 1987.

45. Flinn appears to consider all Highland outmovement after 1846 emigration. Flinn, *Scottish Population History*, p.438.

46. In 1840–2 Levitt and Smout found high emigration and relatively low migration except on the fringes of the Highlands such as southern Argyll. I.Levitt, and T.C.Smout, *The State of the Scottish Working Class in 1843. A statistical and spatial enquiry based on the data from the Poor Law Commission report of 1844* (Edinburgh, 1979), pp.237–40.

47. Devine, *Great Highland Famine*, pp.273–96.

48. The proportion of the Scottish-born population in the Borders region.

Year	Male	Female
1861	8.2	8.2
1911	4.6	4.7

49. The counties in the Borders region with extremes in population densities (inhabitants per sq. mile) in 1891 were:

Roxburgh	80.4
Kircudbright	44.4

50. Dumfries, Kirkcudbright and Wigtown.

51. Female farm labour in Wigtown was exceptional in that it hardly decreased. R.H.Campbell, 'Agricultural Labour in the South-West', T.M.Devine (ed.), *Farm Servants and Labour in Lowland Scotland, 1770–1914* (Edinburgh, 1984), p.67.

52. T.M.Devine, 'Women Workers, 1850–1914', in Devine (ed.), *Farm Servants and Labour*, pp.103 and 113.

53. M.Robson, 'The Border Farm Worker', in Devine (ed.), *Farm Servants and Labour*, p.90.

54. Hunt's analysis includes the counties of Peebles and Selkirk in the region eleven, as well as all the Borders region counties. Hunt, *Regional Wage Variations*, pp.8–9.

55. In 1881–91 male emigrants from the Borders were below the national average.

56. The 1911 English and Welsh census is the only one that tabulates Scottish residents in England and Wales by county of birth.

57. The only Scottish counties that had lost more than 10 per cent of their native population through emigration to England and Wales were Berwick, Dumfries,

Kirkcudbright, Roxburgh and Wigtown. These comprise all the counties in the Borders region and all have a border with England.

58. No proof of the 'long-standing' nature of this pattern can be provided, but neither can any evidence be found to account for this being a recent development. Baines has considered the problem from an English perspective and concluded that there was a considerable movement of people from northern England into Scotland. Baines, *Migration in a Mature Economy*, pp.121–2.

59. Baines also found this pattern.

60. The four closest counties were Cumberland, Durham, Northumberland and Westmoreland. Hunt, *Regional Wage Variations*, pp.43–7.

61. *Ibid*, p.170.

62. Male total mobility from the Borders was only exceeded in the decade 1901–11 by males from the growth region.

63. Male total mobility was highest in the first decade (1861–71), but female losses peaked a decade later (1871–81).

64. The proportion of the Scottish-born population in the 'growth' population region.

Year	Male	Female
1861	28.9	29.0
1911	24.1	25.1

65. The counties in the growth region with extremes in population densities (inhabitants per sq. mile) in 1891 were:

Clackmannan	607.2
Nairn	56.2
Peebles	42.5

66. The definition of an urban county in this study is that 16 per cent or less of the male labour force was employed in agriculture in 1881. All the counties in the Central Lowlands therefore qualified as urban counties, See Erickson, 'Who Were the English and Scots Emigrants?' appendix B, Table 11, p.377.

67. Appendix to ch.1 and Table 1–4 recalculated. Hunt, *Regional Wage Variations*, pp.63–4.

68. Carter considers the north-east to include the counties of Aberdeen, Banff, Elgin, Kincardine and Nairn. I.Carter, *Farm Life in Northeast Scotland. The Poor Man's Country* (Edinburgh, 1979), p.86.

69. M.Harper, *Emigration from North-East Scotland*, vol.I, *Willing Exiles* (Aberdeen, 1988), pp.156–90.

70. R.H.Campbell, *The Rise and Fall of Scottish Industry 1707–1939* (Edinburgh, 1980), p.82.

71. *Ibid.*, p.103.

72. J.H.Treble, 'The Occupied Male Labour Force', in Fraser and Morris (eds.), *People and Society in Scotland*, vol.II, p.170.

73. The growth population region experienced proportions of migration that were well above the national average, whereas emigration was generally below.

74. The proportion of the Scottish-born population in the Central Lowlands population region.

Year	Male	Female
1861	44.7	44.3
1911	61.1	59.7

75. The proportion of the Scottish-born population in the Central Lowlands population region in 1881 was 51.2 per cent of males and 50.5 per cent of females.

76. The counties of Ayr, Clackmannan and Haddington which are in the growth region in this study are also included in region twelve in Hunt's analysis. Hunt, *Regional Wage Variations*, pp.8–9.

77. *Ibid.*, pp.50–3.

78. *Ibid.*, p.177.

79. C.H.Lee, 'Modern Economic Growth and Structural Change in Scotland. The Service sector Reconsidered', *Scottish Economic and Social History*, vol.3, 1983, pp.5–35.

80. Male emigrants were not above the national average in the decades 1891–1911.

81. The emigrant shipping trade was concentrated on Glasgow and Liverpool. Harper, *Emigration from North-East Scotland, vol.I*, p.93.

82. The Borders region had a higher proportion emigrating but its total population was small.

83. See n.6.

84. Differences in the standard errors do not affect these conclusions for male emigrants, but for females there is disagreement. In 1861–71 the peak age band of female loss ranges from 20–34 years; in 1871–81 and 1881–91 it was 20–9 years and in 1891–1901 15–24 years. It is only in the decade 1901–11 that all three sets of data show female emigration concentrated in the 20–4 age band.

85. Anderson and Morse have noted that the English were 'particularly concentrated in the cities'. The peak immigration of Irish into Scotland occurred in the decade 1841–51, and in that year (1851) 18.2 per cent of Glasgow's population were Irish-born. Thereafter the rate of Irish immigration slowed down but the life-time population decreased only slowly. Anderson and Morse 'The People', p.18.

86. Current Irish immigrants into Scotland, 1861–1911. Brock, 'Scottish Emigration', vol.II, appendix XXVII, p.300.

Decade	Males	Females	Male: Female Ratio
1861–71	26,626	18,613	1.4
1871–81	32,656	22,223	1.5
1881–91	11,337	6,685	1.7
1891–1901	33,811	13,678	2.5
1901–11	1,722	3,652	0.5

87. Collins has argued that Irish immigration into Scotland remained fairly constant throughout the study period. This does not conflict with the evidence in the previous footnote, because Collins measured movement into Scotland and in footnote 86 the measurement is current immigration into Scotland minus outmovement from Scotland (whether returning to Ireland or going to a third country). B.Collins, 'The Origins of Irish Immigration to Scotland in the Nineteenth and Twentieth Centuries', T.M.Devine (ed.), *Irish Immigrants and Scottish Society in the Nineteenth and Twentieth Centuries* (Edinburgh, 1991), p.1.

88. Nearly 7,000 children were sent abroad by the Quarrier Homes in the period 1872–1930, and this was only one of several organisations encouraging child emigration. Nevertheless, in every decade this study has estimated that at least 60,000 children aged 0–9 years emigrated from Scotland. The assisted movement of children can therefore account for only a very small proportion of child emigration. Harper, *Emigration from North-East Scotland, vol.I*, p.130.

89. See n.5.

90. Although the United States was the most popular overseas destination for Scots, more people emigrated to other parts of Britain. Flinn, *Scottish Population History*, Tables 6.1.2 and 6.1.7. compared, pp.442 and 451.

91. Erickson, 'Who Were the English and Scots Emigrants?', p.371.

92. See table 5.2.8 for average age at first marriage. Flinn, *Scottish Population History*, p.331.

93. M.Harper, *Emigration from North-East Scotland, vol.II, Beyond the Broad Atlantic* (Aberdeen, 1988), pp.231–88.

94. Harper has provided estimates of the number of female emigrants. It is impossible to determine what proportion of the female emigrants in Table I were Scots, but in Table II the volume was very small, although could possibly be significant in individual decades and age bands. *Ibid.*, Tables I and II, pp.286–7.

95. Erickson, 'Who Were the English and Scots Emigrants?', p.370.

96. Thomas estimates that between 1840 and 1940, 50 per cent of Scottish overseas emigrants were skilled. Thomas, *Migration and Economic Growth*, p.64.

97. It should be borne in mind that the age structure of the emigrant population described by Erickson was for an overseas destination and many Scots emigrants were in fact moving south into the rest of Britain. Although the United States was the most popular overseas destination for Scots, it was not the only one and Flinn has found that the ratios of emigrants of each sex differed according to the country of destination. One may speculate that the age profile of emigrants also differed according to destination. Certainly for the years 1912–13 Flinn has shown that the skilled, unskilled and middle classes were attracted to different countries. Flinn, *Scottish Population History*, pp.452–3 and n.91.

98. Oral evidence of Mrs A.Hepburn, many of whose family moved from Glasgow to Saskatchewan, Canada in the late nineteenth century. An unmarried adult son emigrated first and later his brothers joined him. When they prospered they returned to Lanarkshire to collect first their fiancées and then later their retired father. Harper also cites similar patterns of family movement from the north-east to Canada. Harper, *Emigration from North-East Scotland, vol.I*, pp.209–10.

99. Anderson and Morse, 'The People', p.16.

100. Baines has pointed out that it took at least four or five weeks to cross the Atlantic by sail and steamships were a considerable improvement. However, the contemporary evidence of Stevenson suggests that conditions in steerage class on the steamships were still very unpleasant, although the journey was much quicker. Baines, *Migration in a Mature Economy*, p.33; Stevenson, *Amateur Emigrant*, pp.5–50.

101. This section is based on Baines, *Migration in a Mature Economy*, pp.31–5.

102. Shepperson has argued that prior to 1865, craftsmen and mechanics who recrossed the Atlantic did so because 'of real or imagined dissatisfaction with America and not because they were temporary labourers'. W.Shepperson, 'British Backtrailers', in O.F.Ander (ed.), *In the Trek of the Immigrants* (Rock Island, Illinois, 1964), p.181.

103. Erickson, 'Who Were the English and Scots Emigrants?', p.371.

104. Harper, *Emigration from North-East Scotland, vol.I*, pp.254–9.

105. It should be noted that these people working abroad may have intended to return to Britain, but if they died while still abroad then they became true emigrants.

106. Laslett provides evidence of temporary emigration among men from Lanarkshire

coal mines. J.H.M.Laslett, *Nature's Noblemen: The Fortunes of the Independent Collier in Scotland and the American Midwest, 1855–1889* (Los Angeles, 1983), p.35.

107. Of the twenty-two return emigrant families recorded in 1891, the heads of household in five families were miners and three were in the building trade (two joiners and a builder). The joiners had been in Canada and all the other families in the USA.

108. Stevenson, *Amateur Emigrant*, p.47.

109. M.I.Fewster, 'The Yarmouth Fishing Industry 1880–1960', unpublished M.Phil thesis, University of East Anglia, 1985, p.101.

110. See p.105 above.

111. Baines, *Migration in a Mature Economy*, Table 4.5, p.115.

112. The life-time population refers to the total population living in a place and not the just the most recent arrivals (current emigrants).

113. The number of Scots enumerated in the censuses of England and Wales and Ireland between 1861 and 1911. Brock, 'Scottish Emigration', vol.II, appendix XXVIII, p.301.

	Life-Time Scots-Born Population in England and Wales	Life-Time Scots-Born Population in Ireland
1861	169,202	16,861
1871	213,254	20,318
1881	253,528	22,328
1891	282,271	27,323
1901	316,838	30,101
1911	321,825	38,486

114. Overseas emigration did not exceed that to England and Wales for females in 1891–1901.

115. The estimates in Table 5 for the proportions of total emigrants moving to other parts of Britain are lower than those of Anderson and Morse. They estimated that 'about half' of Scots who emigrated moved south, but included Ireland in their calculations. See Anderson and Morse, 'The People', p.17.

116. Baines did not calculate his data beyond 1901. Baines, *Migration in a Mature Economy*, Table 4.5, p.115.

117. Flinn's estimates of Scottish emigration are to the United Kingdom, which includes Ireland, but they are still probably higher than those of Baines. Flinn, *Scottish Population History*, Table 6.1.2, p.442.

118. It is interesting that Flinn estimated a marked drop in Scots-born emigrants to the rest of the United Kingdom, because the table in footnote 113 shows a slight rise in the life-time emigrant population in England and Wales and a much larger proportional rise in the life-time population in Ireland. However, the majority of these life-time emigrants could have been resident outside Scotland for several decades. See n.113 and 117.

119. Baines estimates of Scottish males in England and Wales fluctuate more than those for females. Baines, *Migration in a Mature Economy*, Table 4.5, p.115.

120. A Scot emigrating to England and then moving abroad could not be measured as an overseas emigrant in the present study, because the movement was outside Scotland. The estimates of Scottish movement into England are those of Baines and his estimations are also net of returns, which means that a person leaving cancels out a new arrival.

121. Thomas, *Migration an Economic Growth*, pp.124–6.

122. Baines, *Migration in a Mature Economy*, pp.213–78.

123. See p.105 above.

124. Return emigrants, letters and published information enabled prospective emigrants to find out about places before they left.

125. Baines, *Migration in a Mature Economy*, p.282. There is Scottish evidence to support this. Bumsted argues that the emigration of 1770–5 provided a 'beachhead' for later movement. J.M.Bumsted, *The People's Clearance: Highland Emigration to British North America, 1770–1815* (Edinburgh, 1982), p.65.

126. Counties with more than 16 per cent of the population employed in agriculture in 1881 have been classified as rural. The rural counties in the growth region were Aberdeen, Banff, Moray, Nairn and Kincardine in the north-east and also Bute, East Lothian and Peebles. Erickson, 'Who Were the English and Scots Emigrants?', appendix B, Table 11, p.377.

127. Current immigrants from England and Wales into Scotland between 1861 and 1911. Brock, 'Scottish Emigration', vol.II, appendix XXVII, p.300.

Decade	Males	Females	Male: Female Ratio
1861–71	12,416	11,687	1.1
1871–81	16,976	16,734	1.0
1881–91	16,324	16,963	1.7
1891–1901	19,440	20,957	0.9
1901–11	28,240	22,887	1.2

128. Current immigrants into Scotland who were not British subjects between 1861 and 1911. Brock, 'Scottish Emigration', vol.II, appendix XXVII, p.300.

Decade	Males	Females	Male: Female Ratio
1861–71	1,024	526	1.9
1871–81	1,759	844	2.1
1881–91	2,1924	1,082	2.0
1891–1901	7,117	3,477	2.0
1901–11	5,593	4,314	1.3

129. See n.86.

130. Collins, 'The Origins of Irish Immigration', p.11.

131. *Ibid.*, pp.11–13.

132. Baines, *Migration in a Mature Economy*, p.279.

133. Harper, *Emigration from North-East Scotland*, vol.I, pp.156–90.

134. The estimates of losses are based on the total population of the country. Ireland and Norway probably had relatively few immigrants, whereas Scotland had a substantial immigrant population. It may therefore be the case that Scotland's losses of her native population are greater than the data suggests. See n.3.

7

The Making of 'Scots on the Make': Scottish Settlement and Enterprise in Australia, 1830–1900

Ian Donnachie

In the colonies those who make money are generally Scotchmen.
(Anthony Trollope, *Australia*, 1873)

Scottish migration to the Antipodes never assumed the scale of that to North America. Nevertheless those Scots who subjected themselves to what the distinguished Australian historian Geoffrey Blainey has described as the 'tyranny of distance' played a significant role in the social and economic development of both Australia and New Zealand.[1] Thanks partly to the Australian Bicentennial celebrating European settlement, historians in both Australia and Britain have been investigating in greater detail than before the contribution of the four national groups from the British Isles to the making of modern Australia. Certainly from very date of foundation in 1788 the Scots were readily identifiable as a distinct ethnic and cultural group which firmly stamped its mark on many aspects of colonial life and continued to exert influence out of all proportion to its number for many generations. Enterprising Scots, universally 'on the make', were naturally associated with success—and for a minority the rewards of either labour or risk-taking were enhanced standards of living and status in a rapidly developing colonial society. Inevitably the story of the Scots in Australia—so far as it can be summarised here—is dominated by the successes of the entrepreneurial minority. It takes little account of the majority of 'invisible' Scots: the women, the criminals, the labourers, the domestic servants, the diggers, the outcasts, not all by any means failures but groups whose history is only just beginning to be investigated in both Scotland and Australia.

This chapter has three main objectives. First, it reviews the developing historiography of the Scottish–Australian connection, with particular reference to what historians have written about the migration of people, skills and capital from Scotland to Australia. Second, it makes some assessment of the extent and nature of Scottish migration to Australia during the formative period of colonial development from 1830 to 1900. Third, it explores the impact of the Scots as a group and as individuals on the economic development of colonial Australia, noting the most favoured regions and sectors.

Before tackling the central themes of this chapter the non-Australian reader might appreciate a brief word of explanation about the development of Australian history since the 1960s. Indeed, some readers will identify the striking parallels between Australian and Scottish historiography which are partly explained by the dominance in scholarship and teaching until the 1950s of British (i.e., English) and imperial or Commonwealth history. Until then the majority of historians in Australia paid little attention to the history of their own country—the exceptions being some rather dull conventional political narratives and a handful of pioneering economic histories which firmly placed Australian political and economic development in an imperial or Commonwealth context. However, there was one important demographic study which has immediate relevance to the present discussion, its concern being immigration (again mainly British) into Eastern Australia before 1851.[2] But new forces were soon at work with the passing of the empire: an assertion of Australian nationalism, identity and history; an increased interest in economic and social history, which embraced new approaches imported from both Britain and the United States; and greater attention than before to regional and local history, which proved to have enormous potential given the vast, and largely untapped, resources of the various state archives in Australia. Coincidentally, archive-linkage between Britain and Australia—never feasible on any scale before—made comparative studies possible and began to generate fresh insights into the interplay between the histories of the two countries and peoples. First and foremost the possibilities of linking records in Britain and Australia seemed to hold out considerable potential for more detailed and sophisticated migration studies and business histories. Into these new attempts at analyses historians have begun to fit the study of Scotland's social, economic and cultural links with Australia.

I

Prior to the post-1950s renaissance in Scottish history, a handful of scholars, addressing the history of the Scots diaspora, devoted some attention to Scottish emigration to Australia. The most prominent was Andrew Dewar Gibb whose *Scottish Empire*, though highly impressionistic, provided the first survey of Scottish involvement in regions of recent settlement overseas.[3] Gibb chose his title to suggest within a short compass 'how Scotland has reacted to the conception of empire and the part she has played in promoting it'. However, it was, said Gibb, an essentially English empire that Scotsmen were helping to build.[4] In what he described rather condescendingly as 'the suburbs of the empire' Gibb was able to catalogue a substantial Scottish input to Australian history and development. A succession of governors, explorers, administrators and politicians inevitably occupied many pages of the story but Gibb also highlighted the Scottish contribution to agriculture, mining and shipping. The squatters of Victoria were commended as 'enterprising men who had ventured out beyond state boundaries and occupied huge tracts of land for pastoral purposes'.[5] As pastoralists, and so charged with care of the predominant industry, they were of supreme importance to the state, though by the 1860s, said Gibb, their opposition to any other than a pastoral use of land was menacing the best interests of the colony. It fell to other Scotsmen to resolve the issue, leading opposition to the squatters and fathering the legislation of the Land ACTS which cramped their pretensions. Gibb also identified a significant Scottish contribution to Australian mining, notably in South Australia, Victoria and Western Australia, where by some remarkable quirk of fate they seem to have pioneered discovery and exploitation—a much exaggerated view of reality. By improved shipping 'Australia was brought nearer to the home country by the ever-shortening journey' and a significant part was played by Scottish masters who drove their vessels remorselessly across the seas on the business of their Scottish owners. 'The bond in those days between Australia and Scotland,' wrote Gibb of the latter half of the nineteenth century, 'was a real and important one, and Scottish hands and brains contributed in a real sense to bind Australia to the empire and to lay the foundations of her prosperity'[6] Gibb's hagiography left much unsaid, making no mention of the nature or scale of Scottish migration and investment.

Nearly thirty years later the first modern account of Scottish emigration to Australia appeared in Gordon Donaldson's study, a *The Scots Overseas*.[7] The author charted the gradual increase in migration from Scotland to Australia after 1820, noting the early involvement of the Australian Company of Edinburgh and Leith, the activities of that great champion of Scottish emigration to Australia, John Dunmore Lang, and the vital role of the colonial emigration agencies. Donaldson also made some efforts to quantify the numbers of emigrants, their origins and destinations, and identifying the fact that Scottish settlers were far and away most numerous in Victoria and New South Wales. He showed how the free settlers, in particular, were often equipped with the appropriate skills and capital which gave them immediate advantages for success in their chosen occupations in the colonies. Access to David Macmillan's early findings allowed Donaldson the opportunity to highlight the importance of Scottish enterprise and investment in Australian land, agriculture manufacturing.

Pioneering work on Scottish settlement in Australia itself was first undertaken by Margaret Kiddle, a researcher at the University of Melbourne, whose bold and imaginative study of the social history of the Western District of Port Philip (later Victoria) from the 1830s to the 1890s, highlighted the leading role of Scots as early squatters and eventually prominent landholders.[8] Indeed, the antecedents of the last Australian Prime Minister, Malcolm Fraser, were among their number. Kiddle showed that while some settlers from New South Wales trekked overland across the Blue Mountains and followed the Murray and Darling River systems and their anabranches, a surprisingly large number crossed the Bass Straits from Van Diemen's Land attracted by apparently empty lands, the possibilities of creating a new society free of the taint of the convict system and the opportunities presented by opening up a district relatively far removed from the authorities in distant New South Wales. The Vandiemonian Scots were to play an important role in the pastoral economy of the region.

More rigorous, less impressionistic and one of the first to rely to any degree on the marriage of archives (especially legal and business records) in both Australia and Scotland was David Macmillan's important and influential study of emigration, commerce and investment in the pioneering era from earliest settlement until the middle of the nineteenth century.[9] The book itself derived from a long-term research project on Scottish enterprise in Australia and earlier publications gave some indication of important new findings.[10] There were three strands to Macmillan's study: first, an examination of Scottish attitudes to Australia at different times before 1850; second, an assessment of the origins and extent of Scottish emigration to Australia; and third, detailed case-studies of the shipping, mercantile and emigration operations of two important Scottish companies, the Australian Company of Edinburgh and Leith and the later Aberdeen Australian Companies. Macmillan's work emphasised the strong and enduring links between Scotland and Australia in the period before 1850 and, like Turrentine Jackson's work on the south-western United States covering a period later in the century, showed that Scottish investment and entrepreneurship contributed much to the success of colonial agriculture and industry.[11]

Meantime, other Australian historians produced major regional studies which, *inter alia*, examined the Scottish contribution to pioneer life. Among the first and most influential of the regional histories were Geoffrey Bolton's *A Thousand Miles Away: A History of North Queensland to 1920*, which indicated a strong Scottish contribution in opening up a then remote tropical zone to coastal shipping, trade, agriculture and mining; and Duncan Waterson's study of New England (originally New Caledonia) and the Darling Downs, major pastoral districts settled by Scots in northern New South Wales and southern Queensland.[12] Other significant studies included that by Don Watson on *Caledonia Australis*, a work which dealt mainly with Highland settlement in Gippsland and neighbouring parts of Victoria and New South Wales; and Paul de Serville's *Port Philip Gentlemen*, a study of élite society in the rapidly expanding city of Melbourne where, from the outset, Scots figured prominently in business, politics, education, the Church and cultural life.[13] Elsewhere in south-eastern Australia Eric Richards and his acolytes looked in some detail at South Australia where Scottish immigration and settlement (including an important Highland contingent) proved to be much more substantial than previously realised. Long regarded as an essentially English colony, South Australia was seen to have strong Caledonian connections, especially in such vital activities as agriculture and mining. Richards then cast his net wider in several general surveys of the Scottish–Australian connection, including a very useful essay in Cage's *The Scots Abroad* and a similar, though more extended treatment in the National Library of Scotland's publication, *That Land of Exiles: Scots in Australia*, produced to accompany a major exhibition for the Australian Bicentennial.[14]

The most important synthesis undertaken by an Australian scholar is seen in the work of Malcolm Prentis, whose *Scots in Australia* provides an overview of Scottish migration and settlement in New South Wales, Victoria and Queensland before 1900.[15] He followed this with a volume in the Australian Ethnic Heritage Series, under the somewhat bizarre title of *The Scottish in Australia*, which ranges even more widely across the continent, embracing Tasmania and Western Australia.[16] Prentis drew on many secondary works, including a growing number of local and regional histories produced in Australia, unpublished theses, parliamentary papers and archival material which had never been examined from the Scottish perspective.

Moreover, further research in both Scotland and Australia has since produced interesting results, particularly regarding migration and the Scots contribution to economic development in the pre-Federation era. Space permits us to cite only a few examples. First, the present author's work on transportation from Scotland to Australia indicates that of a total of 8,000-odd convicts, over a third were despatched after 1840 and that a high proportion were equipped with the same basic skills taken to the colonies by the assisted emigrants.[17] To some extent this confirms the findings of a recent reassessment of Australia's convict migrants which has caused something of a furore in the Australian historical community.[18] Convicts, it contends, were no different from free settlers in that they contributed to the labour market and the majority eventually integrated fully into colonial society. Second, the earliest cohorts of assisted emigrants from the Highlands have been investigated in some detail by Tom Devine who shows how a vigorous and controversial scheme was organised by the Highland and Island Emigration Society in the aftermath of the famine. This resulted in nearly 5,000 persons emigrating to Australia in the 1850s with two-thirds settling in Victoria—by that time virtually a Scots colony. There is little evidence of conspiracy between the colonial emigration authorities and the landlords, though, concludes Devine, this and other migrations greatly reduced the burden of the poor rates and relief payments made by proprietors.[19] Third, Cliff Cumming of Deakin University, Victoria, recently completed a major research project on Scottish settlement, and political activities in the Port Philip District. This important regional study examines the impact of both religion and culture on the apparent cohesion of the Scots community in metropolitan Melbourne and the nascent state of Victoria.[20] Last, as regards financial and entrepreneurial activities, Chris Smitz of the University of St Andrews continues his detailed examination of the rocky road taken by Scottish investment in Australian mining from 1870 to 1920.[21]

It would be remiss in this brief survey of Scottish–Australian historiography to overlook the Aboriginal perspective—which presents an altogether different and indeed tragic story. The findings of Henry Reynolds, brilliantly summarised in *The Other Side of the Frontier*, do the Scots pioneers little credit.[22] Whether the ruthless extermination of the Aborigines by Scottish settlers was any worse than similar atrocities committed by the English, Irish or Welsh is a question that will probably remain unanswered, but it certainly introduces an element of revisionism into Scotland's view of her own past, especially the brutalities suffered by enforced migrants before and during the period under review here.

Most Australian historians have taken the view that the prime characteristic of the Scots in Australia was success and that this could be explained by three main factors: the individually brilliant

Scot; 'clannishness'; and the Protestant work ethic. However, a Scottish scholar, John Fraser, tried to put the facts and controversies about the role of the Scots in a wider context by setting out to test the impressions some Australian historians had given about the role of the English, Irish, Welsh and Scots in Australia and challenging traditional views of why the Scots were apparently so successful. While Scots were seen to be conformist but adaptable, education and skills were invariably of paramount importance.[23] Eric Richards, writing in advance of Prentis's survey (published in 1983) presented a similar case. He threw some fresh new light on Scottish labour, capital and enterprise in Australia, demonstrating that while *success* was readily identifiable and probably widely acknowledged both by contemporaries and historians, *failure* was likely to be much less so.[24] Some obvious questions arise. What proportion failed in pastoral, financing, commercial or industrial enterprise in relation to those who succeeded? One might point, for example, to the downfall of many previously successful individuals during the sustained depression which hit Australia in the 1890s. And there are many other relevant and interesting propositions. How many came, and why? Where did they come from, and where did they end up? Were the Scots more or less successful than other ethnic groups, and if so why? The individuals who had the inbuilt advantages of upper- and middle-class education, upbringing, and wealth could not fail to be achievers (though many did); but they were greatly outnumbered by the labouring class of the Scottish Lowlands or the peasant class of the Highlands. What became of the great majority—largely unrecorded but for names on the ship's passenger or assisted emigration board lists? How was success achieved and was it individual or corporate? For much of the period the Scots contribution to Australian economic development seems to have been orchestrated from Scotland and manipulated by Scots back home in the banks, finance houses, insurance offices, lawyers' and shipping offices of Edinburgh, Leith, Glasgow, Dundee and Aberdeen. Therefore did Scottish entrepreneurship in Australia perhaps derive as much from home as education, culture and the Kirk—those three great manifestations of Scottishness overseas?

This superficial survey can hardly hope to tackle the wider issues of Scottish ethnic and cultural separateness, but nevertheless, as Fraser and others have rightly stressed, they were always somewhere in the background of the successful Scots. But we can explore further the expanding tool-kit of historiography on the Scots in Australia and make some assessment of how fresh knowledge is modifying perceived or received wisdom both of Australian and Scottish history.

II

Turning secondly to social migration, we can readily some perspective on overall numbers and trends from British and Australian census and immigration records, admirably summarised by Prentis. As Table 1 shows, something in the region of $1\frac{1}{2}$ million British and Irish immigrants arrived in Australia between 1788 and 1900. After a slow start the introduction of assisted emigration can be seen in the greatly enhanced numbers migrating during the 1840s. The dramatic upturn of the 1850s, when nearly a third of the total migrant population arrived in Australia, reflected the lure of the Gold Rush and the prosperity brought in its wake, especially to the newly established colony of Victoria. Totals for later decades also directly mirrored economic conditions in the colonies, the 1880s seeing another boom while the 1890s were years of general depression. Over the period with which we are directly concerned here the level of migration at different times was clearly as much a function of prevailing conditions at home as the effectiveness of propaganda issued by vigorous colonial and other emigration authorities. Moreover, several discussants at the Scottish Historical Studies Seminar emphasised that the role and character of bilateral trade between Britain and Australia had a profound impact on the timing and level of migration. The economics of shipping over such vast distances necessitated full holds inward as well as outward bound. Hence convict or emigrant ships—both sail and steam—often doubled as general cargo vessels on the return journey, carrying goods

TABLE 1
EMIGRATION FROM THE UNITED KINGDOM TO
AUSTRALIA, 1788–1900

1788–1820	approx. 700
1821–30	8,935
1831–40	67,882
1841–50	114,761
1851–60	497,636
1861–70	214,318
1871–80	176,333
1881–90	339,943
1891–1900	100,633
Total	1,520,141

Sources: Emigration Returns, in PP, 1830, XXIX;
1833, XXVI; 1851, XLVI; 1899, CVII; Prentis, *Scots in Australia*, p.55.

like whale-oil, wool and, when refrigeration made it possible, meat, which were as valuable, if not more so, than passengers.

Immigration assisted by the colonial authorities was clearly vital to the transformation of New South Wales from a convict to a free society. However, the data in Table 2 indicate that after sustained growth during the 1830s, peaking in 1841 (the year after transportation to New South Wales ended), immigration proceeded by fits and starts largely dictated by the immediate labour needs of the colony. For several years in the later 1830s the Scottish proportion varied between a quarter and two-fifths, but overall averaged around 15 per cent. Accurate figures for unassisted immigrants are elusive but between 1832 and 1850 probably 7,000, or nearly a quarter, were Scots.

As we saw from the data in Table 1 economic conditions acted as the main regulator of the flow of immigration into south-eastern Australia after 1851, statistics for government migrants and the Scottish percentage being seen in Table 3. In the decade of gold in the 1850s Scots accounted for around 90,000 immigrants, 15 per cent of the total, a figure well in excess of the Scottish proportion of the UK population at the time. About a third were assisted immigrants, the majority being free settlers. The former, and almost certainly all immigrants, greatly favoured Victoria—though probably as much for its Scottish connections as the lure of gold. It has been estimated that no less than 80 per cent of Scottish assisted immigrants during the 1850s settled in Victoria.[25] Table 4, derived from the first census of Victoria, gives some indication of the colony's popularity with Scots in the immediate aftermath of the Gold Rush. The Scots, again representing

TABLE 2

ASSISTED IMMIGRANTS TO NEW SOUTH WALES, 1832–50

Year	Number	% Scots	Year	Number	% Scots
1832	792		1842	6,823	11
1833	1,253		1843	11	–
1834	484	10	1844	4,139	4
1835	545		1845	498	2
1836	808		1846	–	–
1837	2,664	44	1847	–	–
1838	6,102	37	1848	7,885	19
1839	8,416	23	1849	15,773	13
1840	6,636	25	1850	6,055	3
1841	20,103	8			

Sources: Returns by New South Wales Immigration Agent, 1841–52 (including Port Philip District and Moreton Bay); Madgwick, *Immigration* pp.223, 241; Macmillan, *Scotland and Australia* pp.265–303; Prentis, *Scots in Australia*, p.61.

TABLE 3
ASSISTED IMMIGRANTS AND SCOTTISH PROPORTION, 1851–1900

Years	New South Wales Total	% Scots	Victoria Total	% Scots	Queensland Total	% Scots
1851–60	71,649	11	87,963	24	–	–
1861–70	18,212	6	45,594	–	62,005	–
1871–80	24,412	9	5,545	–	50,728	–
1881–90	34,079	14	–	–	103,140	–
1891–1900	659	17	–	–	10,509	10
Total	149,001	11	139,104	–	226,382	12

Sources: Immigration Returns, Votes & Papers, NSW, Victoria and Queensland, 1851–1901; Prentis, *Scots in Australia*, p.68.

15 per cent of the total, ranked third behind immigrants from England and Ireland. They were widely distributed throughout the colony, with proportionately more than their number would suggest settled in the up-country pastoral districts and inland towns. Scots accounted for over 18 per cent of all assisted immigrants, their places of origin divided equally between northern and southern counties. A quarter were from the three leading Highland counties of Inverness, Ross and Sutherland, but the Highlanders were greatly outnumbered by those from the highest-ranking Lowland counties of Lanark, Midlothian and Forfar.

The great majority of Scots in Victoria and elsewhere, unlike the Irish, arrived in families and connections of kin played an important role in the chain of immigration throughout the period.

Whatever the weaknesses in the data relative to the Scottish proportion of immigrants before 1900 we know that roughly 250,000 were Scots. They went as convicts, free settlers, and assisted immigrants. The nature and make-up of the immigrants changed considerably over time, though always the bulk were of the labouring class. As Richards indicates: 'The Scots offered a general range of proletarian skills for the benefit of Australian development,' and rightly emphasises that the great mass of Scots migrants were absorbed into the urban labour force or up-country sheep-runs rather than middle-class capitalist occupations.[26] This comes as no surprise, for, as Prentis shows, the bulk of the Scots assisted migrants after 1851 and before 1900 came from industrialised Lowland areas such as Glasgow and Clydeside, Edinburgh, Dundee, West Lothian, Fife and Stirlingshire. The Highland proportion declined everywhere, even in Victoria which, as we have seen, attracted significant numbers from the north of Scotland in the 1850s. Given the distance—as

TABLE 4
DEMOGRAPHIC DATA RELATING TO SCOTS IN PORT PHILIP
DISTRICT/VICTORIA 1854
(i) BIRTHPLACE OF THE PEOPLE

Total	*236,798*	%
Scotland	36,044	15
England	97,943	41
Wales	2,326	1
Ireland	39,728	17
Victoria	29,996	13
Other Aust. cols.	11,237	5
Other places	19,524	8

Source: Census of Victoria, 1854, Table II.

(ii) DISTRIBUTION OF THE PEOPLE

	Total	*Scots*	*% Scots*
Seaport towns & suburbs	105,661	15,873	15
Gold fields	66,698	7,723	13
Inland towns & districts	40,591	6,428	16
Pastoral districts	16,678	3,742	22

Source: Census of Victoria, 1854, Tables V–VIII.

(iii) ASSISTED IMMIGRATION TO VICTORIA, 1854–5

Total	9,254	
Scotland	1,722	
England	4,510	
Ireland	2,906	
Others	116	
Origin of Scots:	A Northern counties	870
	Southern counties	852
By county:	Inverness	306
	Sutherland	58
	Ross	60
	Forfar	132
	Perth	105
	Fife	84
	Lanark	263
	Midlothian	251

Source: Report of Acting Immigration Agent, 1855, Appendix III.

Blainey observed—it is perhaps surprising that as many did make it to Australia, and probably few would have without the emigration schemes.

In one sense the origins and background of the migrants, as Richards says, mirrored the needs of the developing colonial economy: skills in pastoral agriculture, mining, shipping, engineering and manufacture. There was a certain continuity but priorities changed with time, hence the ultimate substitution of the urban artisan or mechanic for the Highland or Border shepherd. For all the attention devoted to migration studies in a country whose people are better documented historically than any other on earth, we still lack detailed knowledge about these waves of selected immigrants and only future research will tell us more about the origins and background of the majority of settlers. Inevitably we know less about the Highland peasant or the Glasgow mechanic in Australia than we do about the free-settling Scots grazier, shipowner or banker made good in the 'Lucky Country'; even this at the current state of knowledge is riddled with myth, half-truths, and certainly lacking detailed analysis.

III

Among the quarter of a million Scots and their immediate descendants was the nexus and potentially élite group of dynamic aspirers about whom most is known—the entrepreneurs—and they constitute the third strand in our discussion. While the critical skills of scarce immigrant labour and abundant capital were clearly vital to successful enterprise, both still need thorough investigation to be properly appreciated. Quantification is likely to pose major challenges but for the moment personal histories give us at least some idea of the qualitative impact made by entrepreneurial Scotsmen on the make. Some had money of their own, brought with them to build up businesses; others had other people's money—much of it from back home in Scotland—to invest in new enterprise. As well as being qualitative this was highly concentrated regionally in Australia, especially so in Victoria and New South Wales, though ultimately extending to Queensland, where sheep-runs and city enterprise alike attracted men and capital. Scottish entrepreneurship was highly dynamic and wide-ranging in such varied activities as pastoralism (an early and abiding interest), shipping, mercantile endeavour, mining, engineering and manufacture, and there are numerous success stories that can be cited. The reply to the query—supposedly from

Irish-Australians in the later nineteenth century—as to what exactly the Scots had achieved in Australia was, 'well, we own it!'[27]

This might seem a bit of an exaggeration but the upper- and middle-class Scots—though again difficult to quantify numerically—certainly brought capital, enthusiasm, entrepreneurial skills, hard work, and a determination to make good in their adopted country. Some were the sons of gentry or merchants sent out with capital to make their own way in the world; others were less lucky in capital, but ambitious individuals willing to work hard and take the risk of new enterprise themselves once they had accumulated enough capital. Still others were part of the new technical and managerial élite created back home by industrialisation: engineers, chemists, manufacturers, accountants, professional managers and, at a lesser level, bookkeepers, clerks and artisans. Lawyers and bankers were also present in modest numbers, taking to Australia the characteristic shrewdness of the Scot. All had certainly been influenced in some measure by domestic institutions back home in Scotland—the most powerful for enterprise being education. Even the Scots convicts, as I have indicated, seem to have been better educated than their English or Irish counterparts.

From the 1830s at least, Scottish capital was exported widely overseas, notably to North America. But Australia became an early and long-favoured beneficiary, mainly of surplus capital deriving from the profits of successful enterprise at home, or of savings—another great Scots virtue. Macmillan's pioneering works showed how this was orchestrated through individuals, commercial firms, pastoral enterprises, investment companies, land companies, banks, and lawyers—all anxious to cash in on the development of the new colonies and the potentially higher returns than were possible at home. Of course there were substantial risks given the tyranny of distance separating Australia from Scotland, and some enterprises were exposed to the periodic slumps and depressions of the latter half of the nineteenth century. But many more survived, their owners becoming wealthy and prominent in politics and the establishment élite of the colonies, especially so in Victoria, New South Wales and Queensland.

There are many success stories that could be cited from such spheres as agriculture, mining, investment, manufacture and shipping, but only a few cursory examples must suffice. Readers anxious for more detail will find that the *Australian Dictionary of Biography* and the works of Macmillan and Prentis bulge with hard-headed, resourceful, and successful Scottish capitalists, whose careers followed similar paths.

From the outset the most obvious field of activity was agriculture in which the Scots were early and remarkably successful pioneers in Van

Diemen's Land and New South Wales, moving later in the 1830s to the Port Philip District and ultimately other areas of wider Victoria, as it became. The Western District and Gippsland, as we have noted, were like Scots colonies, with Melbourne itself a major centre of Scots influence from the beginning. Kiddle and more recently de Serville have shown the success of such pioneers—often ruthless squatters and land-grabbers. These pioneers set the tone for later initiatives after 1850, notably in large-scale pastoralism, when land and capital became increasingly and irretrievably bound up with each other. Macmillan describes how many of these enterprises were controlled either directly or indirectly from Scotland, and later examples in Queensland and Western Australia, while managed by expatriate Scots, continued to attract much of their capital from the homeland.

A high propensity to take risks often brought high returns; such was the case of Gibbs, Ronald & Co, founded in the 1850s, and the precursor of the Australian Mercantile & Finance Co. The leading light was Robert Bruce Ronald, who came from an Ayrshire family with connections in the Liverpool wool trade and settled initially in the rich pastoral district bordering the Barwon River near Geelong. In partnership with Richard Gibbs, another expatriate Scot, he established a remarkably lucrative business in land mortgaging and the provision of capital to the pastoral industry. A splendid example of the Calvinist temperament, Ronald, says Richards, was struck by the *mores* of Australian society, noting of the townsmen that they were 'generally speaking a low mushroom underbred race' but at the same time reflecting that 'business, business is the only thing, money making the only pursuit'—the last probably the view taken by many of his fellow countrymen interested more in self-improvement than criticising those beneath them on the ladder to success. The Scots contribution to agricultural development in Victoria, New South Wales, Queensland and elsewhere was certainly significant and it was backed up in many instances by personal wealth or corporate funds manipulated by finance houses like Gibbs, Ronald & Co.[28]

Intensive farming, rather than extensive land dealing or the management of up-country sheep-runs also brought its special rewards in wine production—an activity generally associated in the Australian mind with German immigrants. The value of Coonawarra's red soil has been recognised since John Riddoch, a Scotsman who made his pile from trading with Victoria's gold miners, established the Penola Fruit Colony in 1890. The land there had already proved itself over forty years as a prime site for the cultivation of fruit trees and vines. Riddoch divided over a thousand acres into ten-acre 'working men's' blocks which were then offered for sale at £5 an acre. Before the decline of the Scotsman winery, which was sold after his death for the production of brandy, there were 348 acres under vine. Riddoch's famous Coonawarra Claret came mainly from the shiraz and cabernet sauvignon grapes. 'An old Scotsman has an acre of garden and orchard which is worth a long journey to see,' commented one newspaper reporter in 1890. 'I do not think I have seen a more productive spot, not even in the irrigated gardens of Spain.'[29]

Scots capital, like Scottish entrepreneurs, was highly mobile and found its way into another significant sphere of the later nineteenth-century Australian economy—mining—at first in coal, later copper, silver, gold and shale oil. The Brown brothers, James, John and Alexander, of East Maitland, New South Wales, are good examples, building up varied enterprises around coal, including pioneering coal exports from Newcastle, NSW. The brothers—as their entries in the *Australian Dictionary of Biography* emphasise—illustrated in their particular business skills two sides of the Scottish business ethic at its best. According to their biographer, James was an 'able and persistent' mine manager, while Alexander was 'a shrewd, enterprising man of commerce'.[30] Likewise when the Broken Hill Proptrietory Co (destined to become one of the largest in Australia) was established, its upper levels of ownership and management were, as Trengove put it, 'thronged with Scots'. More than half the original 1885 board members were Scots, including W.P. McGregor, the chairman from 1886 to 1890, who had at one time engaged his own kilted piper not only to play reveille and curfew but also to provide the music at Highland balls and similar grand Caledonian gatherings.[31]

Success in engineering and manufacturing brought industrial Scotland to prominence as 'Workshop of the Empire' so it is little surprise to find such expertise prominent in the Scottish diaspora. Transferred and adapted technology certainly played an important role, as the heritage of industrial archaeology surviving in many parts of Australia quite dramatically demonstrates to this day. But invention was important too and Scots engineers and manufacturers were leaders in Australian innovation during the period to 1914. Much of the industry was geared to the needs of agriculture or urban markets—as George Parsons has shown with particular reference to Melbourne—while a third and vitally important sphere was transport, railway construction, railway engineering and shipbuilding.[32] Manufacture like mining could generate more mobility than pastoralism or commerce, for the mechanic-artisan could rise to the status of businessman-entrepreneur by dint of inventive genius and hard work. Skills translated from Scotland to Australia brought good profits in iron founding, shipbuilding, agricultural engineering and a wide variety of manufactures where colonial production could be made to pay thanks partly to high shipping and transport costs rather than protection. As one simple example: brewing became a prominent and profitable industry in colonial Australia—as it was at home in Scotland. Robert McCraken was a major entrepreneur in the Melbourne brewing industry, successfully adapting his skills to local conditions and raw materials and innovating in refrigeration and other new techniques at his City Brewery.[33]

Finally there were shipping and trade—spheres long attractive to Scots. Some big names immediately jump from the pages of Australian history, for two of the most famous shipping firms were both fiercely Scottish: McIlwraith McEacharn and Burns Philp, Islay-born Sir Malcolm McEacharn being a director of both firms. The McIlwraiths were a dynamic business family, most prominent being Sir Thomas McIlwraith, the indefatigable businessman turned politician and one-time premier of Queensland. Burns Philp was also a remarkably successful enterprise because, as Bolton put it, the clever Burns was the originator and planner and the cautious Philp the 'copy book apprentice'.[34]

Literally hundreds of examples of Scottish achievement—often in the face of long odds—could be cited, but space hardly permits this here and we must pass on to a few conclusions. While we know about numerous successes in entrepreneurship, as well as in other important fields like the Church, the press, education and politics, the failures are cloaked in the anonymity that many Scots sought in their new environment. Perhaps more critically—as I have suggested here—historians trying to assess the Scottish contribution have inevitably concentrated on the successes of an élite, rather than life and labour of the great majority of essentially proletarian migrants. In a review of Cage's *The Scots Abroad: Labour, Capital, Enterprise, 1750–1914*, which includes the essay by Richards cited here, I noted that there were few endearing characters to be met with in the pages of the book. A rereading of Macmillan, Prentis and more recent work by Cumming and others confirms one's worst fears. Scottish capitalism was as ruthless in Australia as at home, though it clearly brought the same or even greater rewards to a minority. Admittedly some rose from the ranks of Crouzet's artisan class to success in Australia—but one suspects the majority made only marginal gains. Studying the diaspora of the Scots to Australia and other parts of the globe—as this Seminar Series demonstrates—puts Scottish history itself in a new light. Certainly the brutality of the Highland clearances (and indeed migrations on a similar scale from the Lowlands) takes on a slightly different gloss when set against the ruthless treatment meted out by some Scottish settlers, pastoralists, and land companies to the Australian Aborigines—from Tasmania in the south to the far north of Queensland. Moreover the inevitable exploitation of less fortunate Scottish convict settlers by their compatriots is another unsavoury chapter which so far remains untold.

Much of interest remains to be explained in the whole story, but the soundings of recent historical research are opening up a whole new terrain in both Australian and Scottish history. After 1900 (at least till the post-1945 era) Scottish immigration was more modest, though probably just as formative. Could it be that 'Red Clydeside' (another of the great Scottish myths?)—as Australian historian Noel McLachlan suggests—infused infinitely more radical Scots migrants into Australian society than the unhappy victims of the clearances or the unemployed Lowland mechanics? What impact did they have on Australia? Greater perhaps than that of their predecessors?[35]

NOTES

1. G. Blainey, *The Tyranny of Distance: How Distance Shaped Australia's History* (Melbourne, 1966).

2. R.B. Madgwick, *Immigration into Eastern Australia, 1788–1851* (Sydney, 1937, repr. 1969).

3. A.D. Gibb, *Scottish Empire* (London and Glasgow, 1937).

4. Ibid, p.vii.

5. Ibid, p.5.

6. Ibid, p.286.

7. G. Donaldson, *The Scots Overseas* (London, 1966).

8. M.L. Kiddle, *Men of Yesterday: A Social History of the Western District of Victoria 1834–1890* (Melbourne, 1961).

9. D.S. Macmillan, *Scotland and Australia 1788–1850: Emigration, Commerce and Investment* (Oxford, 1967).

10. See in particular 'The Scottish Australian Company, 1840–1850: the Origins and Growth of an Aberdeen Venture in Colonial Development', *Scottish Historical Review*, vol.XXXIX, 1960, pp.16–31; *The Debtor's War: Scottish Capitalists and the Economic Crisis in Australia, 1841–46* (Melbourne, 1960); 'The Beginnings of Scottish Enterprise in Australia: The Contribution of the Commercial Whigs', *Business Archives and History*, vol.II, no.2, 1962, pp.95–106; and 'Scottish Enterprise in Australia, 1798–1879' in P. Payne (ed.), *Studies in Scottish Business History* (London, 1967), pp.319–44.

11. W.T. Jackson, *The Enterprising Scot* (Edinburgh, 1968).

12. G. Bolton, *A Thousand Miles Away: A History of North Queensland to 1920* (Brisbane, 1963); D.B. Waterson, *Squatter, Selector and Storekeeper: A History of the Darling Downs* (Sydney, 1968).

13. D. Watson, *Caledonia Australis: Scottish Highlanders on the Frontier of Australia*

(Sydney, 1984); P. de Serville, *Port Philip Gentlemen and Good Society in Melbourne before the Gold Rushes* (Melbourne, 1980).

14. E. Richards, 'Australia and the Scottish Connection, 1788–1914', in R.A. Cage (ed.), *The Scots Abroad: Labour, Capital, Enterprise, 1750–1914* (London, 1985), pp.111–55; 'Scottish Australia 1788–1914', in E. Richards, A. Howe, I. Donnachie and A. Graves, *That Land of Exiles: Scots in Australia* (Edinburgh, 1988), pp.9–39.

15. M.D. Prentis, *The Scots in Australia: A Study of New South Wales, Victoria and Queensland, 1788–1900* (Sydney, 1983).

16. M.D. Prentis, *The Scottish in Australia* (Melbourne, 1987).

17. I. Donnachie, 'Scottish Criminals and Transportation to Australia, 1786–1852', *Scottish Economic and Social History*, vol.4, 1984, pp.21–38; '"Utterly Irreclaimable": Scottish Convict Women and Australia 1787–1852', *The Journal of Regional and Local Studies*, vol.8, no.2, 1988, pp.1–16.

18. S. Nicholas (ed.), *Convict Workers: Reinterpreting Australia's Past* (Sydney, 1988).

19. T.M. Devine, *The Great Highland Famine: Hunger Emigration and the Scottish Highlands in the Nineteenth Century* (Edinburgh, 1988), pp.245–72.

20. C. Cumming, 'Vision and Covenant; Scots in Religion, Education and Politics in Port Philip, 1838–51', unpublished PhD thesis, Deakin University, Vic., 1989.

21. C. Smitz, 'Scottish Investors and Australian Mining 1870–1920', *Scottish Records Association Conference Report*, vol.10, 1988, pp.22–7. See also his paper 'Howard Smith, Scottish Investors and the Origins of Coal & Allied Industries', *Australian Corporate History Bulletin*, vol.III, no.1, 1987, pp.4–7 for an account of the most profitable single Edinburgh-based Australian mining company, the Caledonian Coal Co.

22. H. Reynolds, *The Other Side of the Frontier: Aboriginal Resistance to the European Invasion of Australia* (Ringwood, Vic., 1982). For a recent assessment of events in the Port Philip District, where Scottish settlement predominated, see A.G.L. Shaw, 'The Aborigines and the Land: Port Philip 1835–48', in C. Bridge (ed.), *New Perspectives in Australian History* (London, 1990).

23. J.M.Fraser, 'Scots in Australia', *British Australian Studies Magazine*, vol.1, no.2, 1984, pp.20–4.

24. See E. Richards's introductory remarks in his 'Australia and the Scottish Connection', pp.112–13.

25. Prentis, *Scottish in Australia*, pp.25–6.

26. Richards, 'Australia and the Scottish Connection', p.135.

27. Bruce Mitchell in a recent review of *That Land of Exiles* (*Australian Studies*, no.4, 1990, pp.122–3) expresses some surprise that Scottish-Australianists have not yet challenged the widely held view that the Irish exercised the greatest influence on the Australian psyche—given the apparent success of the Scots.

28. Richards, 'Australia and the Scottish Connection', pp.143–4, quoting J.D. Bailey, *A Hundred Years of Pastoral Banking: A History of the Australian Mercantile and Finance Company, 1863–1963* (Oxford, 1966), pp.55–66.

29. Prentis, *The Scottish in Australia*, p.44.

30. *ADB*, vol.3, pp.259–61.

31. A. Trengove, *What's Good For Australia!: The Story of B.H.P.* (Stanmore, NSW, 1975), pp.12–16, 48–9.

32. T.G. Parsons, 'Some Aspects of the Development of Manufacturing in Melbourne 1870–90', unpublished PhD thesis, Monash University, 1970.

33. *ADB*, 5, pp.136.

34. *ADB*, 5, pp.160–1; G.C. Bolton, 'The Rise of Burns, Philip, 1873–93' in A. Birch and D.S. Macmillan (eds.), *Wealth and Progress: Studies in Australian Business History* (Sydney, 1967), pp.112, 122.

35. N. McLachlan reviewing Prentis, *The Australian*, 11 February 1984.

8

Migration and Motivation: A Twentieth-Century Perspective

Isobel Lindsay

> Objective conditions do not operate in a vacuum since the institutional roles, expectations, beliefs and values of a society provide a framework within which an individual makes a decision whither to migrate or not.[1]

Migration is one of the areas of social behaviour in which the need to take both a structural and a social action approach is particularly strong. If we exclude forced migration arising from such experiences as famine, natural disasters, severe political repression, then the decision to migrate involves a considerable degree of individual rational decision-making. There is little long-distance migration which can be interpreted as a spontaneous emotional response. Migration involves a series of conscious decisions, weighing up the relative advantages and disadvantages of the current location and of other locations, deciding where and when to go, detaching oneself from existing social networks and from property, planning accommodation and work in the new destination. Because of the high input of concentrated decision-making required, the individual's knowledge, perceptions and aspirations need to be studied in order to understand the broad patterns of migration. But of equal or greater importance are the structural factors within which the individual must operate in making migration choices: work opportunities, financial rewards, housing, lifestyle, legal constraints, the 'climate of mobility', language. It is these structural factors which provide the input for individual decision-making but people's aspirations and their knowledge and confidence may differ within the same structural situation. We need to increase our understanding from both the action and structural perspectives in order to interpret migration patterns.

The principal emphasis in this chapter will be in examining motivation. But first we have to consider the pattern and context of external migration in twentieth-century Scotland. The themes which we shall explore are the growing trend to élitism in external migration, the evidence of some modification of the north–south drift by counter-urbanisation trends, and the interpretation of economic opportunity as frequently an enabling or constraining factor in migration rather than a primary motivator.

The Toothill Report on the Scottish Economy said in 1960:

> Emigration generally means the loss of the more skilled workers and of the younger parts of the population . . . But it is not possible to frame a policy to stop it and indeed it would be short-sighted to do so even if it were. It has gone on at as high proportionate rates through some of the most prosperous periods of our history and we think it is likely to continue in some measure, for we could find no direct relationship between it and unemployment rates.[2]

These comments encapsulate many of the long-established attitudes to Scottish migration loss: an acceptance that it is a constant fact of Scottish life about which little can be done, a recognition that there is a qualitative as well as quantitative loss and that explanations cannot be provided on the basis of socio-economic trends within Scotland. These are assumptions that we should examine.

Until 1989–90 there has only been one year this century (1932–3) in which Scotland has experienced any net gain from migration. Inter-censal losses have varied but have always been substantial.[3] Scotland

	000
1901–11	254
1911–21	238
1921–31	390
1931–51	220
1951–61	282
1961–71	326
1971–81	151
1981–89	116

	UK	*Overseas*
1921–31	330	60
1931–51	210	10
1951–61	140	142
1961–71	169	157
1971–81	52	99
1981–9	70	47

will have experienced a net migration loss of around 2 million in the twentieth century, a substantial figure for a small population. The direction of migration loss between overseas and the rest of the UK has varied considerably since figures were first produced in 1921.[4]

The one thing which is immediately apparent, as Toothill commented, is that there is no simple relationship between net migration loss and economic developments within Scotland; certainly lower levels of unemployment do not correlate with lower levels of migration loss. Indeed if there is any pattern, it is that improved economic conditions in Scotland are more likely to be associated with high net migration loss than conditions of recession. The key variables are clearly related to developments furth of Scotland. This does not mean that what happens in Scotland is unimportant but that its importance is comparative not absolute. Hollingsworth's conclusion that there was a 'relatively stable Scotland, greatly influenced by booms and slumps elsewhere'[5] may exaggerate the extent of the stability but it is a plausible hypothesis for the purposes of explaining variations although it is less helpful in explaining absolute levels.

Perhaps the single most important change which took place in the post-Second World War period was the legal/economic one which altered the policies of traditional receiving countries abroad. The 1950s and 1960s were a period in which the encouragement of migration by countries like Canada, Australia, South Africa, Rhodesia was very strong and improved prosperity in Scotland gave more Scots the resources required to undertake the long-distance migration with some confidence. The result was the net loss overseas of 300,000 in twenty years. The peak pre-war period for migration loss, 1921–31, was heavily weighted towards England rather than overseas. The active recruitment of able-bodied whites turned into a much more restrictive immigration strategy with the recession of the early 1970s. Domestic unemployment became a priority for countries like Canada and Australia and they became highly selective in the migrants they would accept. Only those with skills in short supply were considered and these legal restrictions on movement to the most popular receiving countries abroad have become increasingly tight. The popular white-dominated African states became less attractive because of political change. Therefore in relation to overseas migration the international context in which Scots made choices in the 1980s was markedly different from that of the 1960s.

Migration within the UK has not, of course, been subject to legal restraints but there were important changes in the labour market. The period following both world wars saw the development of a broader industrial base in the Midlands and South-East England with the take-off of fast-growing sectors like chemicals, vehicles, light engineering. There was also the development of what has been called the 'new spatial division of labour'[6] in which, rather than regional specialisation in which each place contained all the tasks involved in the production of a range of goods and services, areas became differentiated by the role they played in the production process. Strategic management jobs, production jobs, research and development jobs, were increasingly geographically separate, reducing the relative opportunities for certain types of jobs in some areas and increasing them in others. The result was that even when employment opportunities improved in Scotland, they were even greater in parts of England. Until the 1970s, this applied to skilled and semi-skilled jobs. There was a strong labour market for a range of manual work. The radical de-industrialisation which has taken place in the past two decades has severely reduced the employment opportunities for manual workers in England but has still left opportunities for the highly trained. Therefore just as migration opportunities for the less skilled have been cut off by the popular receiving countries abroad, so migration opportunities for those less skilled have also become impracticable in relation to England. Even where low-level service jobs have been available, housing costs have been prohibitive for anyone on low incomes. There has been no recent net flow of manual workers from north to south and Scotland had a lower inter-regional outmigration of manual workers than other northern regions.[7] Therefore external migration has become increasingly the activity of the skilled élite, with few opportunities for those with low qualifications.

As far as we can assess, the more skilled have always been represented in migration loss in a higher proportion than the home population[8] but before the 1970s, outmigration appears to have had quite a broad social mix. But as we move towards the end of the century, there is a closure of opportunity for lower socio-economic groups and little prospect of this changing. Growing European Community integration is unlikely to alter this trend. There will be greater ease of movement for the higher technical, professional, managerial workers, although this is greatly inhibited by language and cultural differences. But the existing surplus of 'guest workers' and the potential supply of good quality cheap labour from eastern Europe, offers little hope for the manual worker or routine clerical worker who would have been readily welcomed into Toronto, Sydney or Coventry thirty years ago.

The classical equilibrium model of migration as a means of equalising labour demand and supply has little relevance in situations of highly differentiated labour and housing markets. In creaming off those in whom there has been a high educational investment, but not offering opportunities for those who are unemployed or on low incomes, migration may act primarily as a reinforcement of regional imbalance.

The north–south population drift has been one of the most significant UK demographic trends, accentuated since the late 1970s. It has affected not only Scotland but northern England.[9] The four regions of the south were already ahead of others in population growth in the 1970s and this gap has increased in the 1980s largely through migration.

Migration has produced a situation of population decline in Scotland since the mid-1970s combining as it has done with declining birth-rates, now lower than those of England and Wales instead of at the traditionally higher levels. But the Scottish position is not one of consistent north–south drift. While that has been the dominant trend in relation to England, within Scotland population change has been closer to the counter-urbanisation pattern typical of Western developed countries from the 1960s onwards.[10] Although in the decade 1976–86 Scotland as a whole had a net loss of 152,000 people, some regions within Scotland gained. Borders, Dumfries and Galloway, Grampian, Highland, Orkney and the Western Isles all gained from a combination of movement from inside and outside Scotland. The great losers were the urbanised areas of Strathclyde, where the net loss was 172,360 over the decade, greater than the net Scottish loss despite the input into urban regeneration during those years.[11]

The most interesting case is the Highlands and Islands which has produced an exceptional example of migration reversal. It is interesting not because the migration gains are high but because of the contrast to the previous 150 years. The Highlands gained over 8,000 between 1976 and 1986, 4,390 of this gain coming from other parts of Scotland and 3,750 from outside Scotland. Previously the Highlands had experienced substantial population decline while Scotland as a whole was still undergoing slow population growth. Between 1921 and 1961 the area lost about a quarter of its population.[12] By 1961 the population had fallen to 302,000 from its level of 424,000 in 1851. Population levels started to stabilise after the mid-1960s and then slowly increased, primarily through migration but now with a birth-rate slightly higher than the Scottish average. While oil developments were a factor in this recovery along with three other major projects at Dounreay, Lochaber, Invergordon, this was not the only reason. The turn-around had started before oil, and population gain has been widely dispersed in different areas of the Highlands.[13] It has also been sustained despite the closure of two of these large developments and the run-down of oil-related employment. Nor can it be explained by the retired 'white settler' category since the percentage of people in the young adult category has increased. The fact that other less urbanised areas have also gained suggests that there is a more general factor at work.

If there is a counter-urbanisation process taking place either for lifestyle reasons or because of developments in occupational structure towards the service sector, might this eventually have implications for Scotland as a whole. Because Scotland is a country of low population densities and with most of its land area populated by small communities, might those economic pressures which have produced the north–south drift be somewhat modified by an increased counter-urbanisation trend? The past two years have seen an historically atypical net gain from migration, coming largely from a sharp increase in inmigration. An obvious reason is recession in southern England which one would have expected to increase return migration and reduce outmigration. Return migration has always been a significant factor,[14] one which is sensitive to changing economic conditions. But if new inmigration has increased as well as return migration, explanations are more complex since Scotland still has above average unemployment. It will be some years before we can assess whether this is an aberration or the sign of a developing trend.

We have looked at some aspects of change in migration patterns in the twentieth century. These have illustrated a number of structural features, primarily economic, in which migration decisions have operated. But we cannot understand migration by simply looking at structural changes and assuming that individuals respond like automatons to structural stimuli. The attempts by economists to produce models of inter-regional migration related to standard indices of employment, earnings, etc. has produced only weak linkages.[15] Subjective interpretations and aspirations have to come in to any equation. Hart has suggested that 'a migrant does not migrate merely to take advantage of better economic welfare conditions in another region at a given point in time but rather he is motivated by the fact that he expects the better conditions to remain constant or increase in the forseeable future.'[16] In other words even in a primarily economic interpretation, complex areas of knowledge, expectation, aspiration must form a vital part of any explanation. Nor can we take for granted that the role of economic motivation is overwhelmingly dominant. It may in many cases be a constraining factor or an enabling factor rather than a primary motivating factor. People may wish to experience change and variety and be constrained or enabled by economic factors, without these economic opportunities themselves being the prime objective.

A very limited amount of survey work has been done on motivation in Scottish migration:

> Very little information yet exists about the characteristics of migrants—
> the varied motives which prompt them to move, the number of moves
> they make, or the respects in which they differ from their static friends
> and relatives . . . and very little attempt has been made to relate the
> characteristics of migrants to the social contexts in which the migration
> occurred.[17]

There are difficulties in finding appropriate samples, particularly with
external migration. Once people have decided to migrate and have gone,
their settlement choices are diverse. Before they have made definite
decisions, they are not easy to identify unless with a large sample or
with concentration on only a specific sub-group.

Probably the most substantial study, in terms of scale, of migration
motivation in Scotland was that sponsored by the Government Social
Survey in 1948.[18] This was concerned with outmigration in rural
areas and was prompted by the problems of rural depopulation.
While it did not focus primarily on outmigration from Scotland,
it did examine motives and characteristics of migrants and potential
migrants. A total of 6,656 were interviewed in south-west Scotland,
the Tweed basin, Aberdeenshire and Banff. In addition, information
was collected from the sample about people who had moved from the
area during the previous thirty years and over 300 in this category
returned questionnaires. Of the total sample, 10 per cent expressed
a desire to move. This rose to 20 per cent of professional, clerical
and managerial workers. The most migration-prone group were the
16–29-year-olds. Apart from age and occupation, there appeared to be
little objectively different in the circumstances of the potential migrants
and others. Eighty per cent of the reasons given for wishing to move
fell into three categories: 35 per cent wanted a better job, 25 per cent
wanted to escape from stagnation, loneliness, 20 per cent indicated
an unspecified desire for change. The remainder of the reasons were
principally related to change in personal circumstances, e.g. marriage.
What is interesting is that just over a third of the answers related
specifically to economic/occupational advancement. The desire for
change and new experience seemed to be at least as important as the
narrowly economic.

We cannot, of course, assume that people's conscious interpretation
of their motivation is actually what motivates them but we have to take
their own interpretation seriously. Of those people who had left the area
and could be traced, there was clear evidence of upward mobility both
in relation to their previous occupations and the occupational structure
in the areas they had left. When asked why they had moved, a much

higher proportion gave employment-related reasons than those currently wishing to migrate. Employment reasons were given by two-thirds, 22 per cent gave social relationships, 12 per cent housing amenities and 10 per cent to broaden outlook. Fifty per cent said that if a better choice of job had been available, they would have remained in their old districts. Several reasons might explain the differing importance of occupational and 'change' reasons between the original sample and the migrant respondents. The migrants were not a statistically selected sample, but more important may be the fact that this group had actually moved whereas the others aspired to move. Those with specific occupational aspirations may have found it easier to translate their wishes into practice or been more positively motivated.

Illseley *et al.* examined the characteristics and motivation of migrants in Aberdeen as part of a wider medical sociology study of women having their first child between 1951 and 1959 and their families.[19] Their progress was followed over five years. This, of course, was a specific population category and the migration streams examined were primarily within Scotland. What did emerge was a strong occupationally determined pattern of outmigration. The highest rate of outmigration occurred in social class I—63 per cent within five years. The rate fell sharply with decreasing status to 33 per cent in class II, 19 per cent in class III and 10 per cent in classes IV and V. These broad variations conceal some interesting differences within occupational groups. Among managerial groups the rate is high among employees of large-scale national or multi-national organisations but low in local resource industries such as fish processing or granite quarrying, and in small businesses. Similar considerations applied to clerical workers, with employees of banks, insurance companies and similar organisations being most likely to move.

Among manual workers those with the highest propensity to move were skilled mechanics, fitters, electricians:

> Educationally, socially and physically, these engineers are the aristocrats of local manual work and they may be particularly susceptible to the attractions of a higher standard of living elsewhere when they find their occupational pathway blocked locally. They are very largely Aberdonian in origin, not earlier inmigrants from the countryside. They differ sharply in their rate of outmigration from other skilled engineers in the city, many of whom are employed in shipbuilding, an industry which is stationary or declining throughout the country and which is not conspicuously more prosperous in other areas than in Aberdeen. The engineering industry thus provides an excellent example of the impact of both local and national conditions on rates of migration, of

the push-pull forces which have received so much attention in migration research.

Illseley *et al.* concluded that structural factors in the economy, combined with levels of aspiration, substantially explained migration patterns. But family factors were also of some significance in influencing repeat migration and the direction of movement.

Both the Illseley and Hutchison studies highlighted the higher levels of migration of professional and higher administrative workers. This is an accepted generalisation from much migration research.[20] But it is worth giving some consideration to a category of Scots migrant at the opposite end of the socio-economic spectrum. While this does not represent mainstream migration, it has been highlighted during the 1980s as an increasing social problem. The young homeless in London include a higher proportion of Scots than would be justified by UK population share.[21] By definition this is not a group which is easy to enumerate or to study methodically because of their impermanence. The Shelter charity, however, has carried out a small project with seventy young Scots who were sleeping rough.[22] It is tempting to interpret the migration of the low-skilled young Scots coming to London without resources as an example of irrational migration or at least ill-informed migration. Looked at objectively it would appear that no careful weighing up of advantages and disadvantages could have taken place, no attempt to find accurate information. But this may be a misinterpretation. Unstable family backgrounds characterised many of these young people, with 44 per cent having been in residential care at some time. Social attachments in Scotland were either weak or negative for many. The majority had been unemployed before coming to London. For those who had not moved directly from a family home to London, there had been a high level of housing instability with an average of over four locations in a year. In weighing up losses and gains in the migration process, they did not in general have much to lose either economically or socially. The reasons they gave for migrating were not so very different from the undergraduates we will examine later. The most frequent reason given was employment related, but the next most important category of reasons came under the heading of desire for change, independence, adventure. Unlike the more socially stable low-skilled, this group of young people were not integrated into supportive social relationships and often had much to escape from in that respect. Despite the severe problems they had experienced in London, a third of the sample definitely did not want to return to Scotland. Therefore while the trend towards élite migration appears to be predominant, there are exceptions, not numerically large but socially significant because of the problems they represent for the receiving area.

It is, however, the migration of the high-skilled which represents the mainstream, and the socio-economic significance of that migration differs greatly depending on the relative balance of migration streams and the location of net gains and losses. If the in and outmigration of highly educated sections of the labour force is in balance, then the economic impact is likely to be neutral, although there might be social stresses e.g. if the cultural background of inmigrants differs from outmigrants. But if there are significant quantitative differences in migration streams of the highly skilled, this raises a range of important issues. Human capital investment is as much a key economic factor in modern societies as any other form of capital, some might argue more so since in the advanced industrial societies the dependency on knowledge-based systems is paramount.[23] The net loss of a highly trained section of the labour force is both a real or 'accounting' loss because of the very high level of expenditure which goes into education and it is also a qualitative loss in that one might expect the people involved to be competent and aspiring in areas beyond the narrowly occupational. For those places experiencing the gain of highly educated workers, the position is of course reversed. They gain people in whom substantial resources have been invested by others, and they normally gain them when they are young since migration is predominantly the activity of young adults.[24] They gain all the benefits which a highly skilled labour force can provide and they improve their tax yields from better-paid workers. So the migration of the skilled is of particular concern. If this migration takes place within the same political unit, e.g. the same local authority area, then the economic effects will be limited. But if movement is to a different state or even to a different local authority, then there are very clear winners and losers.

It cannot be argued without qualification that if the area of loss has high unemployment, then there are gains from migration loss. The well educated will probably not find great difficulty in getting work although it may not be at their level of qualification. By depleting the skill base of the community and improving it elsewhere, the effect may be to reinforce the relative attractions of more successful areas for employers. Therefore both because of their high mobility and their economic importance, those with higher education are especially worthy of study.

Scotland, with its high levels of migration loss and its traditionally higher proportion of young people in universities, makes it particularly vulnerable to graduate migration. One common conclusion reached by various studies of Scottish graduate migration is that no matter how substantial the current losses may be, it is no worse than in the past. Scotland has historically not only been an exporter of people but of highly trained people. McKay's study of Aberdeen graduates over the period 1860–1960 [25] was prompted by the brain-drain concerns of the 1960s. His two principal conclusions were that the problem was long-standing and that the likelihood of graduates leaving Scotland was strongly related to the degree taken. In effect some skills were internationally marketable and others less so or not at all. Some found a ready local demand, others found difficulty in finding opportunities in Scotland for specialised areas of employment. The average proportion of Scots-born Aberdeen University male graduates over the century who had their principal place of work in Scotland was 53 per cent, with 29 per cent going to England and Wales and 18 per cent to the rest of the world. Only 25 per cent of all male medical graduates worked principally in Scotland, 35 per cent of engineers and 46 per cent of scientists. In contrast over 80 per cent of the divinity and law graduates remained in Scotland. Although there is return migration, the extent of outmigration increases and the net effect was that more graduates were working outside Scotland in their last reported job than in their first. The differences in the degree distribution among those going and those remaining were too great to suggest that there was any prior disposition in the selection of degree courses by those prone to move or to stay. Movement appeared to be strongly market-led.

Other evidence supports both the high historical and contemporary outflow of graduates. A survey carried out for the Toothill Committee by Glasgow University's Appointments Committee of graduates going into industry during 1954–9, found that two-thirds of the arts graduates and three-quarters of the science graduates found their first employment outside Scotland.[26] Forsyth and Merler compared the characteristics of emigrant and non-emigrant Scots-domiciled graduates from six Scottish universities who had graduated between 1966 and 1969 and gone into manufacturing industry.[27] Forty-four per cent left Scotland for other parts of the UK. The study concentrated on the structural factors which might have influenced these decisions. The industry mix in Scotland did not correspond with the graduate mix but the discrepancy was not great enough to be other than a partial factor. The proportion in which migrant and non-migrant graduates took up jobs was similar in the field of production and research and development, but more emigrants took up jobs in marketing and finance, probably a reflection of changes in occupational distribution brought about by concentration of economic control. Starting salaries were on average higher for those who left Scotland but there were wide variations within the average.

The differentials for post-graduates were greater. Given the costs of relocation, starting salaries were not seen as a decisive factor in explaining outmigration. There was considerable variation in disciplines in levels of outmigration. A majority of those going into industry with pure science, maths and social science degrees left Scotland but the figures for others was lower, reflecting the greater opportunities at that time in e.g. engineering in Scotland. It appeared to be partly occupational structures and partly perceptions of future potential which were more important than immediate advantages such as salary.

The most comprehensive review of Scottish graduate migration has been that carried out by the Scottish section of the Association of Graduate Career Advisory Services (MacAGCAS).[28] It does not include figures for graduates who get their first jobs abroad but this is a small proportion of the total for first employment. For 1988–89 70 per cent of Scottish-domiciled graduates from Scottish universities for their first job in Scotland. The proportion was the same for colleges and central institutions. But while around 30 per cent of Scottish graduates got their first job in England and Wales, only 0.3 per cent of English- and Welsh-domiciled graduates from universities in England and Wales got their first job in Scotland (see Table 1A).

The type of employment which Scottish graduates go into gives a strong indication of the structural factors influencing the graduate flow. Forty-four per cent of Scottish graduates who took up work in England and Wales did so in the manufacturing sector, in contrast to 24 per cent of those who remained in Scotland. The average percentage of UK graduates who went into manufacturing was 27 per cent (see Table 1B). Thirty-five per cent of those going to England and Wales went into

TABLE 1A

SCOTTISH UNIVERSITIES—SCOTTISH DOMICILE GRADUATES—
BREAKDOWN OF EMPLOYED UK

	Employed Scotland	Employed Rest of UK	Total
1981–2	2,259 (74%)	795 (26%)	3,054
1982–3	2,496 (76%)	774 (24%)	3,270
1983–4	2,713 (74%)	937 (26%)	3,650
1984–5	2,712 (72%)	1,042 (28%)	3,754
1985–6	2,452 (70%)	1,096 (30%)	3,548
1986–7	N/A	N/A	N/A
1987–8	2,629 (70%)	1,152 (30%)	3,781
1988–9	2,428 (70%)	1,064 (30%)	3,492

Source MacAGCAS.

TABLE 1B

SCOTTISH UNIVERSITIES – SCOTTISH DOMICILE GRADUATES ONLY; TYPES
OF EMPLOYED AND TYPE OF WORK SUMMARY

Type of Employes	Scotland	Rest of UK	Total	(Total UK%)
Public service	596 (72%)	223 (28%)	819	
	(23%)	(20%)	(22%)	(15)
Health service	493 (87%)	75 (13%)	568	
	(19%)	(6%)	(15%)	(15)
Manufacturing	627 (55%)	501 (45%)	1,128	
	(24%)	(44%)	(30%)	(27)
Finance	507 (75%)	170 (25%)	677	
	(20%)	(15%)	(18%)	(20)
Commerce/other	364 (67%)	178 (33%)	542	
	(14%)	(15%)	(14%)	(23)
Totals	2,587 (70%)	1,147 (30%)	3,734 (100%)	
	(100%)	(100%)	(100%)	(100)
Business/managerial	985 (66%)	497 (34%)	1,482	
	(38%)	(43%)	(40%)	(48)
Scientific/technical	551 (58%)	399 (42%)	950	
	(21%)	(35%)	(25%)	(21)
Public/social Serv.	833 (86%)	134 (14%)	968	
	(32%)	(12%)	(26%)	(23)
Cultural/other	218 (65%)	116 (35%)	334	
	(8%)	(10%)	(9%)	
Totals	2,587 (70%)	1,147 (30%)	3,734 (100%)	
	(100%)	(100%)	(100%)	(100)

Source: MacAGCAS.

scientific and technical work but only 21 per cent of those who stayed in
Scotland. It would appear that there is a shortfall in the job opportunities
available in Scotland in scientific, technical and industrial management
areas in relation to the numbers of students we produce with these
qualifications. These graduate losses at the stage of first employment
are likely to increase with second and third jobs.

Some evidence suggest that the availability of graduate employment
in general in Scotland, i.e. not just new graduates, declined during the
1980s. The Labour Force Survey found that in 1983 Scotland had 9.4
per cent of British graduate population in employment. By 1987 this
was seven per cent, i.e. 14,000 fewer despite little change in the total
numbers in employment in Scotland. Over this period the number of
graduates working in Britain went up by 283,000 and the numbers
increased or remained static in every other region.[29] Graduate migration
loss is clearly of historical and contemporary significance, representing

as it does the élite section of the labour force and it deserves particular consideration.

To study the attitudes of undergraduates towards migration is comparatively straightforward. They are an easily defined and accessible group. To study graduates who have left Scotland is obviously difficult. Because of dispersal and lack of contact, putting together a representative sample presents problems. It was decided to carry out a research project on graduate migration among present and former students of Strathclyde University. The object of the research was to examine characteristics and motivation. The undergraduate project was based on a sample of twenty per cent of Scottish – domiciled third-year undergraduates during the session 1989–90. The response rate to the questionnaire was sixty per cent, 202 replies. All were currently Scottish domiciled and ninety-seven per cent had been brought up solely or mainly in Scotland. Eighty-four per cent were from the Central Belt of Scotland; the sex ratio was fifty-seven per cent male: forty-three per cent female. Eleven per cent were mature students over twenty-five. Eighty-six per cent had relatives living outside Scotland, a reflection of the high migration loss of the past.

The most striking figure is the very low preference, just over two per cent, who positively wished to work in other parts of the UK. It would appear that those undergraduates who are attracted by migration have a clear preference to go abroad rather than to England. But preferences and expectations are far from being similar. There is a sharp contrast between the preferred location for employment and their expected location.

Students are clearly pessimistic about their job opportunities in Scotland. While sixty-five per cent would positively like to stay, only thirty-one per cent feel confident about getting work in Scotland. The rest think it either unlikely or uncertain. There is greater pessimism about the chances of getting employment in Scotland than the actual figures for graduate employment indicate.

Looking more closely at those students expressing a preference to work outside Scotland, are there differences in objective characteristics? There was a marginally higher proportion of males, sixty-two per cent as opposed to fifty-seven per cent in the total sample. Students from a working-class background were under-represented among those who would prefer to leave Scotland, thirteen per cent as opposed to twenty-seven per cent in the total sample. Intermediate non-manual are the most over-represented, twenty-nine per cent as opposed to nineteen per cent. There would appear to be some social class factors affecting preferences.

The single most important factor which makes students want to stay in Scotland is that of social relationships—almost sixty per cent gave that

UNDERGRADUATES
OCCUPATIONAL CLASS OF FATHER/GUARDIAN

	%
Managerial/professional	53
Intermediate non-manual	19
Manual	27

COURSE TAKEN

	%
Arts/Social Science	11
Engineering	26
Science	32
Business studies, law, accountancy	26
Hotel school and others	5

PREFERRED WORK LOCATION

	%
Scotland	65
Rest of UK	2
North America	8
Australia/New Zealand	2
Europe	10
Other	1
No preference	11

EXPECTED WORK LOCATION

	%
Scotland	31
Rest of UK	29
Abroad	14
DK	24

as their principal reason. The most important factor which makes them want to leave is the prospect of work opportunities, forty-seven per cent. But lifestyle factors are of significant and similar importance in both categories—as a reason for going and a reason for staying. Environment and social attitudes are a positive factor for some students who would prefer to remain in Scotland and 'broadening horizons', the change and experience reason, is the second in importance for those wishing to

UNDERGRADUATES
PREFERRED SECTORS OF EMPLOYMENT

	%
Manufacturing	23
Independent professional	18
Social services	10
Banking, finance	9
Energy, water	5
Other services	4
Public administration, defence	3
Construction	3
Other	1
No preference	8

PRINCIPAL REASON FOR PREFERRING
TO WORK IN SCOTLAND

	%
Family/social relationships	59
Lifestyle	19
Environment	8
Work opportunities	7
Social attitudes	5
Children's upbringing	1

PRINCIPAL REASON FOR PREFERRING
TO WORK OUTSIDE SCOTLAND

	%
Family/social relations	1
Work opportunities	47
Lifestyle	19
Social attitudes	1
Broaden horizons	21
Money	7
Climate	3
Children's upbringing	1

For those preferring to work in Scotland, What
Factors Might Make Them Change Their Mind?

	%
None	7
Lack of employment opportunities	44
Lack of employment with career prospects	32
Money	6
Personal relationships	8
Other	3

GRADUATE MIGRANTS
SUBJECT OF FIRST DEGREE

	%
Arts/social studies	15
Engineering	37
Science	31
Business studies, law, accountancy	14
Other	5

46 per cent had a second degree and 64 per cent a
professional qualification.

FATHER/GUARDIAN'S OCCUPATION

	%
Managerial/professional	43
Intermediate non-manual	30
Manual	25

LOCATION OF FIRST JOB

	%
Scotland	53
Rest of UK	19
Abroad	28

LOCATION OF SECOND JOB WHERE APPLICABLE

	%
Scotland	23
Rest of UK	17
Abroad	61

LOCATION OF THIRD JOB WHERE APPLICABLE

	%
Scotland	13
Rest of UK	7
Abroad	80

leave. Or those who would prefer to stay in Scotland, three-quarters might change their mind if they found problems in getting work or work with career opportunities. So there is a potentially larger pool of migrants than the preference figures suggest. It is not primarily economic factors which make students want to stay in Scotland, nor is it economic factors which are the main incentive for almost half of those students who would prefer to leave. But lack of economic opportunity may, in practice, prove decisive if graduates find their job prospects poor.

A survey of graduates who had left Scotland and were working abroad was also carried out. Strathclyde University distributes an alumni magazine to around 5,000 former students who are now overseas. A questionnaire was included in this for graduates who were originally Scottish domiciled. Many of the 5,000 would not have been Scottish students originally but logistical problems made it difficult to separate them. Two hundred and twenty-three valid responses came from forty-four different countries. The response rate is difficult to judge since the proportion of the total distribution who were not Scottish was not known and some of this type of mailing will not reach its destination or will be unopened. We can make no claims to a properly representative sample but it does provide material of interest.

Only twenty per cent of respondents were women. Part of the explanation for this is the strongly male-dominated gender structure of the university in the past because of its technological emphasis.

Just as McKay's Aberdeen study showed, it is not the location of the first job after graduation which gives an accurate picture of graduate loss but movement in subsequent jobs. Of those giving work as their main reason, sixty-two per cent said it was career opportunities which influenced them, twenty-three per cent money and fourteen per cent to get employment.

Although work opportunity was the reason given by half the respondents, the desire for experience, change etc. was also an important motivating factor.

Only a minority would appear to have serious intentions of returning; although a much larger group have a degree of ambivalence about return migration, one suspects much of it is of a sentimental rather than intentional nature.

Both the undergraduate and graduate studies predictably find that employment-related reasons were the single most important. Both studies also found that a significant minority gave apparently non-economic reasons. There is close similarity in the proportion giving economic reasons (job opportunities or money) among graduates abroad

GRADUATE MIGRANTS
PRINCIPAL REASON FOR LEAVING SCOTLAND

	%
Broaden horizons	27
Work opportunities	47
Family/social relationships	12
Money	3
Lifestyle	4
Social attitudes	1
Other	4

PRINCIPAL REASON FOR NOT
RETURNING TO SCOTLAND

	%
Broaden horizons	3
Work opportunities	39
Climate	3
Family/social relationships	21
Money	10
Lifestyle	18
Health	1
Social attitudes	2
Children's upbringing	2

WISH TO RETURN TO SCOTLAND

	%
Yes	15
No	34
Maybe	50

WHETHER LIKELY TO RETURN

	%
Yes	14
No	41
Maybe	32
Only when retired	13

and undergraduates, fifty per cent and fifty-four per cent respectively. There is also similarity in the second most popular reason, i.e. 'to broaden horizons', twenty-seven per cent and twenty-one per cent for undergraduates. The next significant category of preference for undergraduates was that of lifestyle/social attitudes, twenty per cent, but this was given by only five per cent of those who lived overseas as the initial reason for leaving. Personal relationships were higher in importance for graduates, twelve per cent, than undergraduates, one per cent.

What these responses suggest is that although the most important single reason for leaving or wishing to leave is work and to a marginal extent money, this constitutes only around half of the reasons given. So other factors appear to play a significant role—the desire for experience, adventure, perceptions of more attractive ways of life elsewhere. This may be reinforced by the fact that so many have relatives in other countries—eighty per cent of the undergraduates. Migration is a mainstream not a deviant tradition in the Scottish context. It may also reflect the 'gravity' effect of a country with small population finding it more difficult to offer some of the attractions of countries with larger populations. It may reflect factors in the socio-political structures in Scotland which fail to fulfil the aspirations of young Scots. More in-depth research into motivation would be required to identify the specific non-economic factors which are most influential.

This cannot, however, be presented as a simple pattern of economic/non-economic motivation. Whatever people's primary motivation may be, the structural factors of economic opportunity play a crucial role in enabling people whose motivation is non-economic to move and in preventing people whose motivation is economic from moving. Even if people's motivation is economic, their reasons for staying away may become primarily social as they are integrated into new social networks. We need, therefore, to develop a model in which employment opportunities are the central structural determinants but are modified by social, cultural and personal factors.

NOTES

1. G.J. Lewis, *Human Migration* (London, 1982).
2. *Toothill Report on the Scottish Economy*, The Scottish Council (Development and Industry) (1961).
3. Annual Reports of the Registrar General Scotland.
4. *Ibid.*

5. T.H. Hollingsworth, *Migration* (Edinburgh, 1970).

6. A. Fielding, 'Population Redistribution in Western Europe', in P. Congdon and P. Batey (eds.), *Advances in Regional Demography*, (London, 1989).

7. T. Champion, 'Internal Migration and the Spatial Distribution of Population', in H. Joshi (ed.), *The Changing Population of Britain*, (Blackwell, 1989).

8. Hollingsworth, *Migration*.

9. Champion, 'Internal Migration'.

10. Fielding, 'Population Redistribution'.

11. Annual Reports of Registrar General.

12. C. Walker and A. McCleery, 'Economic and Social Change in the Highlands and Islands', *Scottish Economic Bulletin*, no.35, 1987.

13. *Ibid.*

14. D. Bell and F. Kirwan, *Return Migration in a Scottish Context*, Fraser of Allander Institute Occasional Paper, 1977.

15. R.A. Hart, 'Economic Expectations and the Decision to Migrate', *Regional Studies*, vol.7, 1973.

16. *Ibid.*

17. R. Illseley, A. Finlayson and B. Thompson, 'The Motivation and Characteristics of Internal Migrants' in C. Jansen (ed.), *Readings in the Sociology of Migration* (London, 1970).

18. I.B. Hutchison, *Depopulation and Rural Life in Scotland*, Government Social Survey for Department of Health, Scotland, Summary, 1963.

19. Illseley, *et al.*, 'Internal Migrants'.

20. R. Shaw, *Migration Theory and Fact* (Regional Science Research Institute, 1975).

21. Centrepoint Soho, *No Way Home* (1987); *Homeless and Hungry* (1989).

22. *Living on the Borderline* (Shelter, 1991).

23. A number of writers have emphasised this point. It is particularly associated with D. Bell, *The Coming of Post-Industrial Society* (London, 1974) and J.K. Galbraith, *The New Industrial State* (London, 1967).

24. Shaw, *Migration Theory*.

25. D. McKay, *Geographical Mobility and the Brain Drain* (London, 1969).

26. *Toothill Report.*

27. D. Forsyth and G. Mercer, 'The Emigration of Graduates from Scotland 1966–69', *Regional Studies*, vol.7, 1973.

28. Contained in MacAGCAS Conference Report, June 1990.

29. S. Creigh and A. Rees, 'Graduates and the Labour Market in the 1980s', *Employment Gazette*, January 1989.

INDEX